Anonymous

Verney's Almanac

Anonymous

Verney's Almanac

ISBN/EAN: 9783337341138

Printed in Europe, USA, Canada, Australia, Japan

Cover: Foto ©Thomas Meinert / pixelio.de

More available books at **www.hansebooks.com**

VERNEY'S

ALMANAC

1899

JULY, SEVENTH MONTH. [1899.

PHASES OF THE MOON.

	D.H.M.		D.H.M.
New Moon	8 6.31 a.m.	Full Moon	23 7.41 a.m.
First Quar.	16 9.59 a.m.	Last Quar.	29 10.42 p.m.
Perigee,	11 2.4 a.m.	Apogee,	23 9.7 p.m.

ASTRONOMICAL PHENOMENA.

July 4 Sun in Apogee, 7 p.m.
" 6 Venus in con. with moon, 1 p.m.
" 7 Jupiter in con. with moon, 4 a.m.
" 10 Mercury in conjun. with moon, 1 p.m.
" 13 Mars in conjun. with moon, 1 p.m.
" 20 Saturn in conjun. with moon, noon.

ASTRONOMICAL NOTES.

	1st—H.M.	15th—H.M.
♀ Venus rises	5 7 a.m.	rises 5 28 a.m.
♂ Mars sets	9 36 p.m.	sets 9 18 p.m.
♃ Jupiter sets	1 33 a.m.	sets 0 40 a.m.
♄ Saturn sets	5 16 a.m.	sets 4 17 a.m.

Venus morning star.

The times of rising and setting of the sun and moon are for the upper limb corrected for parallax and refraction. Brisbane standard time.

Date.	Day.	MEMORANDA AND DIARY.	The Sun Rises.	Sets.	The Moon Rises.	Sets.	High Water on Brisbane Bar. Morn.	Aftrn.
			H. M.	H. M.	A.M.	A.M.	H. M.	H. M.
1	S	Battle of the Boyne 1690	6 39	5 4	0 18	11 52	3 21	3 56
2	S	5th Sunday after Trinity.	6 39	5 4	1 18	P.M.	4 37	5 18
3	M	Electric tramcars com. run. in Bris.1897	6 39	5 4	2 18	1 13	5 50	6 19
4	Tu	Declar. of American Independence 1776	6 39	5 5	3 16	1 59	6 47	7 14
5	W	East India Company formed 1698	6 39	5 5	4 13	2 49	7 39	8 13
6	Th	Duke of York married 1893	6 39	5 5	5 6	3 41	8 25	8 47
7	F	First Land Sale at Moreton Bay 1842	6 39	5 6	5 55	4 33	9 9	9 29
8	S	● Right Hon. J. Chamberlain born 1836	6 39	5 6	6 39	5 29	9 49	10 8
9	S	6th Sunday after Trinity.	6 39	5 7	7 19	6 23	10 26	10 45
10	M	Melbourne University founded....1854	6 39	5 7	7 55	7 16	11 3	11 19
11	Tu	Sir P. A. Jennings, K.C.M.G., died 1897	6 39	5 7	8 28	8 8	11 38	11 54
12	W	Crimea evacuated 1856	6 38	5 8	8 58	8 59		0 11
13	Th	First iron casting made in Qld. ...1862	6 38	5 8	9 29	9 50	0 27	0 46
14	F	Bastille (Paris) stormed........1789	6 38	5 9	9 59	10 43	1 4	1 23
15	S	St. Swithun.	6 38	5 9	10 31	11 37	1 43	2 5
16	S	☽ 7th Sunday after Trinity.	6 37	5 10	11 5	A.M.	2 29	2 55
17	M	Brisbane and Gympie Railway op. 1891	6 37	5 10	11 44	0 33	3 27	4 1
18	Tu	Infallibility of Pope declared ...1870	6 37	5 11	P.M.	1 33	4 43	5 25
19	W	Indooroopilly Railway Bridge op. 1895	6 37	5 11	1 20	2 34	5 59	6 30
20	Th	Spanish Armada defeated 1588	6 36	5 12	2 18	3 37	7 2	7 31
21	F	Battle of Shrewsbury 1403	6 36	5 12	3 23	4 37	8 0	8 27
22	S	Union of England and Scotland 1705	6 35	5 13	4 32	5 35	8 54	9 19
23	S	○ 8th Sunday after Trinity.	6 35	5 13	5 43	6 27	9 13	10 7
24	M	Gibraltar captured 1704	6 34	5 14	6 52	7 13	10 31	10 54
25	Tu	St. James. Beenleigh Rail. op. 1885	6 34	5 15	7 59	7 56	11 15	11 38
26	W	First Insurance Company estab. 1700	6 34	5 15	9 4	8 35	11 59	
27	Th	Duchess of Fife married 1889	6 33	5 16	10 8	9 13	0 20	0 42
28	F	Robespierre guillotined 1794	6 32	5 16	11 10	9 52	1 5	1 29
29	S	St. Peter.	6 32	5 17	A.M. 0 10	10 31	1 54	2 20
30	S	9th Sunday after Trinity.	6 31	5 17	0 11	11 13	2 49	3 22
31	M	First Queensland Railway opened 1865	6 30	5 18	1 11	11 58	3 59	4 43

Potted Eggs.—Boil six eggs hard; remove the shells, and rub them through a hair-sieve with one ounce of butter. Mix with them two dessertspoonfuls of anchovy sauce, pepper, and mace; place in dishes, and pour melted butter or lard over the top.

Potato Stew.—Boil one pound of salt pork in two quarts of water; when done, take out, score, and brown it in the oven. Add to the liquor ten sliced raw potatoes, and two onions also sliced; stir in one teacupful of milk and one beaten-up egg; boil it up, pour it over the meat, and serve.

AUGUST, EIGHTH MONTH. [1899.

PHASES OF THE MOON.

	D.H.M.		D.H.M.
New Moon	6 9.48 p.m.	Full Moon	21 2.45 p.m.
First Quar.	14 9.54 p.m.	Last Quar.	29 9.57 a.m.
Apogee,	7 8.2 a.m.	Perigee,	21 7.6 a.m.

ASTRONOMICAL PHENOMENA.

Aug. 5 Venus in conjun. with moon, 10 p.m.
,, 8 Mercury in conjun. with moon, 2 p.m.
,, 11 Mars in conjun. with moon, 6 a.m.
,, 13 Jupiter in conjun. with moon, 4 p.m.
,, 16 Saturn in conjun. with moon, 8 p.m.

ASTRONOMICAL NOTES.

	1st—H.M.	15th—H.M.
♀ Venus rises	5 48 a.m.	rises 5 55 a.m.
♂ Mars sets	8 58 p.m.	sets 8 42 p.m.
♃ Jupiter sets	11 35 p.m.	sets 10 47 p.m.
♄ Saturn se's	8 7 a.m.	sets 2 11 a.m.

Venus morning star.

The times of rising and setting of the sun and moon are for the upper limb, corrected for parallax and refraction. Brisbane standard time.

Date	Day	MEMORANDA AND DIARY.	The Sun Rises	Sets	The Moon Rises	Sets	High Water on Brisbane Bar Morn.	Aftrn.
			H. M.	H. M.	A.M.	P.M.	H. M.	H. M.
1	Tu	*Lammas Day*—Bank Holiday.	6 30	5 18	2 8	0 46	5 25	5 58
2	W	Thames (N.Z.) Goldfield opened 1867	6 29	5 19	3 2	1 37	6 27	6 55
3	Th	Maryborough (Q). lit with gas 1879	6 29	5 19	3 52	2 30	7 20	7 45
4	F	Battle of Weissenburg 1870	6 28	5 20	4 38	3 24	8 6	8 28
5	S	Atlantic Cable completed 1858	6 27	5 20	5 19	4 18	8 48	9 7
6	⬤	*10th Sunday after Trinity.*	6 26	5 21	5 56	5 11	9 25	9 43
7	M	Rev. Dr. Lang died 1878	6 26	5 21	6 30	6 3	10 0	10 17
8	Tu	S.S. Catterthun wrecked 1895	6 25	5 22	7 1	6 55	10 34	10 50
9	W	First Land Sale held in Brisbane ..1843	6 24	5 22	7 32	7 46	11 6	11 22
10	Th	Greenwich Hospital founded 1675	6 23	5 23	8 2	8 38	11 39	11 55
11	F	Earthquake in Tasmania 1897	6 23	5 23	8 33	9 31	—	0 13
12	S	Brisbane Tramway opened 1885	6 22	5 24	9 6	10 25	0 30	0 50
13	☽	*11th Sunday after Trinity.*	6 21	5 24	9 42	11 22	1 10	1 31
14	M	☽ Sir Colin Campbell died 1863	6 20	5 25	10 23	A.M.	1 56	2 22
15	Tu	Ipswich (Q). lit with gas 1878	6 19	5 25	11 10	0 21	2 51	3 27
16	W	Royal Princes arrived at Brisbane ..1881	6 18	5 26	P.M.	1 21	4 6	4 56
17	Th	Earthquake in Melbourne 1855	6 17	5 26	1 3	2 21	5 38	6 13
18	F	Ben Tillett visited Brisbane 1897	6 17	5 27	2 9	3 18	6 46	7 17
19	S	New Exhibition Building, Bris., op. 1891	6 16	5 27	3 18	4 12	7 47	8 13
20	☽	*12th Sunday after Trinity.*	6 15	5 28	4 27	5 1	8 38	9 3
21	M	◯ 1st Q'land State Trial (Reg. v Pugh) 1861	6 14	5 28	5 36	5 46	9 26	9 48
22	Tu	Battle of Bosworth Field 1485	6 13	5 29	6 44	6 27	10 10	10 32
23	W	Lamington Bridge, Marybro., opd..1896	6 12	5 29	7 50	7 7	10 53	11 13
24	Th	*St. Bartholomew.*	6 11	5 30	8 55	7 47	11 35	11 56
25	F	Destructive fire at Charleville (Q)...1897	6 10	5 30	9 58	8 27	—	0 18
26	S	Battle of Cressy 1346	6 9	5 31	11 1	9 9	0 40	1 3
27	☽	*13th Sunday after Trinity.*	6 8	5 31	A.M.	9 54	1 29	1 55
28	M	☽ Eruption of Krakatoa, ...1883	6 7	5 32	0 1	10 37	2 24	2 55
29	Tu	Oliver Wendell Holmes, poet, born 1809	6 6	5 32	0 57	11 33	3 29	4 8
30	W	Battle of Plevna 1877	6 5	5 33	1 49	P.M.	4 52	5 32
31	Th	Gold Rush at Charters Towers 1872	6 4	5 33	2 36	1 20	6 2	6 30

Stewed Macaroni.—Add to 1 tablespoonful of butter mixed with 1 of flour, 4 tablespoonfuls each of stock and sweet cream ; season with salt and white pepper, add 2 ozs. boiled macaroni ; let it boil up, and serve hot.

Kentucky Cod.—Cut the cod into pieces about two inches square, season with pepper and salt, and roll in corn-meal (if this cannot be obtained use oatmeal). Fry some thin rolls of bacon, and arrange them round a hot dish. Fry the fish brown in the bacon fat ; if there is not enough in the pan, add some lard. Drain the fish, and arrange it in a pile on a hot dish with the fried bacon round.

SEPTEMBER, NINTH MONTH.   [1899.

Telephone 379.

QUEENSLAND MODEL DAIRY, Turbot Street.

PHASES OF THE MOON.
D.H.M.   D.H.M.

New Moon 5 1.33 p.m. | Full Moon 19 10:31 p.m.
First Quar. 13 7.49 a.m. | Last Quar. 27 1.2 a.m.
Apogee, 3 11 4 a.m. | Perigee, 18 4·9 p.m.
Apogee, 30 10 p.m.

ASTRONOMICAL PHENOMENA.
Sept. 4 Mercury in con. with the moon, 1 a.m.
 ,, 5 Venus in conjun. with the moon, noon
 ,, 8 Mars in conjun. with the moon, 11 p.m.
 ,, 10 Jupiter in con. with the moon. 5 a.m.
 ,, 13 Saturn in conjun. with the moon, 4 a.m.

ASTRONOMICAL NOTES.
1st—H. M.   15th—H. M.

♀ Venus rises 5 56 a.m. rises 5 51 a.m.
♂ Mars sets   8 26 p.m. sets 8 12 p.m.
♃ Jupiter sets 9 52 p.m. sets 9 8 p.m.
♄ Saturn sets 1 4 a.m. sets 0 11 a.m.
Venus morn. star.   Venus close to sun.

The times of rising and setting of the sun and moon are for the upper limb corrected for parallax and refraction. Brisbane standard time.

Date.	Day.	MEMORANDA AND DIARY.	THE SUN Rises	THE SUN Sets	THE MOON Rises	THE MOON Sets	High Water on Brisbane Bar Morn.	High Water on Brisbane Bar Aftrn.
			H. M.	H. M.	A.M.	P.M.	H. M.	H. M.
1	F	Great Earthquake in New Zealand 1888	6 3	5 34	3 18	2 13	6 56	7 19
2	S	Moreton Bay Settlement founded ..1824	6 2	5 34	3 57	2 6	7 41	8 2
3	S	14th Sun. after Trinity.	6 0	5 35	4 31	3 59	8 21	8 39
4	M	French Republic proclaimed 1970	5 59	5 35	5 4	4 51	8 56	9 14
5	Tu	● First American Congress assembld 1773	5 58	5 36	5 35	5 42	9 30	9 48
6	W	Brisbane proclaimed a Municipality 1859	5 57	5 36	6 5	6 34	10 3	10 19
7	Th	H.M.S. Captain found., 500 lost ..1870	5 56	5 36	6 37	7 27	10 36	10 58
8	F	Sebastopol taken 1855	5 55	5 37	7 9	8 21	11 10	11 27
9	S	Mirani Bridge, Mackay, opened....1897	5 54	5 37	7 44	9 17	11 46	—
10	S	15th Sunday after Trinity.	5 53	5 38	8 23	10 14	0 4	0 24
11	M	Rioting in Brisbane 1866	5 51	5 38	9 7	11 13	0 45	1 9
12	Tu	S.S. Dandenong foundered 1876	5 50	5 39	9 57	A.M.	1 33	2 1
13	W	☽ Battle of Tel-el-Kebir..........1882	5 49	5 39	10 53	0 11	2 31	3 6
14	Th	Duke of Wellington died 1852	5 48	5 40	11 54	1 7	3 45	4 33
15	F	Cairo occupied 1882	5 47	5 40	P.M.	2 1	5 20	5 58
16	S	First Railway opened 1830	5 46	5 41	2 6	2 50	6 30	7 1
17	S	16th Sunday after Trinity.	5 44	5 41	3 13	3 36	7 28	7 55
18	M	Revolution in Spain.............1868	5 43	5 41	4 21	4 18	8 18	8 41
19	Tu	○ President Garfield died 1881	5 42	5 42	5 27	4 58	9 4	9 26
20	W	Delhi taken 1857	5 41	5 42	6 34	5	9 46	10 8
21	Th	St. Matthew. Sir W. Scott died ..1832	5 40	5 43	7 39	6 19	10 29	10 50
22	F	Lord Denman died 1854	5 39	5 43	8 44	7 1	11 12	11 34
23	S	Perth, W.A., constituted a city 1856	5 38	5 44	9 46	7 46	11 55	—
24	S	17th Sunday after Trinity.	5 36	5 44	10 46	8 35	0 19	0 42
25	M	Ipswich Grammar School opened ..1862	5 35	5 45	11 41	9 26	1 6	1 32
26	Tu	First N.S.W. Railway opened.....1855	5 34	5 45	A.M.	10 19	2 8	2 28
27	W	☾ George Cruikshank, arti-t, born ..1792	5 33	5 46	0 31	11 13	2 59	3 32
28	Th	Professor Louis Pasteur died.....1895	5 32	5 46	1 15	P.M.	4 10	4 50
29	F	St. Michael.—Michaelmas Day.	5 31	5 46	1 55	1 1	5 27	5 56
30	S	Lord Nelson born...............1758	5 30	5 47	2 32	1 53	6 21	6 44

Veal Pie.—An excellent dish for a plain home dinner is made by stewing some veal until it is tender; thicken the gravy with flour, and season with pepper and salt, and put in enough butter to flavour it; then make a nice crust-like biscuit dough. Put the veal and gravy into an earthen pudding dish, and cover the dish with the crust. Bake and serve hot.

Good Breakfast Dish.—Cut thin slices of cold roast beef, and lay them in a tin saucepan set in a pot of boiling water. Cover them with a gravy made of three tablespoonsful of melted butter, one of walnut ketchup, a teaspoonful of vinegar, a little pepper and salt, a spoonful of currant jelly, one of made mustard and some warm water. Cover tightly, and steam half an-hour, keeping the water in the outer vessel on a hard boil.

OCTOBER, TENTH MONTH. [1899.

<table>
<tr><td colspan="2">PHASES OF THE MOON.</td></tr>
<tr><td>D. H.M.</td><td>D. H.M.</td></tr>
<tr><td>New Moon 5 5.14 a.m.</td><td>Full Moon 19 8.4 a.m.</td></tr>
<tr><td>First Quar. 12 4.9 p.m.</td><td>Last Quar. 26 7.40 p.m.</td></tr>
<tr><td>Perigee, 16 8.3 p.m.</td><td>Apogee, 28 3.3 p.m.</td></tr>
</table>

ASTRONOMICAL PHENOMENA.

Oct. 5 Mercury in conjun. with moon. 4 p.m.
" 5 Venus in conjun. with moon, 9. p.m.
" 7 Mars in conjunction with moon, 4 p.m.
" 7 Jupiter in conjun. with moon, 8 p.m.
" 10 Saturn in conjun. with moon, noon.
" 12 Mars in conjunction with Jupiter, 3 a.m.
" 30 Venus in conjun. with Jupiter, 11 a.m.

ASTRONOMICAL NOTES.

1st – H.M.   15th—H. M.
♀ Venus sets 6 4 p.m. sets 6 28 p.m.
♂ Mars sets 7 58 p.m. sets 7 48 p.m.
♃ Jupiter sets 8 19 p.m. sets 7 37 p.m.
♄ Saturn sets 11 8 p.m. sets 10 18 p.m.
Venus evening star.
The times of rising and setting of the sun and moon are for the upper limb, corrected for parallax and refraction. Brisbane standard time.

Date.	Day.	MEMORANDA AND DIARY.	The Sun Rises	Sets	The Moon Rises A.M.	Sets P.M.	High Water on Brisbane Bar. Morn. H. M.	Aftrn. H. M.
			H. M.	H. M.	A.M.	P.M.	H. M.	H. M.
1	S	*18th Sunday after Trinity.*	5 28	5 47	3 5	2 45	7 7	7 28
2	M	1st train, Brisbane and Gladstone..1897	5 27	5 48	3 36	3 37	7 47	8 5
3	Tu	Bible first translated into English..1535	5 26	5 48	4 7	4 29	8 23	8 41
4	W	Earthquake at Nelson, N.Z. 1870	5 25	5 49	4 38	5 21	8 58	9 15
5	Th	● Torrens Dam destroyed 1867	5 24	5 49	5 11	6 ●	9 33	9 50
6	F	Lord Tennyson died............1892	5 23	5 50	5 45	7 11	10 8	10 26
7	S	1st Brisbane School of Arts opened 1851	5 22	5 50	6 24	8 9	10 45	11 5
8	S	*19th Sunday after Trinity.*	5 21	5 51	7 6	9 7	11 25	11 46
9	M	Sir A. Musgrave, Gov. of Q'land, d. 1888	5 20	5 51	7 54	10 6	———	0 8
10	Tu	Great fire at Coolgardie, W.A. 1895	5 19	5 52	8 48	11 2	0 30	0 55
11	W	Sydney University inaugurated 1852	5 18	5 53	9 47	11 55	1 21	1 50
12	Th	☽ America discovered by Columbus ..1492	5 17	5 53	10 49	A.M.	2 19	2 52
13	F	General R. E. Lee, C.S.A., died....1870	5 15	5 54	11 53	0 44	3 29	4 12
14	S	Battle of Hastings 1066	5 15	5 54	P.M.	1 30	4 57	5 36
15	S	*20th Sunday after Trinity.*	5 13	5 55	0 3	2 12	6 9	6 38
16	M	British Houses of Parliament burnt 1834	5 12	5 55	3 8	2 51	7 6	7 30
17	Tu	Gold Creek Reservoir completed ..1885	5 11	5 56	4 13	3 30	7 55	8 17
18	W	St. Luke. Pettigrew's Sawmill burnd.1874	5 10	5 56	5 17	4 10	8 40	9 3
19	Th	○ Dean Swift died 1745	5 9	5 57	6 23	4 51	9 23	9 45
20	F	J. A. Froude, historian, died 1894	5 8	5 58	7 27	5 35	10 7	10 29
21	S	Battle of Trafalgar 1805	5 8	5 58	8 29	6 23	10 51	11 14
22	S	*21st Sunday after Trinity.*	5 7	5 59	9 28	7 14	11 36	11 59
23	M	First cable message London to Bris. 1872	5 6	6 0	10 21	8 8	———	0 21
24	Tu	Fort Macquarie, Sydney, completed 1803	5 6	6 0	11 9	9 3	0 44	1 9
25	W	Battle of Balaclava 1854	5 4	6 1	11 51	9 58	1 32	1 59
26	Th	☾ S.S. Royal Charter wrecked 1859	5 3	6 2	A.M.	10 53	2 25	2 51
27	F	Capture of Metz............. 1870	5 2	6 2	0 29	11 48	3 21	3 54
28	S	*St. Simon and St. Jude.*	5 1	6 3	1 4	P.M.	4 29	5 4
29	S	*22nd Sunday after Trinity.*	5 0	6 3	1 36	1 29	5 34	6 0
30	M	1st dir. shipmnt. Bris. to Manch'st'r 1895	5 0	6 4	2 7	2 21	6 23	6 45
31	Tu	St. Patrick's Cathedral, Melb., op...1897	4 59	6 5	2 38	3 13	7 7	7 28

Mushroom Salad.—Cut the mushrooms into small pieces, and cook them in a little olive oil ; allow them to simmer for a quarter of an hour ; put in a teaspoonful of lemon-juice, and let them stand and cool.   When cold, place them in a salad-bowl, and season with salt, pepper, and chopped parsley ; two drops of onion-juice should be rubbed round the salad-bowl.   Pour over all a nice mayonnaise dressing and serve.

NOVEMBER, ELEVENTH MONTH. [1899.

PHASES OF THE MOON.

D.H.M.   D.H.M.

New Moon 3 8.26 p.m. | Full Moon 17 8 18 p.m.
First Quar. 10 11.35 p.m. | Last Quar. 25 4.34 p.m.
Perigee, 12 10.3 p.m.   Apogee, 25 noon.

ASTRONOMICAL PHENOMENA.

Nov.   4 Jupiter in conjun. with moon, 1 p.m.
"   4 Venus in conjun. with moon, 11 p.m.
"   5 Mars in conjun. with moon, 10 a.m.
"   5 Mercury in conjun. with moon, 11 a.m.
"   6 Saturn in conjun. with moon, 10 p.m.
"   16 Venus in conjun. with Mars, 10 p.m.
"   28 Venus in conjun. with Saturn, 7 a.m.

ASTRONOMICAL NOTES.

1st—H. M.   15th—H. M.

♀ Venus sets 7   0 p.m.   sets 7 27 p.m.
♂ Mars sets 7 38 p.m.   sets 7 30 p.m.
♃ Jupiter sets 6 47 p.m. rises 4 49 a.m.
♄ Saturn sets 9 17 p.m. sets 8 29 p.m.

Venus evening star.

The times of rising and setting of the sun and moon are for the upper limb, corrected for parallax and refraction. Brisbane standard time.

Date	Day	MEMORANDA AND DIARY.	THE SUN Rises	THE SUN Sets	THE MOON Rises	THE MOON Sets	High Water on Brisbane Bar. Morn.	High Water on Brisbane Bar. Aftrn.
			H. M.	H. M.	A.M.	P.M.	H. M.	H. M.
1	W	*All Saints.*— Valley Railway opened 1890	4 58	6 6	3 10	4 7	7 47	8 7
2	Th	Cleveland Railway opened........1889	4 57	6 6	3 44	5 2	8 26	8 46
3	F	St. Jean D'Acre taken 1840	4 57	6 7	4 22	6 0	9 5	9 24
4	S	Famine in Paris 1870	4 56	6 8	5 3	6 59	9 44	10 5
5	☽	*23rd Sunday after Trinity.*	4 55	6 8	5 51	7 59	10 26	10 49
6	M	Peace with America............1783	4 54	6 9	6 44	8 57	11 11	11 34
7	Tu	First *Gazette* published 1665	4 54	6 10	7 41	9 52	11 57	—
8	W	John Milton died 1674	4 53	6 11	8 43	10 43	0 21	0 46
9	Th	Prince of Wales born 1841	4 53	6 11	9 47	11 28	1 11	1 38
10	F	☽ Masonic Hall, Brisbane, consc. .1886	4 52	6 12	10 51	A.M.	2 6	2 36
11	S	*Martinmas—Half-Quarter Day.*	4 52	6 13	11 54	0 10	3 9	3 45
12	☽	*24th Sunday after Trinity.*	4 51	6 14	P.M.	0 50	4 25	5 6
13	M	Cable Id. set. C. York and T. Island 1886	4 51	6 15	1 59	1 28	5 41	6 11
14	Tu	Sir H. W. Norman left Brisbane .1895	4 50	6 15	3 2	2 6	6 39	7 6
15	W	Great fire at Charleville.........1897	4 50	6 16	4 6	2 45	7 30	7 55
16	Th	John Bright born 1811	4 49	6 17	5 9	3 27	8 18	8 41
17	F	☉ Suez Canal opened...........1869	4 49	6 18	6 12	4 12	9 4	9 26
18	S	Cardinal Pole died 1558	4 48	6 18	7 12	5 2	9 48	10 10
19	☽	*25th Sunday after Trinity.*	4 48	6 19	8 9	5 54	10 33	10 55
20	M	Great fire at Melbourne 1897	4 48	6 20	8 59	6 50	11 17	11 38
21	Tu	Lord Hampden arr. at Sydney 1895	4 48	6 21	9 45	7 46	11 59	—
22	W	River Amazon discovered 1540	4 47	6 21	10 25	8 41	0 20	0 42
23	Th	Duke of Edinburgh arr. in Melb. ..1867	4 47	6 22	11 1	9 36	1 3	1 25
24	F	Tasmania discovered 1642	4 47	6 23	11 35	10 29	1 46	2 10
25	S	☾ John Knox died 1572	4 46	6 23	A.M.	11 20	2 33	2 57
26	☽	*26th Sunday after Trinity.*	4 46	6 24	0 6	P.M.	3 26	3 54
27	M	Alexander Dumas, novelist, died ..1895	4 46	6 25	0 37	1 3	4 29	4 59
28	Tu	Great flood at Melbourne.......1849	4 46	6 26	1 8	1 55	5 33	5 59
29	W	Cardinal Wolsey died...........1530	4 46	6 27	1 41	2 50	6 22	6 46
30	Th	*St. Andrew.*—Bank Holiday.	4 46	6 27	2 16	3 47	7 10	7 33

Chicken Pie for Invalids.—Skin and cut a fowl into joints, put into a deep pie-dish with a little pepper and salt, one hard-boiled egg cut into slices, and two slices of bacon; fill the dish with water, then cut thick slices of bread, remove the crust, moisten with water, and dredge with flour; then cut and fit the bread to form a crust, cover the dish, and bake in a moderate oven till of a nice brown colour. This crust is very easy of digestion.

DECEMBER, TWELFTH MONTH. [1899.

PHASES OF THE MOON.

D.H.M.	D.H.M.
New Moon 3 10.47 a.m	Full Moon 17 11.31 a.m
First Quar. 10 7.2 a.m.	Last Quar. 25 1.57 p.m
Perigee, 7. 4.2 p.m.	Apogee, 23 9 a.m

ASTRONOMICAL PHENOMENA.

Dec. 2 Jupiter in conjun. with moon, 8 a.m.
,, 9 Mercury in conjun. with moon, 11 p.m.
,, 3 Sun eclipsed; invisible in Q'land.
,, 4 Mars in conjunction with moon, 7 a.m.
,, 4 Saturn in conjun. with moon, 11 a.m.
,, 4 Venus in conjun. with moon, 12 p.m.
,, 17 Moon eclipsed; invisible in Q'land.
,, 30 Jupiter in conjun. with moon, 4 a.m.
,, 31 Mercury in conjun. with moon, 9 a.m.

ASTRONOMICAL NOTES.

	1st — H. M.	15th — H. M.
♀ Venus sets	7 57 p.m.	sets 8 17 p.m.
♂ Mars sets	7 22 p.m.	s ts 7 14 p.m.
♃ Jupiter rises	3 59 a.m.	rises 3 14 a.m.
♄ Saturn sets	7 24 p.m.	sets 6 46 p.m.

Venus evening star.
The times of rising and setting of the sun and moon are for the upper limb corrected for parallax and refraction. Brisbane standard time.

Date.	Day.	MEMORANDA AND DIARY.	The Sun Rises	The Sun Sets	The Moon Rises	The Moon Sets	High Water on Brisbane Bar Morn.	High Water on Brisbane Bar Aftrn.
			H. M.	H. M.	P.M.	A.M.	H. M.	H. M.
1	F	Princess of Wales born 1844	4 46	6 28	2 56	4 46	7 56	8 18
2	S	River Brisbane first explored 1823	4 46	6 29	3 42	5 46	8 41	9 3
3	☽	●Advent Sunday.	4 46	6 30	4 33	6 46	9 26	9 49
4	M	Thomas Carlyle born 1795	4 46	6 30	5 31	7 44	10 12	10 36
5	Tu	Mozart died 1795	4 46	6 31	6 33	8 37	11 0	11 23
6	W	Louis Blanc died at Cannes 1882	4 46	6 32	7 38	9 26	11 46	
7	Th	Baron de Lesseps died 1894	4 46	6 33	8 43	10 10	0 10	0 34
8	F	Hon. W. Hobbs, M.D.,M.L.C. died 1890	4 46	6 33	9 48	10 50	0 58	1 22
9	S	S.S. Keilawarra wrecked 1886	4 47	6 34	10 51	11 27	1 47	2 15
10	☽	☾2nd Sunday in Advent.	4 47	6 35	11 53	A.M.	2 48	3 14
11	M	S.S. Fitzroy wrecked............ 1897	4 47	6 35	P.M. 0 6	3 49	4 29	
12	Tu	Terrible Explosion at Ch. Towers ..1897	4 47	6 36	1 56	0 44	5 10	5 44
13	W	Toowoomba Telephone Exch. op... 1897	4 48	6 37	2 58	1 24	6 14	6 42
14	Th	Church Institute, Brisbane. op. ...1897	4 48	6 37	4 0	2 7	7 9	7 55
15	F	Rockhampton procl. municipality.. 1860	4 48	6 38	5 0	2 53	8 0	8 23
16	S	Canterbury (N.Z.) settled.........1850	4 48	6 39	5 57	3 44	8 47	9 10
17	☽	○3rd Sunday in Advent.	4 49	6 39	6 50	4 38	9 32	9 54
18	M	Pialba Railway opened 1896	4 49	6 40	7 38	5 33	10 15	10 35
19	Tu	Twofold Bay discovered by Bass ..1797	4 49	6 40	8 20	6 30	10 56	11 15
20	W	First Sod Mackay Railway turned..1883	4 50	6 41	8 59	7 25	11 35	11 53
21	Th	St. Thomas.	4 50	6 41	9 33	8 19	——	0 12
22	F	Marion Evans (George Eliot) died 1880	4 51	6 42	10 5	9 11	0 30	0 49
23	S	Lord Romilly died 1874	4 51	6 42	10 36	10 3	1 8	1 28
24	☽	4th Sunday in Advent.	4 52	6 43	11 7	10 50	1 47	2 8
25	M	☾Christmas Day.—Bank Holiday.	4 52	6 43	11 38	11 45	2 31	2 55
26	Tu	St. Stephen.—Bank Holiday.	4 53	6 43	A.M. 0 37	3 22	3 52	
27	W	St. John.	4 54	6 44	0 12	1 32	4 28	5 4
28	Th	Innocents Day. Lord Macaulay died, 1859	4 54	6 44	0 49	2 29	5 38	6 7
29	F	Tay Bridge destroyed by storm 1879	4 55	6 45	1 31	3 28	6 35	7 2
30	S	Sydney Exchange opened 1857	4 55	6 45	2 19	4 28	7 29	7 55
31	☽	Sunday after Christmas.	4 56	6 45	3 14	5 28	8 20	8 46

Chicken and Parsley Pie.—Cut up, wash, and dry a chicken; season with salt. Pick and scald some parsley, then squeeze it quite dry; mince it, and lay in a pie-dish. On this lay some of the chicken until the dish is full. Pour in milk almost to the top of the dish; cover with a nice paste, and bake. When cooked, pour off some of the milk, and add half-a-pint of cream. Serve very hot.

Queensland Official Grocers' Price List

H. V. BIRCHLEY'S

GROCERIES LIST.

For High-class Teas, Groceries and Provisions,

All prices subject to market fluctuations,

Any article on this List not in stock can be procured.

Acid—   s. d.
- Acetic .. .. per bottle
- Carbolic .. .. ,,
- Citric .. .. per lb
- Tartaric, Powdered .. .. .. ,,
- Salicylic .. .. ,,

First | Taylor and Sons' Jams | Prize

Avena .. ..

Almonds—
- Jordan .. .. per lb
- Soft Shell .. .. ,,

Alum, Lump .. .. ,,

Annatto—Barnekow's .. .. .. per bottle

Arnica .. .. ,,

Arrowroot—1lb packets .. .. .. per lb
- Crescent, 1lb packets .. .. .. ,,
- Red Cross ,, ... ,,
- Atlas .. .. ,,
- Sun ... . ,,
- Lahey's, 1lb packets .. .. ..
- Lahey's ½lb packets .. .. ..

Asparagus—2lb tins .. .. .. per tin

Baking Powder—See Powders

Balsam—
- Friar's .. .. per bottle
- Powell's .. .. ,,

Barley—
- Patent, Robinson's .. .. .. per tin
- Pearl .. .. per lb

Beans—Haricot .. .. per lb

Beeswax .. .. ,,

We Recommend SQUATTER WHISKY.

s. d.

Beef—Baynes Bros. Luncheon, square tins, 1lb   per tin

     "   "   "   2lb   "

     Fitzroy   "   "   1lb   "

     "   "   "   2lb   "

Biscuits—Hiron's Arrowroot, Almond Rings,   per lb

     Afternoon Tea, Cabin, Cheese Crackers, Cocoa Nut, Cracknells, Currant Lunch, Extra Coffee, Extra Fancy Mixed, Ginger Nuts, Lemon Cream, Ladies' Fingers, Milk Arrowroot, Milk, Soda, Sultanas, Sutton Rusks, Thin Captains, Water, Wine

     Huntley & Palmer   ..   ..   ..   "

     Rankin & Morrow   ..   ..   ..   "

     Robertson's Mixed, Arrowroot, &c.   ..   "

     Arnott's   ..   ..   "

     Bouchard's   ..   ..   "

     Medcraf's   ..   ..   "

     Witham's   ..   ..   "

Bitters—Philadelphia   ..   ..   .. per bottle

Blue—

     Colman's   ..   ..   per lb

     Freeman's, 1oz. squares   ...   ..   per doz

     Keen's   ...   .   per lb

First | Taylor and Sons' Jams | Prize

     Maison's   ...   .   per lb

     Reckitt's   ...   .   per doz

Blue Stone—

Blacking—

     Atlas ..   ..   per doz

     Day & Martin's   ...   .   "

     Jacquot, No. 4   ...   .   each

     Peerless Gloss   ..   ..   ..   "

     Miller's Harness Dress   ...   .   "

Boards—

     17in Wood Wash   ..   ..   "

     17in Wood and Zinc   ..   ..   "

Borax—

     Lump   ...   .   per lb

     Powdered   ..   ..   "

Brosemeal— ..   ..   per bag

Brooms—

     Millet   ..   ..   each

     Hair and Bass, various, splendid values   ...   "

Bricks—Bath   ..   ..   "

Butter--Best   ..   ..   per lb

Cakes—

     Hiron's Christmas Cakes, seed, in 1lb, 2lb, and 4lb tins or card boxes   ..   ..

We Recommend SQUATTER WHISKY.

	s. d.

CAKES—
    Canterbury Cakes, Hiron's, 1lb in foil paper,
        2lb in boxes   ..   ..
    Square Cakes, special for picnics or meetings,
        Hiron's, made to order   ..   ..

Camphor— ..   ..

Camomile Flowers—1oz packets .. per doz

Candles—
    Apollo ..   .. per packet
    Bougie's ..   .. ,,
    Cab or Lamp, 12's ... . ,,
    Carriage, 8's ... . ,,
    D.R.J., 5 Medal ..   ..   .. ,,
    Moulds ..   ..   ..   each
    Electricine ..   ..   .. per packet

Capers ..   .. per bottle

Cassia ..   ..   .. per lb

Cement ..   ..   .. per bottle

Cheese—The finest qualities always on hand

Chicory—Ground ..   .. per lb
    Crescent ..   ..   .. ,,
    Atlas ..   .. ,,

Chlorodyne ..   ..   .. per bottle

Chutney—Sweet Sliced Mango, &c. .. ,,
    ,,   Vencatachellum ..   .. ,,

First | Taylor and Sons' Jams | Prize

Cinnamon—Whole ..   ..   .. per lb

Cloves ..   .. ,,

Cocoa—
    ¼lb and ½lb tins, Van Houten's ..   .. per tin
    ¼lb tins, De Rooy's ..   ..   .. ,,
    ¼lb tins, Cadbury's ..   ..   .. ,,
    ¼lb tins, Fry's ..   .. ,,
    Gold Star ..   .. ,,

Cocoanut—Desiccated ..   .. ¼lb, each
    ,,   ,, ...   ½lb, ,,

Coffee—Pure Ground, in tins ..   .. ¼lb, each
    ,,   ,,   ,, ...! ½lb, ,,
    ,,   No. 1 Turkish ..   ..   ..
    ,,   No. 2 Turkish ..   ..   ..
    ,,   Single Crescent ..   ..   ..
    ,,   Double Crescent ..   ..   ..
    ,,   Blue French ..   ..   ..
    ,,   Red   ,, ...
    ,,   Plantation ..   ..   ..
    ,,   Mocha ..   ..
    ,,   Genuine Pure Mocha ..   ..
    ,,   Atlas ..   ..
    ,,   Egyptian..   ..   ..   ..
    ,,   Cowley's ..   ..

We Recommend SQUATTER WHISKY.

TELEPHONE No. 163.
TELEGRAPHIC ADDRESS "HIRON," TOOWONG.

● ● ●

GEORGE HIRON,

STEAM BISCUIT AND CONFECTIONERY MANUFACTURER AND FLOUR MILLER,

Toowong, Brisbane.

MAKER OF THE QUEEN'S JUBILEE CAKE.

Awarded 4 Gold Medals ......
Queensland International Exhibition, 1897.

Special Gold Medal for Biscuits
Gold Medal for Confectionery
Special Gold Medal for Cakes
Gold Medal for Icing Sugar

※

ASK YOUR GROCER FOR HIRON'S SPECIAL GOLD MEDAL BISCUITS, AND SEE THAT YOU GET THEM.

MILK ARROWROOTS.	RASPBERRY SANDWICHES.	EXTRA FANCY MIXED.
LEMON CREAMS.	EXTRA COFFEE.	MARIES.
	FAIRY CAKES, &c., &c.	

WEDDING, BIRTHDAY, AND TEA MEETING CAKES TO ORDER.

My 1lb. and 2lb. tins of Biscuits, and Fruit Cakes in round tins or card boxes, very suitable for Picnic Parties and for sending to friends at a distance.

When next ordering from your grocer ask for my latest speciality, FAIRY CAKES, they are delicious

Owing to the great demand last year you are respectfully asked to order early my ICED XMAS CAKES as the festive season approaches.

s. d.

Coffee Beans .. ..
    Atlas .. ..

Cornflour .. ..   per lb
    Cornflour or Maizena (Lahey's), 1lb packets.
    ,, ,, ,, ½lb packets.

Confectionery—Crystallised Fruits ..
    Hiron's Fancy Packets, assorted ..
    Hiron's Assorted Animals (dogs, cows, etc.)
    Liquorice (stick, cakes, wire, etc.) ..
    Candies (sugar, assorted colours) .. ..
    Jujubes (all sorts) .. .. ..
    Chocolate Creams, Cakes, etc. .. ..
    Peppermint and Coltsfoot Sticks .. ..
    Lozenges—Peppermint, Cough no More,
      Conversation, Extra Strong Mint ..
    Mixtures—London, Scotch ..
    Rings, Comfits, Sugared Almonds, Aniseed
      Balls, Thousands, Butter Scotch, etc., etc.
    Rankin & Morrow's .. .. ..
    Medcraf's .. ..
    Witham's .. ..
    Bellotti's .. ..
    Bouchard's .. ..
    Treagle's .. ..
    Alexander & Co.'s .. .. ..

Cream of Tartar .. .. ..   per lb
    Atlas .. ..

First | Taylor and Sons' Jams | Prize

Curry—Morton's .. .. per bottle
  ,,   Vencatachellum .. .. per tin
  ,,   Crescent .. .. ,,

Disinfectants Condy's Fluid .. .. per bottle
  ,,   Dr. Fitsch's .. 1lb tins, each
Egg Powder—Royal .. .. .. per packet
  ,,   Atlas .. .. ..
  ,,   Sanbergue's .. ..
Essences—1oz bottles, assorted .. .. each
  ,,   Atlas . .. .
Essence of Coffee and Chicory—
    Symington's 10oz .. .. .. ,,
    ,,   5oz .. .. .. ,,
    Jenkins' .. .. ,,
    Star .. .. ,,
Eucalyptus Oil .. .. .. per bottle
Exterminator—Steele's Cockroach .. per packet
  ,,   Steele's White Ant ..
  ,,   Street's White Ant ..
Extract of Meat—Liebig's .. .. each
  ,,   2oz, Fitzroy, ... ,,
  ,,   4oz, ,, ... ,,

We Recommend SQUATTER WHISKY.

QUEENSLAND MODEL DAIRY, Turbot Street. Telephone 379.

s. d.

For High-class Butter, Telephone 379.

Fish—Anchovies in Oil	..	..	..	tins, each	
,, Bloaters ..	..	..	..	tins, ,,	
,, Findon Haddocks	..	..	..	tins, ,,	
,, Herrings, Fresh	..	..	..	tins, ,,	
,, Herrings, Morton's	..	..	..	tins, ,,	
,, Herrings, Bruce's	..	..	...	tins, ,,	
,, Herrings, Maconochie's	..	..	tins, ,,	
,, Herrings, Kippered	..	..	..	tins, ,,	
,, ,, ,, Morton's	..	tins, ,,	
,, ,, ,, Bruce's	..	tins, ,,	
,, ,, ,, Maconochie's	..	tins, ,,	
,, Herrings, Red	..	..	..	tins, ,,	
,, ,, ,, Morton's	..	tins, ,,	
,, ,, ,, Bruce's	..	tins, ,,	
,, Herrings, Salt	..	..	..	tins, ,,	
,, Lobsters, good brands	..	canned, ,,	
,, Ling	..	..	..	per lb	
,, Mackerel, Fresh	..	..	canned, each	
,, Oysters, Fresh	..	..	canned, ,,	
,, Salmon, Fresh	..	..	canned, ,,	
,, Sardines	..	..	..	canned, ,,	
TOORBUL FISH COMPANY—					
Tinned Schnapper	..	..	..	,,	
,, Bream	..	..	..	,,	
,, Jew Fish	..	..	..	,,	
,, Whiting	..	..	..	,,	

First | Taylor and Sons' Jams | Prize

Tinned Mullet	..	..	..	each	
,, Oysters	..	..	..	,,	
,, Prawns	..	..	..	,,	
,, Crabs	..	..	..	,,	
DR. BANCROFT—Mullet	..	..	..	,,	
Flour—20lb bags	..	..	..	,,	
,, 50lb ,,	..	..	..	,,	
,, 100lb ,,	..	..	..	,,	
,, ..	..	..	..	per ton	
,, Self-raising, 2lb packets	..	..	per packet	
,, Crescent Self-raising	..	..	,,	
,, Atlas Self-raising	..	..	..	
Food—Allen & Hanbury's	..	..	per tin	
,, Benger's	..	..	..	,,	
,, Mellin's	..	..	..	,,	
,, Neave's	..	..	..	,,	
, Nestle's	..	..	..	,,	
Fruit—Currants, prime fruit	..	..	per lb	
,, Prunes	..	..	..	,,	
,, Sultanas	..	..	..	,,	
., Dates, prime fruit	..	..	,,	
,, Elemes, prime fruit	..	..	,,	
,, Figs, 12oz boxes, prime fruit	..	per box	
,, Muscatels, prime fruit	..	..	per lb	
,, Apples, Dried	..	..	..	,,	
,, Peaches, Dried	..	..	..	,,	

We Recommend SQUATTER WHISKY.

s. d.

Fruit Salt—Eno's	..	..	.. per bottle	
Fuller's Earth	..	..	.. per packet	
Gelatine—Nelson's, 1oz packets	..	..	each	
Ginger—Ground	..	..	..	per lb
„ Crescent	..	..	..	„
„ Whole, Bleached	..	..	..	„
„ 1lb tins, Dry	..	..	..	„
Gloss—Bon Ton	..	..	..	each
„ Peerless ..	..	..	..	„
„ Satin Polish, Brown's	..	..	..	„
„ Tan Polish	..	..	..	„
Glaze, Starch	..	..	.. per packet	
Glycerine—1oz bottles	..	..	..	each
„ 4oz „	..	..	..	„
Groats—McKenzie's	..	..	..	per tin
„ Robinson's (English)	..	..	..	„
„ Harper's	..	..	..	„
„ Atlas ..	..	..	..	„
Grease (Axle)—Bidwell's	..	..	..	„
„ Crescent	..	..	..	„
Gum—Small Bottles	..	..	..	

First | Taylor and Sons' Jams | Prize

Ham—Devilled ..	..	..	canned, each	
„ for counter cutting	..	..	per lb	
„ Pineapple	..	..	..	„
„ Corn Cob	..	..	..	„
Herbs (Dried)—Atlas ..	..	..		
"Hire's" Root Beer	..	..	.. per packet	
Honey—Finest, bottles (pickle)	..	..	each	
„ „ tins, 2lb, lever lids	..	..	„	
„ Orange Blossom..	..	..		
„ Harper's	..	..		
„ Atlas ..	..	..		
Hops—Bavarian, ½lb packets	..	..	per packet	
„ „ 1lb „	..	..	„	
„ Crown ½lb „	..	..	„	
„ „ 1lb „	..	..	„	
Ink—Miniature, glass bottles	..	..	per doz	
„ ½ pint bottles	..	..	each	
Insectibane—McBrair's Blattabane	..	per tin		
Insecticide—Crescent ..	..	..	„	
„ Keating's Powder	..	..	„	
„ Atlas ..	..	..	„	
Isinglass—1oz packets, Swinbourne's	..	per doz		

We Recommend SQUATTER WHISKY.

We Ship Butter to all parts F.O.B. Brisbane. QUEENSLAND MODEL DAIRY.

Gold Medal Condensed Milk. VERNEYS, Agents.

		s.	d.
Jams—Barnes', assorted	each		
" "	per doz		
" Cairns'	each		
" "	per doz		
" C. & B.	each		
" "	per doz		
" Eclipse, 1lb, assorted	each		
" "	per doz		
" Reis Bros.,' 1lb, assorted	each		
" " " "	per doz		
" Gray's	each		
" "	per doz		
" New England	each		
" "	per doz		
" "Cannon," 1lb tins assorted	each		
" " " "	per doz		
" Bain's, assorted	each		
" " "	per doz		
" Balgownie	each		
" "	per doz		
" Crown	each		
" "	per doz		
" Duthie's	each		
" "	per doz		

First | Taylor and Sons' Jams | Prize

JAMS — N.S.W.	each		
" "	per doz		
" Elms Bros.' Yacht Brand	each		
" " "	per doz		
" Diamond	each		
" "	per doz		
" Jubilee	each		
" "	per doz		
" Atlas	each		
" "	per doz		
" Deane's	each		
" "	per doz		
" Imperial	each		
" "	per doz		
" Taylor & Sons', tins	each		
" " "	per doz		
" " glass jars			
" Britannia, tins	each		
" " "	per doz		
" " glass jars			
Jellies—Calves' Foot			
Taylor & Sons', tins			
" " glass jars			
" Britannia, tins			
" " glass jars			
" Atlas			

QUEENSLAND MODEL DAIRY Deliver Butter Daily throughout City and Suburbs.

We Recommend SQUATTER WHISKY.

TAYLOR & SONS JAMS

Ask For

✳

TAYLOR & SONS

✳

TAYLOR & SONS' JAMS

Jams,

Jellies and

Marmalade.

✳ ✳ ✳

First and Special Prizes, Exhibition, 1897.

SPECIALITIES:

MELON AND LEMON, MARMALADE, CAPE GOOSE-
BERRY, WHOLE FRUIT STRAWBERRY CONSERVE,
MULBERRY; ALSO, TIP-TOP TOMATO SAUCE AND
TOMATO KETCHUP.

TAYLOR & SONS JAMS

TAYLOR & SONS,
Jam Manufacturers,

BRISBANE.

For High-class Butter, Telephone 379.

			s.	d.
JELLIES—				
,,	Pioneer ..			
,,	Imperial			
,,	Crown ..			
,	Elms Bros.'			
Ketchup—Tomato, Tip Top Brand		per bottle		
,,	Oldmeadow & Co.	,,		
Lead—Black, Reckitt's, 1oz Eclipse				
,,	,,	,,	1oz Zebra	
,,	,,	1oz		
Lentils		per lb		
Lemon Juice		per pint		
		per quart		
Lime Juice		per pint		
,,		per quart		
,,	Montserrat	per pint		
		per quart		
,,	Rose's	per pint		
Lime Juice Cordial—		per pint		
,,	,,	per quart		
Linseed		per lb		
,,	Crushed	,,		
Liquorice		,,		
Lines—Clothes, Flax and Manilla, al zes ..				
,,	Wire, 50 feet —100 feet			

First | Taylor and Sons' Jams | Prize

Lights—Clarke's Night		per doz	
,,	Field's	,,	
Mace—Ground		per lb	
,,	Whole	,,	
Macaroni		,,	
,,	Morton 7lb. tins	,,	
Magnesia—Bishop s Citrate		per bottle	
,,	Kruse's Fluid	,,	
,,	Powdered, 1oz packets	per doz	
Matches—Plaid Vestas, Bell & Black's		,,	
,,	,, 250's ,,	,,	
,,	Safety, Vulcan, large	,,	
,,	Helmet, 250's, No. 4	,,	
Marmalade—C. & B., glass jars		each	
,,	,,	per doz	
,,	Dundee, in tins	each	
,,	,, ,,	per doz	
,,	,, n glass jars	each	
,,	,, ,,	per doz	
,,	Robertson's Shred Jelly	each	
,,	,, ,,	per doz	
,,	Taylor & Sons', tins	each	
,,	, ,,	por doz	
,,	,, glass jars	each	
,,	,, ,,	per doz	

We Recommend SQUATTER WHISKY.

14

MARMALADE—

					s. d.
	Britannia, tins	..	..	each	
"	" "	..	..	per doz	
,	" glass jars		..	each	
	" "		..	per doz	
"	Atlas	..	..	each	
"	"	..	..	per doz	

Maizena .. .. per lb

Meal—Barley, Munn's .. .. .. per cwt
   " Oat, McKenzie's, 7lb bags .. .. per bag
   " " Granuma .. .. .. "
   " " Model .. .. .. "
   " " New Zealand, 7lb bags .. .. "
   " " Atlas .. .. .. "
   " " Star .. .. .. "
   " " Crescent .. .. .. "
   " Maize .. .. .. per lb
   " Wheat, 7lb bags .. .. per bag
   " " 3lb .. .. .. "

Meat and Fish Paste—glass jars C. & B.,
Anchovy, Bloater, Ham, Ham and Chicken,
&c., &c. .. ..

Meats—Baynes Bros., assorted ..
   Fitzroy .. .. ..
   Queensland Meat Export Co.'s 1lb.
    and 2lb. Corned Beef ..
   Ox Tongues .. .. ..

First | Taylor and Sons' Jams | Prize

C. & B. Potted Meats and Fish ..
Extract Fitzroy, 2oz, 4oz .. ..
Liebig's, 2oz, 4oz.. .. ..

Milk, Condensed—Nestle's .. .. per tin
   " Milkmaid .. .. .. "
   " Gold Medal .. .. .. "
   " Queen of Holland .. .. .. "
   " Atlas .. .. .. "

Mince Meats—1lb, Swallow & Ariell .. per lb

Mustard—Colman's D.S.F., ½lb tins .. each
   " " ¼lb tins .. "
   " Keen's " ½lb tins .. "
   " " ¼lb tins .. "
   " McKenzie's D.S.F., ½lb tins .. "
   " " ¼lb tins .. "

Nuts—Almonds .. .. .. per lb
   " Barcelona .. .. .. "
   " Brazils .. .. .. "
   " Walnuts .. .. .. "

Nutmegs .. .. .. per oz
   " .. .. .. per lb

Oats—Aunt Abbey's Rolled .. .. per packet
   " McKenzie's " 2lb packets .. "
   " Provost " 2lb cartoons .. "

We Recommend SQUATTER WHISKY.

The Ideal Food for All Climates, and for All Seasons.

Provost

A Treat from Home. OATS

Prepared in **Scotland** from the finest SCOTCH grain only,

Oats grown in **Scotland far excel** all others in Nutrition and Flavour, therefore eat PROVOST OATS.

They make more **Porridge** than equal weight of American Oats, and COST NO MORE, therefore Britons, support your own kith and kin.

PROVOST OATS make strong Men and Women and Bonnie Bairns.

They are less **heating** than the ordinary Oatmeal, and suitable for the most delicate, young or old, in all seasons or climates.

PROVOST OATS have the Largest Sale of Scotch Rolled Oats in the World, solely on their merits.

They are partly **cooked**, and make perfect Porridge in ten minutes.

Invaluable up **country**, where good Food is costly or difficult to obtain. Always **keep** them at hand.

Sold in 2lb. Cartoons at all Stores.

R. ROBINSON & SONS, SOLE MANUFACTURERS, ANNAN, SCOTLAND

WHOLESALE OF **MAXWELL** BROS., 17 HOUT STREET, CAPE TOWN, **AND** JOHANNESBURG.

●●●●●●●●●●●●

THOS. BROWN & SONS, Limited, Brisbane,

SOLE AGENTS FOR QUEENSLAND.

Gold Medal Milk—The Best. VERNEYS, Agents.

QUEENSLAND MODEL DAIRY Deliver Butter Daily throughout City and Suburbs

		s.	d.
OATS—			
,, Provost, Rolled 6lb bags ..	per bag		
Ointment—Holloway's	per box		
Oil—Castor, Morton's, 5oz	per bottle		
,, ,, ,, 10oz	,,		
,, ,, draught	per drum		
,, Colza			
,, Dugong	,,		
,, Kerosene, 150°	per case		
,, ,, Royal Diamond, Light of the Age, etc.	per tin		
,, Lucca, C. & B.	per bottle		
,, Linseed	,,		
,, ,, Crown	,,		
,, Machine, 2oz	,,		
,, Eucalyptus	,,		
,, Neatsfoot, reputed quarts	,,		
,, ,, ...	,,		
,, Salad, Morton's, 5oz	,,		
,, ,, ,, 10oz	,,		
,, ,, Heaton's, 5oz	,,		
,, ,, ,, 10oz	,,		
,, ,, Higgins' 5oz	,,		
,, St. Jacobs	,,		
Olives—French, Morton's, $\frac{1}{4}$-pts.	,,		
,, Spanish ,, $\frac{1}{2}$-pts.	,,		

First | Taylor and Sons' Jams | Prize

OLIVES—Spanish, Morton's, $\frac{1}{4}$-pts.	per bottle		
Pain Killer—Perry Davis'	each		
Paste—Glass Jars, C. & B. Anchovy, Bloater, &c.	,,		
,, Bloater, Morton's, 4oz tins	,,		
,, Anchovy, ,, 4oz tins	,,		
,, Assorted, 1oz tins, Maconochie's ..	,,		
,, ,, ,, ,, ..	per doz		
,, Fitzroy Ham and Tongue, 4oz ..	each		
,, ,, ,, ,, 8oz ..	,,		
,, Fitzroy Ham and Chicken, 4oz	,,		
Peas—Split	per lb		
,, Blue, good boilers	,,		
Peel—Lemon	,,		
,, Orange	,,		
,, Citron	,,		
,, Rankin & Morrow's	,,		
,, Medcraf's	,,		
,, Atlas	,,		
Pegs—Wood Clothes	per doz		
Pepper—Cayenne, 1oz castors	per oz		
,, Corns, Black	,,		
,, ,, White	,,		
,, Pure Ground, Black	per lb		
,, ,, ,, White	,,		

We Recommend SQUATTER WHISKY.

QUEENSLAND MODEL DAIRY, Turbot Street. Telephone 379.

			s.	d.
PEPPER—				
,,	Mixed Black, loose	per lb		
,,	,, White, loose	,,		
,,	,, Black, 4oz tins	each		
,,	,, ,, 8oz tins	,,		
,,	,, White, 4oz tins	,,		
,,	,, ,, 8oz tins	,,		
,,	Crescent, Mixed Black			
,,	,, Pure ,,			
,,	,, Mixed White			
,,	,, Pure ,,			
,,	,, Red Cross Black			
,,	,, ,, White			
,,	Atlas			

Peppermint Cordial .. .. per bottle
Perfumery .. .. .. ,,
Pipes— Clay, various ..
Pimento – Ground .. .. per lb
,, Whole .. .. ,,
Pickles—Morton's, assorted .. per bottle

,,	St. James'	,,
,,	Capt. White's (C. & B.)	,,
,,	Albert White, assorted	,,
,,	London Assorted	,,
,,	Harrison's	,,
,,	Atlas	,,

First | Taylor and Sons' Jams | Prize

Pills—Beecham's .. .. .. per box

,,	Cockle's	,,
,,	Fletcher's	,,
,,	Holloway's	,,
,,	Safe Cure	,,
,,	Seigel's	,,
,,	Whelpton's	,,
,,	Pink, Williams'	,,
,,	Bile Beans	,,

Polish—Knife, Oakey's .. .. per tin
,, ,, (Protector Brand) .. ,,
,, Boot, Spooner's .. .. per bottle
Powder—Baking, Waugh's .. per tin

,,	,, Crown	,,
,,	,, Boomerang	,,
,,	,, Ward's, 6oz	,,
,,	,, Royal	,,
,,	,, Atlas	,,
,,	,, Empire	,,
,,	Custard	per packet
,,	Egg	,,
,,	Egg, Atlas	,,
,,	Egg, Perfection	,,
,,	Fruit, Cunningham's	,,
,,	Seidlitz	per doz

We Recommend SQUATTER WHISKY.

				s.	d.
POWDER—					
,,	Soothing, Steedman's	..	.. per doz.		
,,	Violet ..	.. ..	.. per packet		
Potatoes—Edwards', Preserved, 7, 14, 28 and 56lb tins					
Puddings - 1lb tins, Swallow & Ariell	..	per lb			
,,	2lb tins, ,,	..	..	,,	
Produce—Bacon, Flitches, best factory	..	,,			
,,	Middles	,,	..	,,	
,,	Rolls	,,	..	,,	
,,	Sides	,,	..	,,	
Barley, Cape	..	..	..	,,	
Bran..	..	..	. per bushel		
Butter, best	..	..	.. per lb		
,, seconds	..	..	,,		
Cheese, New Zealand	..	..	,,		
,, Queensland	..	..	,,		
Chaff, Lucerne, bags	..	.. per cwt			
,, bales	..	..	,,		
,, Mixed bags	..	..	,,		
,, ,, bales	..	..	,,		
,, Oaten bags, prime N. Zealand	,,				
,, ,, bags, Queensland	..	,,			
Eggs, Finest Farmer's Fresh	..	per doz			
Hay, Lucerne, in bales	..	per cwt			
,, Oaten ,,	..	..	,,		
Lard ..	..	..	.. per lb		
Maize, prime	..	..	market rates		

First | Taylor and Sons' Jams | Prize

Oats, Feed	..	..	.. per bushel	
,, Seed	..	..	,,	
,, ,, Black Tartarian	..	,,		
Onions	..	..	.. per cwt	
Pollard	..	..	.. per bushel	
Potatoes, Queensland Blue Skins	market rates			
,, Circular Heads	,,			
,, New Zealand	..	,,		
Pig's Heads	..	..	.. each	
Rye ..	..	..	.. per bushel	
Wheat, Good Chick	..	..	,,	
,, Medium Chick	..	..	,,	
Stanley's Artificial Food	..	per bag		
Preserves—Plums	..	..	per lb	
,, Pears, canned	..	..	each	
,, Apricots, canned	..	..	,,	
,, Tinned, Assorted	..	..	,,	
,, Pineapples, canned,	..	..	,,	
,, Atlas, Assorted, canned	..	..	,,	
,, Morton's Bottled, assorted	..			
Rennet - Barnekow's, quarts	..	.. per bottle		
,, Tablets, in bottles	..	..	,,	
Rice—Ground ..	..	..	per lb	
,, ,, Crescent Brand	..	..	,,	
,, Queensland	..	..	..	,,
,, Rangoon ..	..	..	..	,,

Elms Bros.

WATER AND COSTIN STS., VALLEY,

BRISBANE.

MANUFACTURERS OF:

JAMS, JELLIES, CONSERVES, PICKLES, SAUCES AND PRESERVES,

HAVE much pleasure in notifying their customers and the general public that all their goods bearing their name are GUARANTEED PURE, and true to name, and also that cleanliness is strictly observed, and all goods are manufactured under their personal supervision.

❧ ❧ ❧

ELMS BROS.,

Manufacturers of the celebrated brands of Jellies and Jams, which were awarded GOLD and SILVER MEDALS at the International Exhibition, 1897.

SOLE AGENTS FOR THE

"Eclipse" Jams and Marmalade.

s. d.

Salt—Bottled	..	..	..	..	per bottle
„ Coarse	..	..	..	..	per cwt
„ „ Black Horse		..	..		„
„ Epsom, 1oz packet, 7lb boxes	..	?B???	..		„per doz
„ Fine	..	..	..	..	per lb
„ Rock	..	..	..	..	per cwt
Sauce—Anchovy Ess., C. & B.		..		..	per bottle
„ „ „ ½-pts			..		„
„ Atlas	..	..	..	..	„
„ Catsup, Mushroom, C. & B., ½-pts			..		„
„ Capers, 4oz. Morton's		..		..	„
„ Congreve's, pints	..		..	..	„
„ Chutney, Atlas	..		..	..	„
„ Colonial, ½-pts	..		..	..	„
„ „ pints, loose		..		..	„
„ Hunter's Paw Paw			..	..	„
„ Holbrook's, pints	..		..	..	„
„ Lea & Perrin's, small			..	..	„
„ „ medium		..		..	„
„ Atlas	..		..	..	„
„ Tomato, Chance's	..	..	..	..	„
„ Crescent	..	..	..	..	„
„ Tomato Sauce, Tip Top Brand			..		„
„ „ „ Atlas			..	..	„
„ „ „ B. & S.		..		..	„
„ Tomato Ketchup, „ „			..	..	„

First | Taylor and Sons' Jams | Prize

SAUCE — Verney's	..	..	..	..	per bottle
„ Yorkshire Relish	..	..			„
Saltpetre	..	..	•..	..	per lb
Salts of Lemon		..	..	..	„
Sago—Fine Seed Pearl		..	..	..	„
Semolina—3lb bags		..	..	..	per bag
Senna Leaves—1oz packets			..	..	each
„ „ „			..	..	per doz
Seed – Canary	..	..	..	..	per lb
„ Carraway	..		..	..	„
„ Hemp	..		..	..	„
„ Lucerne	..		..	..	per bushel
„ Panicum	..		..	..	„
„ Rape	..	..		..	per lb
„ Bird, Crescent Brand		..		..	„
Seidlitz Powders			..	..	per box
„ Crescent Brand		..		..	„
„ Atlas		..		..	„
Soap—Anchor	..	..	..	..	per bar
„ Apollo	..	..	..	..	„
„ Barilla	..	..	..	..	„
„ Borax	..	..	..	..	„
„ Brown Windsor, 7 to lb		..		..	per lb
„ Carbolic	..	..	..	..	per bar
„ Campbell's Superfine		..		..	„

We Recommend SQUATTER WHISKY.

V.:& S. Tomato Sauce Leads. VERNEYS, Makers.

Left margin: *QUEENSLAND MODEL DAIRY, Turbot Street. Telephone 379.*

Soap—		s.	d.
,, Calvert's No. 5 Carbolic	per bar		
,, Cuticura, tablets	each		
,, Eucalyptus	per bar		
,, Globe	,,		
,, Kerosene	,,		
,, Lotus	,,		
,, Maypole, tablets	each		
,, Monkey ,,	,,		
,, Pears' Unscented, tablets	,,		
,, ,, Oatmeal and Glycerine, tablets	,,		
,, ,, Transparent Glycerine, ,,	,,		
,, Pride of the Kitchen, tablets	,,		
,, Powder, Extract	per packet		
,, Sand Soap, tablets	each		
,, Sapolio ,,	,,		
,, Soft, in 1lb tins	per lb		
,, Sunlight, tablets	each		
Soups—Skinner's Turtle Soup, pint			
,, ,, ,, ,, ½ pint			
Soda—Bicarbonate	per lb		
,, Caustic	,,		
,, Crystals	,,		
Spice—Mixed, 1oz packets	per oz		
,, Crescent Brand			
,, Atlas, assorted			
,, Clark's Horse and Cattle	per bag		

First | Taylor and Sons' Jams | Prize

Starch—Reckitt's	per lb		
,, Colman's	,,		
,, Cream	per box		
,, ,, assorted colours, ¼lb boxes	,,		
,, Hoffman's, packets	per packet		
,, ,, 1lb boxes	per box		
,, ,, ½lb boxes	per box		
,, Huemann's ½lb boxes	per box		
,, ,, 1lb boxes	,,		
,, ,, large papers	per doz		
,, ,, Rainbow, 7 colours	,,		
,, Reckitt's, assorted colours	,,		
,, Atlas, packets	per packet		
,, Silver Star	,,		
Sulphur	per lb		
,, Roll	,,		
Sugar—Colonial Sugar Co.'s No. 3	,,		
,, ,, No. 2	,,		
,, ,, No. 1A	,,		
,, ,, No. 1x	,,		
,, Fine White, sundry mills	,,		
,, Brown Ration, fine to grainy	,,		
,, Yellow, grainy	,,		
,, Grey	,,		
,, Icing, Crescent Brand	,,		
,, Atlas	,,		

We Recommend SQUATTER WHISKY.

		s. d.
SUGAR—		
,,	Harper's	per lb.
,,	Hiron's Silk Dressed	,,
,,	Loaf	
Syrup—Lemon		per bottle
,,	Golden, Colonial Sugar Co.'s 2lb tins	each
,,	,, ,, 7lb tins	,,
,,	,, Millaquin 2lb tins	,,
,,	,, ,, 7lb tins	,,
,,	,, Atlas	
,,	,, Crescent	
,,	,, Bingera	
,,	Raspberry	per bottle
,,	Winslow's Soothing	,,
,,	Seigel's	,,
Tapioca—Pearl		per lb.
,,	Flake	,,
Tea—Koo-oola		,,
,,	Koo-lana	,,
,,	OO-Pack	,,
,,	Cock Brand	,,
,,	Favorite	,,
,,	Excelsior	,,
,,	Ossington	,,
,,	Finest Panyong	,,
,,	Ceylon	,,
,,	Orange Pekoe	,,

First | Taylor and Sons' Jams | Prize

		per lb
TEA — Pekoe		per lb
,,	Oriental	,,
,,	Empire	,,
,,	Our Family	,,
,,	C.A.N.	,,
,,	Billy	,,
,,	Society	,,
,,	Spring Blossom	,,
,,	Rupee	,,
,,	Victory	,,

We guarantee to give you as good value as any House in Queensland, as we buy for Cash in the best market.

		per lb.
Tongues—Sheep's, 1lb. tins, Fitzroy		per lb.
,,	G.B.H.	,,
,,	Baynes Bros.'	,,
,,	Lunch, Fitzroy	,,
Tobacco—Derby 4's, 7's, 14's to lb.		,,
,,	Cameron's Two Seas, 7's, 14's	,,
,,	Williams "Victory" 14's	,
,,	,, Welcome Nugget	
,,	Lambert & Butler's "Viking," 4oz	per tin
,,	Mascotte, 8's	per lb
,,	Boomerang, twists and flats, all sizes	,,
,,	Capstan, Wills' 4oz. tins	per tin

We Recommend SQUATTER WHISKY.

26

Pure

Ceylon

TEA

OF THE FINEST GROWTH, GROWN AND MANUFACTURED ON **Mukelana** AND . . **Ossington** ESTATES.

Guaranteed Pure and Direct from the Tea Gardens.

SOLE AGENTS:

THOS. BROWN & SONS, Ltd., Brisbane.

NOTHING BETTER!!!

THAN

Yankee Doodle ✳ ✳

The Latest American.

American Eagle ✳ ✳

An Ideal Smoke.

Challenge ✳ ✳ ✳

Bright
And Dark Aromatic.

" They surpass all other brands of Tobacco."—
BRIAR.

			s. d.
TOBACCO—			
,,	Challenge (dark), 8's	per lb.	
,,	,, 6's, Bright Texas Twist ..	,,	
,,	Luxury, 8's	,,	
,,	Yankee Doodle, the latest American	,,	
,,	American Eagle, the "new" tobacco	,,	
,,	My Pet, dark, bright and Aromatic	,,	
,,	Tiger	,,	
	(All sizes, twist and flat, and in packages to suit the trade).		
Cigars—	Manilla-la-Linda		
,,	Royal		
,,	Borneo		
,,	Aristocrato		
,,	Portagas		
,,	Flor de Naves		
,,	Murias		
Treacle—	7lb. tins, patent lever lids ..	per tin	
,,	2lb. tins	,,	
,,	7lb. tins, Crescent Brand	,,	
,,	Billy Cans, loose	per can	
Vaseline—	½lb. tins	per tin	
,,	1lb. ,, ...	,,	
Vermicelli	.. ..	per lb.	
Vinegar—	Bottled, Champion's Brown ..	per bottle	

First | Taylor and Sons' Jams | Prize

VINEGAR—	Bottled, Champion's White	..	per bottle	
,,	,, Date ..	..	..	,,
,,	,, Crawford's	..	..	,,
,,	,, Crescent	..	..	,,
,,	,, James'	..	..	,,
,,	,, XXX ..	..	..	,,
,,	,, *Fairfield	..	..	,,
,,	,, Concentrated	..	..	,,
,,	,, Atlas, Malt	..	..	,,
,,	Raspberry ..	..	..	,,
,,	Pineapple, Harrison's	..	..	,,
,,	Battle Axe ..	..	..	,,
Wax—	Bees	..	per lb.	
,,	Atlas Bottling	..	..	
Whiting	.. ..	..	..	,,

IRONMONGERY
AT LOWEST RATES.

Adzes ..	..	..	..	..
Axes—	Collins, 4½ to 6lb ..	..	..	
,,	Kelly's ,,	..	..	
,,	King's ..	..	..	

We Recommend SQUATTER WHISKY.

Bolts and Nuts—A large stock of all sizes.
Bits – Cobra-nail, all sizes, 3 to 8/32's   ..
  ,,   Scotch Pattern, twist, all sizes   ..
  ,,   Boker, ¼in ..   ..
Basins—Tin Hand   ..   ..   ..
Black, Brunswick—bottles, ¼-pints   ..
    ,,   ,, ½ ,,   ..
Blinds—Bamboo, outside splits, complete with
       Pulleys   ..   ..   ..
Bedsteads—4-post, 1in pillars, ornamented ..
    ,,   Half-tester, 1in pillars orna-
       mented, brass mounts   ..
Brushes—Fibre Banister, special line   ..
Brooms—Hair ..   ..
Colors—Dry and Ground, in all shades   ..
Chimneys—"La Bastie," Unbreakable   ..
    ,,   "Corona" brand   ..   ..
    ,,   "Bismark," 10 line, fireproof ..
    ,,   Duplex, fireproof   ..   ..
Cases—Eley's Cartridge—Brown, blue, green
Camp Billies—Strong Tin   ..   ..
Dressing, Harness, Miller's, 1-pint tins ..
Dishes—Stamped Tin Baking   ..   ..
Files—Millsaw ..   ..

First | Taylor and Sons' Jams | Prize

FILES — Handsaw ..   ..
Forks—Digging, Strong, 4-prong   ..   ..
    ,,   Medium 4-prong   ..   ..   ..
    ,,   3-prong ..   ..
Galvanised Iron—10ft. Sheets ..   ..
    ,,   ,,   9ft. ,, ...
    ,,   ,,   8ft. ,, ...
    ,,   ,,   6ft. ,, ...
Holloware—Tinned, Siddon's Patent Strainer
Hooks—Reaping ..   ..
Hinges—Butt, Kendrick's, all sizes in stock ..
    ,,   Japanned T, all sizes in stock   ..
Jars—Spring Top, 1 quart ..   ..   ..
    ,,   Wide mouth, 2 quart   ..   ..
    ,,   ,, 1 ,, ...
    ,,   Lightning, 1 pint ..   ..   ..
Kettles—Best, tinned inside   ..   ..
Lamps—Glass Hand, asstd. patterns, complete
    ,,   Table ..   ..
Lead, White—Champion's Genuine, in 28lb
       and 56lb Kegs ..   ..   ..
    ,,   Storer's   ,, ..
Mattresses—Best Ceylon Fibre, Plain or
       Fancy Ticks ..   ·   ..
    ,,   Double-wove, Steel Wire   ..
Mincer—Enamelled Enterprise, No. 10   ..

We Recommend SQUATTER WHISKY.
31

Mugs—Enamelled .. .. ..
Nails—in 7lb packets, all gauge to 12 inclusive
,, Patent Lead Head for Roofing ..
Oil—5-gal drums, Blundell, Spence & Co., Raw
,, ,, . Boiled
,, ,, Storer's Raw
,, ,, ,, Boiled
,, ,, ,, Neatsfoot, Extra Refined ..

Pans—Tinned Frying, all sizes .. ..
Paints—mixed ready for use, all colours, 1lb tins
,, ,, ,, ,, 2lb tins
Pastry Rollers—Enamelled Handles ..
Plates—Enamelled .. .. ..
Saws—Cross-cut .. ..
,, Hand .. ..
,, Meat .. ..
Stoves—Kerosene, "The Aurora," 4in wick ..
Spades—"Climax," solid steel .. ..
Shovels—No. 4, Navvy, Skelton's .. ..
,, ,, Parkes .. ..
Screws—All sizes, ⅜ to 4in .. ..
Shot—Patent .. ..

First | Taylor and Sons' Jams | Prize

Spouting and Ridge Capping—all sizes
Tar .. . . per gallon
Tomahawks—Handled, No. 2 .. ..
Tacks—Blued in packets of 1000, ⅜in ¼in ..
Turpentine .. ..
Varnish—Mander's, Oak, gallons and halves
Wire—No. 8, Japanned Steel .. ..
,, ,, 10 ,, ...
,, Barb, 4 point, thick set, "Iowa" Brand

GLASS AND EARTHENWARE.

Cups and Saucers—Best White and Gold,
Breakfast size ..
,, Printed, assor. patterns
Jugs—Sets of 3, printed or banded and gilt ..
Tumblers—Pressed .. .. ..
,, Etched .. .. ..
Toilet Sets—Assorted patterns and shapes,
6-piece sets .. ..
,, Assorted patterns and shapes,
5-piece sets .. ..
Dishes—Glass Butter, a special line ..
,, ,, Sugars to match .. ..
Teapots—Assorted patterns .. ..

VIEWS OF TOOWOOMBA

CHILDS' TOOMBUL
WINES.

Awarded 40 FIRST PRIZES,
GOLD, . . .
SILVER and BRONZE MEDALS.

PRICE LIST.

WHITE WINE:

CHAMPAGNE, 50s. per doz. qts.
SPARKLING MOSELLE, 30s. per doz. qts.
CHABLIS ⎫
HOCK ⎭ Dry 18s. per doz. qts. Bu'k.
PINEAU ⎫
VERDEILHO ⎭ Sweet, 18s. per doz. qts., 6s. per. gal.
SHERRY, 22s. per doz. qts., 8s. per gal.

RED WINE:

PORT   22s per doz. qts., 8s. per gal.
ESPAR, SWEET 18s. „   „   „   6s.   „
CLARET, DRY, 18s. „   „   „   6s.   „

●●●●●●●

These Wines are thoroughly matured and are highly recommended by the medical profession.
TRIAL ORDER MADE UP IN ASSORTED DOZEN IF DESIRED.

ADDRESS: **D. J. CHILDS,**

TOOMBUL VINEYARD, NUDGEE

QUEENSLAND MODEL DAIRY deliver Butter daily throughout City and Suburbs.

Time of Sun's Rising and Setting throughout the Colony.

Corrected for refraction, will answer for all ensuing Almanacs, being the means of 4 years.

		JAN.		FEB.		MARCH.		APRIL.		MAY.		JUNE.		JULY.		AUG.		SEPT.		OCT.		NOV.		DEC.	
		1	15	1	15	1	15	1	15	1	15	1	15	1	15	1	15	1	15	1	15	1	15	1	15
Boolburra, Gladstone and Springsure, 24°	Rises. Sets.																								
Bowen, 20°	Rises. Sets.																								
Bundaberg and Tambo, 25°	Rises. Sets.																								
Cardwell, 18½°	Rises. Sets.																								
Charleville, Roma, and Gympie, 26½°	Rises. Sets.																								
Clermont, 22¾°	Rises. Sets.																								
Cooktown, 15½°	Rises. Sets.																								
Cape York, 10½°	Rises. Sets.																								
Gayndah, Taroom, and Maryborough, 25½°	Rises. Sets.																								
Mackay, 21¼°	Rises. Sets.																								
Normanton, 17¾°	Rises. Sets.																								
Rockhampton, 23½°	Rises. Sets.																								
St. Lawrence, 22½°	Rises. Sets.																								
Townsville and Gilberton, 19½°	Rises. Sets.																								

For any other place, take the same line as the town in the same latitude as the place wanted.

RECIPES.

Stock for Soups.—To form stock for soups—put into a stewpan all odd pieces of meat—such as tops of ribs, the brisket, ox-cheek, sirloin bones, pieces of mutton, bacon, ham, trimmings of turkey, fowl, or veal, &c.; cover well with cold water; add carrots cut into rings, herbs, onions, pepper, salt and spices. Let it almost boil, then let it simmer for about 6 hours. Remove to a cool place, and skim off all the fat. To clarify stock whisk the whites of 2 eggs with half a pint of water for 10min., then pour in very gently 4 quarts of stock, boiling and whisking all the time. Place the stewpan over the fire; skim it clear; when on the point of boiling whisk it all well together, then draw it to the side and let it settle till the whites of the eggs become separated. Strain it through a fine cloth placed over a sieve.

Vermicelli Soup.—Make 2 quarts of Stock hot, add ¼lb. of vermicelli, simmer for half an hour—if boiled quickly vermicelli will burst.

Pea Soup.—Boil pint and a-half of split peas, tied up in a cloth, until they are quite tender; slice 2 carrots, 3 turnips, 3 large onions, 2 heads celery, add pepper. Let these warm in Beef Stock until they are thoroughly soft; rub the peas and stewed vegetables through a sieve; add to them Beef Stock to render the soup of the desired consistence; boil for half an hour, stir frequently and serve with fried diced bread and powdered mint.

Mock Turtle Soup.—Procure half a calf's head, scald it, bone it, then cut up a knuckle of veal or shin of beef, which put into a stewpan with ¼lb. of lean ham, 1oz. of salt, a carrot, turnip, three middling sized onions, a head of celery, a bunch of parsley, and bay leaf; add half a pint of water; set it upon the fire, moving it round occasionally until the bottom of the stewpan is covered with a white glaze; then add 6 quarts of water and put in the half calf's head or scalp; let it simmer upon the side of the fire for 2½ hours, or until the scalp is tender, then take it out and press it between two dishes; pass the stock through a sieve. Then put into a stewpan a ¼lb. of butter, let it boil, and as soon as it begins to colour add 6oz. of flour, and keep stirring over a sharp fire for a few minutes; let it stand off the fire for a few minutes to cool, then add the stock. Stir over the fire till boiling, draw to the side and skim off all the fat, and pass through a hair sieve into another stewpan; cut the scalp into pieces 1in. square, but not too thick, and put them into the soup and make quite hot; season with a little cayenne pepper and add two glasses of sherry and some forcemeat balls.

Eels.—They must be simply boiled—either whole or crimped—and eaten with parsley or butter sauce. Another method is by placing them to the fire on a steel wire, or fine spit. This is the more preferable method with large eels. When done in this method they may be served with ketchup, anchovy or caper sauce. They may be also fried, when they are to be dipped in beaten egg, and covered with crumbs of bread and chopped sweet herbs.

Bream or Mullet must be boiled with the same precaution as directed for Whiting; it is more equally dressed when split, or cut into moderately sized pieces. Put some salt in the water; when it boils take off the scum; boil it very gently. Bream or Mullet require almost as much boiling as meat, viz., a quarter of an hour to every pound of fish.

Shrimps on Toast.—Put into a small saucepan a dessertspoonful of butter; when hot stir in a dessertspoonful of rice flour and a gill of milk; stir until it commences to thicken, then add half a pint of shrimps; season with salt and pepper, stir slowly until thoroughly heated. Serve on toast garnished with parsley, or celery heads.

Salmon Pudding.—One tin salmon, 2 eggs, 1 tablespoonful anchovy sauce, pepper and salt, 1 pint melted butter sauce. Open the tin and strain away the liquor, chop up the salmon and season nicely, beat in the eggs and one gill melted butter sauce. Put into a buttered mould, boil for three-quarters of an hour, turn out and pour over the rest of the melted butter sauce.

Broiled Mutton Chops.—Cut the chops from either the loin or the best end of the neck, trim them neatly and take off some of the fat if requisite. Pepper them lightly; put them on the gridiron over a clear fire. Turn the chops three or four times. When done, sprinkle a little salt over them, and lay a few small bits of butter on them.

Stewed Loin of Mutton—to eat like venison. The bones are taken out and boiled for gravy, which is put into the stewpan with the mutton, rolled up and tied; add half a pint of red wine, an onion, and some dried mushrooms. Season with pepper and salt on the inside of the mutton before it is rolled. The mutton must be stewed for two hours, and when taken out a little mushroom ketchup should be added to the gravy, thickened with butter and flour.

Tripe and Onions.—Method: Tripe bought at tripe shops is already cooked, and will only require re-cooking in some suitable sauce. If bought in the raw state, it must be soaked in salted water and then cooked gently for several hours. Supposing the tripe to be already prepared, boil it up again, and simmer gently until quite tender; drain it well, cut it into convenient sized pieces for serving, and cover with good onion sauce. This is one of the nicest ways of preparing tripe.

A Dish of Calf's Feet.—Parboil two feet until you can remove the bones from them. Put the meat into a stewpan with a gill of the stock in which it was boiled, with two ounces of butter. Boil three eggs hard, cut off the whites in halves, rub the yolks smooth, with a seasoning of pepper, salt, and chopped parsley. Let the whole simmer together for ten minutes; garnish the dish with sippets and the whites of the eggs.

Scrambled Eggs with Milk.—Butter a saucepan well. Proportion your eggs to your milk according to your supplies of each. Three eggs to a cupful of milk will do very nicely, but 4, 5 or 6 can be used. Add the eggs to the cold milk, turn into the cooking dish; stir constantly till it thickens, and remember that the utmost care is necessary to remove it from the fire at exactly the right instant, when it is just done or it will "whey," and the sooner more milk is used the better. In scrambling eggs plain, if you are a little short of eggs, a few spoonfuls of milk can be added and nobody will know the difference. Like scrambled eggs, the foregoing dish can be used plain or over toast, or a dish the children will like amazingly can be made by dipping pieces of very stale bread into hot salted water, buttered lightly, and adding the eggs when cooked.

Scrambled Mutton.—Two cupfuls of cold chopped mutton, two table-spoonfuls of hot water, and a piece of butter as large as a walnut. When the meat is hot break into it three eggs, and cook until the eggs begin to stiffen, stirring it constantly; season with pepper and salt.

Beef Tongues.—A salted tongue, if dried, must be soaked for some hours previous to being dressed; then put into cold water and gently brought to boiling; clear the scum, and remove saucepan from fire, allowing it to simmer gently; if dried, a tongue will require four hours; if simply salted only three hours' boiling. While hot the outer skin should be peeled off. Boiled turnips usually accompany boiled tongue.

Rump Steak Pie.—Cut 1½ lb. of steak into thin slices, each about 4 inches long; sprinkle them with pepper, salt and flour, and into each slice put a tiny bit of fat; roll it up and lay it in the dish. Continue in this way till it is full, laying slices of hard boiled egg between the meat at intervals, using 2 eggs for the quantity specified, and putting in 6 small rolls of lean ham or bacon. These give a most delicious flavour. Nearly fill the dish with good gravy, or water if no gravy is procurable,

taking care that the pie funnel is in good working order, that the liquor may not boil over the pastry. Cover with a good crust, and set in a tolerably quick oven, that the pastry may not be dried. When this is sufficiently brown, cover with buttered paper, and put the pie in a part of the oven where it will gently simmer only. It should take 1½ hours at least, and the more gently it is cooked after the pastry is browned the richer and better it becomes.

Brawn.—Ingredients ; To a pig's head weighing 6lb. allow 1¼lb. lean beef, 2 tablespoonfuls of salt, 2 teaspoonfuls of pepper, a little cayenne, 6 pounded cloves. Mode : Cut off the cheeks and salt them, unless the head be small, when all may be used. After carefully cleaning the head, put it on in sufficient water to cover it with the beef, and skim it just before it boils. A head weighing 6lb. will require boiling from 2 to 3 hours. When boiled enough to come off the bones easily, put it into a hot pan, remove the bones and chop the meat with a sharp knife before the fire, together with the beef. It is necessary to do this as quickly as possible to prevent the fat settling on it. Sprinkle in the seasoning, which should have been previously mixed. Stir it well, and put it into a brawn tin if you have one ; if not, a cake tin or mould will answer the purpose if the meat is well pressed with weights, which must not be removed for several hours. When quite cold, dip the tin into boiling water for a minute or two, and the preparation will turn out and be fit for use. The liquor in which the head was boiled will make good pea soup, and the fat, if skimmed off and boiled in water and afterwards poured into cold water, answers the purposes of lard.

The following table gives the average time for cooking meat :—

	h.	m.					h.	m
Beef, round of, 30lbs.	6	0	Chicken				0	20
Beef, round of, 8lbs	3	0	Fowl				0	40
Beef, round of, 5lbs.	2	0	Fowl (large) or Capon			1	0
Beef, brisket of, 10lbs.	3	0	Partridge				0	20
Beef, aitchbone of, 14lbs.	3	0	Pigeon				0	20
Beef, thin flank rolled, 10lbs.	5	0	Rabbit				0	45
Pork, leg of, 8lbs.	3	0	Greens, kept boiling			0	25
Pork, hand of, 6lbs.	2½	0	Cabbage ,,			0	25
Ham, 12lbs.	4½	0	Asparagus ,,			0	25
Ham, piece of, 6lbs.	3	0	Artichokes ,,			0	35
Bacon, 2lbs.	1½	0	Artichokes, Jerusalem		0	30
Pig's Cheek	2½	0	Spinach				0	12
Pig's Feet	3	0	Sprouts, Brussels			0	15
Ox Tongues, fresh	4	0	Beetroot				2½	0
Ox Tongues, dried and soaked	4½	0	Cauliflower				0	20
Mutton, leg of, 9lbs.	2½	0	Sea Kale, young			0	20
Mutton, neck of, 7lbs.	2	0	Sea Kale, large			0	45
Veal, breast of, 7lbs.	2½	0	Parsnips				0	35
Veal, neck of, 5lbs.	2	0	Onions, moderate size, whole	1	0
Veal, knuckle of, 7lbs.	2½	0	Broccoli				0	20
Calf's Head	3	0	Kidney Beans, young			0	15
Calf's Feet	3	0	Kidney Beans, large			0	30
Turkey, small	1½	0	Turnips				0	45
Turkey, large	2	0	Green Peas				0	20

The liquor in which fresh animal food has been boiled should on no account be wasted, but should be used for making stock for soup and sauces.

Potato Salad.—Cut up a pint of boiled potatoes while hot, mix half a teaspoonful each of chopped onion and parsley, put all in a salad bowl. Make a dressing of vinegar, oil, pepper, and salt, pour over, mix well, allow it to set well, and serve very cold.

Spinach.—Take some spinach and boil it till it becomes quite tender; press all the water away, and then chop the leaves very fine; next mince an onion very finely, fry it in beef dripping till quite done and add it to the spinach, stirring together with a tablespoonful of flour, a little pepper and a dash of sugar; then into a small stewpan or fryingpan put a tablespoonful of butter and put it in the spinach, stirring well till it is quite hot; put in the middle of a hot dish, and garnish it with sippets of toast.

Mushroom Sauce.—Wash, peel and quarter a cupful of fresh mushrooms; roll in flour, and cook for five minutes in 2 tablespoons of butter with a little chopped onion; then add 1 pint of brown sauce made of one-fourth of a cup of butter, one-third of a cup of flour and one pint of brown stock. Season with salt and pepper. Cook for five minutes and serve.

Bread Sauce.—Put a teacupful of bread crumbs into a saucepan, pour over half a pint of milk, add one onion and a dozen black peppercorns; boil and stir well together, then simmer until it becomes stiff; take out the onion and pepper, and with butter and cream reduce the bread to a proper consistence.

Caper Sauce.—Chop a tablespoonful of capers very small and boil them up in melted butter.

Tomato Sauce.—Stew 6 large ripe tomatoes in a pint of beef gravy, with two teaspoonfuls of minced eschalots; when tender mash through a sieve. Set this on a moderate fire, with a glass of sherry or white wine added. When it has acquired a proper consistence, add pepper, salt and a little lemon juice.

Stewed Celery.—Clean the heads thoroughly. Take off the coarse, green outer leaves, cut in small pieces, and stew in a little broth. When tender, add a cupful of sweet cream, a teaspoonful of flour, and a piece of butter the size of a bean. Season with pepper and salt.

Snow Eggs.—This is a simple, delicious sweet. Boil in a porcelain-lined saucepan a quart of milk, 2 tablespoonfuls of sugar and yellow peel of half a lemon cut in shreds. Whip to a very stiff froth the whites of 6 eggs, setting aside the yolks for sauce. Mix with these whites 4 tablespoonfuls of powdered sugar. Take a tablespoonful of the whites and drop it gently on the boiling milk. Do not put in enough spoonfuls at a time to crowd them. Let the eggs cook very slowly on the boiling milk till they are firm, which will require about four or five minutes. Dish up the eggs with a skimmer, and continue till all the whites are used. Pile the snow eggs thus formed on a handsome low glass platter, if you have one, and prepare a rich boiled custard of the yolks and the boiled milk.

Canadian Fruit Cake.—Ingredients: One pound of flour, half a pound of butter, three-quarters of a pound of sugar, half a pound of currants, quarter of a pound each of chopped dried apples and raisins, two ounces of chopped pine cones, four eggs, a gill of milk, a few drops of almond flavouring. Cream the butter and sugar, beat in the eggs one at a time, add the milk and salt. Now stir in the flour, and then the remainder of the ingredients. Bake in a paper-lined mould, and, when done, ice over the top.

Fig Pudding.—Required: Half a pound of scraps of bread, quarter of a pound of chopped suet, half a pound of figs, one egg, three ounces of moist sugar. Method: Soak the bread in water till quite soft, squeeze it dry. Add the chopped suet, the sugar, the figs chopped quite small, and the beaten egg. Boil the pudding in a well-greased pudding basin for an hour and a-half. Serve with custard sauce.

Lemon Cheese Cakes.—Rasp the rind of a large lemon with four ounces of fine sugar, then crush and mix with the yolks of three eggs, and half the quantity of whites, well whisked; beat these together thoroughly; add to them four tablespoonful of cream, a quarter of a pound of oiled butter, the strained juice of the lemon, which must be stirred quickly in by degrees. If the lemons are not large, take two. Line some patty pans with thin puff paste, half fill them with the mixture, and bake them thirty minutes. The extra whites can be placed upon the tops after the cheese cakes are baked and placed again in the oven for a few minutes.

Curd Cheese Cakes.—Take 1½ pint of new milk, and curdle it with a teaspoonful of strong rennet. Break the curd with a wooden spoon and drain the whey from it. Add to the curd one well-beaten egg, a dessertspoonful of brandy, a tablespoonful of sugar, currants, and chopped candied peel. Flavour with grated lemon rind to taste. Line some patty pans with good puff paste, fill with the mixture, and bake.

Banana Fritters.—Required : ¼lb. of flour, 1 tablespoonful of salad oil, 1 gill of tepid water, the white of an egg, bananas, lemon juice, sifted sugar. Method : Put the flour in a basin, make a hole in the centre, pour in the oil and the water gradually, stir till smooth ; add the white of an egg, first beaten to a stiff froth. Cut the bananas in slices lengthways, rub them over with lemon juice, immerse them in the batter, and fry in plenty of hot fat. Drain well and sprinkle with sifted sugar.

Cream Cakes.—Slightly melt 2oz. butter ; add 2oz. of sugar and 2oz. of flour, about a teaspoonful of apricot jam, half an egg, and a tablespoonful of cream ; mix it all up well, and drop small quantities of the mixture on a baking-tin ; remove from the oven when they are a light brown. If liked, they can be rolled directly they are baked, while they are still soft. To keep them nice and crisp they should be put in a closely-shut tin.

Cream Pudding.—One quart milk, 4 eggs, 3oz. sugar, 6oz. flour, nutmeg. Mix the flour to a smooth paste with a little of the milk, put the rest on to boil, with a strip of lemon peel added ; when nearly boiling pour in the flour and stir well ; let it boil two or three minutes, then remove from the fire and beat in the yolks of the eggs ; return to the fire and cook till it comes to boiling point ; beat for two or three minutes ; pour into a dish, grate a little nutmeg on the top, and serve cold.

Tartlets.—Roll out a good sized piece of puff paste, and therewith line some patty pans; then take small pieces of the paste, roll them out in shapes about 2 inches in diameter ; into these put a lump of apricot jam, then fold the paste over, dip them into fine sugar, place them in the paste-lined patty pans, and bake them in an oven until the tartlets become light golden in color. Serve them quite hot.

Cheese Patties.—Puff pastry, 2oz. grated cheese, 2 eggs, 4oz. butter, ½ gill thick white sauce, pepper and salt. Line some small patty pans with pastry, put the cheese, yolks of eggs, butter, sauce, and seasoning into a saucepan and stir till thick ; take the saucepan from the fire and stir in the whites of the eggs beaten to a stiff froth ; put into lined patty pans, bake for eight minutes ; serve warm.

Orange Jelly.—Squeeze the juice of six oranges into one pint of water, put in their peel, which must be taken out when flavoured enough ; add half an ounce of powdered sugar, and let it boil gently. Dissolve one and a-half ounce of isinglass, and add, then strain and pour into moulds.

Blanc Mange.—Dissolve one ounce of isinglass in one and a-half pint of raw milk, some sugar to taste, and two or three laurel-leaves or a few bitter almonds ; let it boil a few minutes ; when flavored nicely, take out the leaves and strain into moulds. This looks very dainty if slightly coloured with a few drops of cochineal. When cold, turn out in a glass dish.

Sponge Cake.—Kentish Recipe : The weight of 5 eggs in sugar, 3 in flour. Beat well the yolks, add the powdered sugar and flour, still beating well, lastly the whites beaten to a froth. Beat all well together. Bake immediately in a quick oven. Yorkshire Recipe : Seven eggs, leaving out three whites, beat well ; ¾lb. loaf sugar, on which grate the rind of a lemon ; dissolve in a teacup of cold water, place in a saucepan until nearly boiling, pour on the already beaten eggs ; beat again for 20 minutes ; then beat in by slow degrees 9oz. of flour ; add at the last moment before baking the juice of half a lemon. Bake in a quick oven. The following recipe for a sponge cake is a very good one. Boil ¾lb. of loaf sugar in a quarter pint of water ; beat the yolks of 8 eggs and the whites of 2 a little ; pour the sugar and water boiling hot on the eggs, stirring all the time with a whisk. Beat for an hour ; then strew in gradually ½lb. of finely sieved flour, stir a little, and add the peel of one lemon grated. Bake for an hour, and lay paper on the top to prevent its burning.

Sponge Pudding. - Put a layer of jam into a buttered pie-dish, and cover it with sponge fingers. Continue alternate layers until the dish is full. Make a pint of nice custard flavoured with vanilla, pour this over the biscuits, and let it stand for three-quarters of an hour. Whisk the whites of two or three eggs to a stiff froth, pile this on the pudding, and brown before a hot fire for a few minutes. Serve cold.

Tunbridge Cakes.—Rub 6oz. of butter into 1lb. of flour and 6oz. of white sugar, moisten with two well-beaten up eggs, and make it into a paste; roll it out very thin, and cut it into any shape; prick with a fork, and sprinkle over them some carraway seeds; brush with the white of an egg, sprinkle sifted sugar over them, and bake on a baking-tin for ten minutes.

Bachelor's Cake.—One pound flour, ½lb. sugar, ¼lb. butter or lard, four wine-glassfuls of milk, ¼lb. of sultana raisins, ¼lb. of currants, ¼lb. candied peel, a quarter of a nutmeg, two teaspoonfuls of ground ginger, one of cinnamon, and one of carbonate of soda. These ingredients being well mixed, and slowly baked for one and a-half hour, will form a very nice cake.

Steamed Pudding.—One cup flour, 1 cup currants, 1oz. sugar, ½ cup milk, 1 teaspoonful baking powder, nutmeg or lemon to taste. Mix the flour, currants, sugar and baking powder together, add a little grated lemon peel or nutmeg for flavouring, and mix into a thick batter with the milk; turn into a buttered basin and steam for two hours. Serve with butter or sugar and custard sauce.

Rich Plum Cake.—One and a-half pound of butter, one and a-half pound of fine sugar, one and three-quarters pound of flour, three-quarters pound of mixed peel, half pound of blanched almonds, four pounds of blanched currants, fourteen eggs, half glass of brandy, half teaspoonful of mixed spice, one table-spoonful of rose water, a salt spoonful of carbonate soda. Beat butter and sugar together, beat eggs and add gradually. Then add soda, spice, rose water, and brandy. Then add the flour and beat well. Then add the fruit, mix well together, and put in well buttered tins and bake in a slow oven.

Plain Plum Pudding.—Ingredients: Two pounds each of suet, raisins, sugar and currants, one pound of sultanas, half a pound of mixed peel, two ounces of spice, one pound of bread crumbs, the same of flour, one grated nutmeg, six eggs, and sufficient milk to give consistency.

Ginger Cakes. - Mix well together ½lb. of flour and 6oz. of butter, then add ¼lb. of moist sugar, one egg, a teaspoonful of ginger, and two tablespoonfuls of golden syrup; stir them all well together, and drop tablespoonfuls of the batter on the baking tin, and bake till done.

Ginger Snaps.—Three-quarters of a pound of flour, half a pound of treacle, half a pound of moist sugar, half a pound of butter, and one ounce of ginger. Put the sugar and ginger in the flour, then treacle and butter melted, beat well together, and drop pieces the size of a walnut on tins to bake. If preferred rolled, take them out when nicely brown, let them lie a second, and then roll up.

A Nice Currant Cake. - One pound of self-raising flour, six ounces of fine sugar, six ounces of butter, six ounces of currants, three eggs (well beaten), one and a half ounces of lemon peel, a little milk or water. Beat the butter and sugar together, next add the eggs, beat well, then the flour gradually, now the currants and peel; lastly, the water or milk; beat all together thoroughly and put into a lined tin; bake for an hour.

Vienna Bread. - Sift in a tin pan 4lb. flour, bank it up against the sides, pour in one quart of milk and water, and then mix in sufficient flour to form a thin batter, then quickly and lightly add one pint of milk in which is dissolved 1oz. salt, and 1½oz. compressed yeast. Leave the remainder of the flour against the sides of the pan; cover the pan with a cloth, and set it in a place free from draught for three-quarters of an hour. Then mix the rest of the flour and knead until the dough will leave the sides and bottom of the pan, then let it rise for two hours and a half. Finally divide the mass into 1lb. pieces, to be cut in turn into 12 parts each. This

gives square pieces about 3 inches and a-half, each corner of which is taken up and folded over to the centre; then the cakes are turned over on a dough-board to rise for half an hour; after which they are put into a hot oven and baked for 10 minutes.

Light Tea Cake.—Mix thoroughly a teacupful each of flour and sugar, with a dessertspoonful of baking powder; beat 3 eggs till light with a little milk, mix them quickly with the flour, &c., till quite smooth; line some tea cake rings with buttered paper, pour in the batter, and bake in a moderate oven.

Rainbow Cake.—Mix quarter pound butter with half pound sugar, add three eggs, half cup of milk and half pound of flour with two teaspoonfuls of baking powder. Divide mixture into three parts, bake one plain, colour one with cochineal, and the third with chocolate (or cocoa and sugar); bake, and stick the three colours in layers with icing before cold. Ice the top.

Cocoanut Cakes.—Take two cocoanuts and grate them very finely, and to them add their weight in fine sugar, with half a teacupful of ground rice and three eggs. Beat the eggs till quite in a froth, then mix the other ingredients with a fork. Put the mixture in small rough lumps in a baking tin, and bake in a moderate oven.

Cocoanut Biscuits.—Mix seven tablespoons of sugar with two tablespoons of butter, break in two eggs, add seven tablespoons of desiccated cocoanut and two tablespoons of milk; mix one teaspoonful cream of tartar with half teaspoonful carbonate of soda and add to the above mixture, then add sufficient flour to stiffen to a paste, when roll out and cut; bake in a quick oven.

Half Pay Pudding.—One cup each of suet, flour, currants, raisins, breadcrumbs and milk. Add candied peel, two tablespoons of treacle and pinch of salt. Boil three or four hours in small basin.

Bachelor's Pudding.—Take some slices of sponge-cake, and lay in the bottom of your glass dish; soak well with some sherry, well sweetened, then pour some custard over it, cover with cream, and put a few heaps of jelly on the top.

Sugar Ice for Plum Cake.—When the cake is almost cold, beat and sift eight ounces of fine loaf sugar, with four spoonfuls of rose water, the juice of a lemon, and the whites of two eggs beaten to a froth and strained. Mix these well together, and cover the cake over with it. Set the cake in a cool oven to dry the icing, but not to discolour it; an hour will harden it.

Macaroons.—Ingredients: Quarter pound sweet almonds, four spoonfuls of orange flower water (if approved of), six whites of eggs, and one pound sifted sugar. Blanch and pound with some of the whites of eggs. Whisk the whites and add them gently to the pounded almonds. Sift the sugar into the almonds till the whole forms a paste, not too stiff to be dropped on wafer pap r, which must be spread ready to receive them on an oven plate. When dropped, wet a spoon that the paste may not adhere to it, and round each macaroon till of a good shape. Bake in a slow oven.

Cheese Straws.—Half a pound of flour, two ounces of butter, two ounces of good cheese, two eggs. Rub the butter in the flour, grate the cheese, and add; season well with cayenne and salt, and mix with the yolks of the eggs and the white of one. Roll out very thin, and place on a buttered tin, and cut into narrow strips, about four inches long, with a paste-cutter. Bake in a moderate oven for ten minutes.

Quince Jam.—Peel the quinces, core them, slice them into a preserving-pan, and pour over as much water as will barely cover them. Let them simmer very gently until they are soft, stirring them occasionally to keep them from burning to the pan, then beat them to a pulp with a wooden spoon. Weigh the fruit, and for each 1lb. allow ¾lb. of sugar. Put the sugar into a preserving-pan with as much water as will moisten it, and boil it to a clear syrup. Put in the fruit, and boil it until smooth and thick. Stir frequently whilst it is being boiled. The jam will be

done enough if it jellies when dropped upon a plate. Put it whilst hot into glasses or jars, and when it is cool cover in the usual way with paper dipped in the white of egg.

Quince Jelly. Choose the quinces that are ripe and yellow, but quite sound. Wash, but do not peel them; cut them into slices, and put them into a preserving-pan; shake them well down, barely cover them with water, and let them boil gently until they are soft, but they must not be allowed to remain so long as to deepen their colour. Turn them into a jelly-bag, and let the juice drain from them without pressure; filter it two or three times if necessary, till clear and bright. Measure the juice, and boil it quickly for 20 minutes. Take it from the fire, and stir into it till dissolved 12oz. of powdered lump sugar for each pint of juice. Boil it again, and carefully remove the scum as it rises. Let it boil until it will jelly when a little is put on a plate. Pour it at once into glasses or small moulds. The jelly ought to boil quickly, or the colour will not be good. The pulp left in the jelly-bag may be boiled with moist sugar for common use; ½lb. of sugar will be sufficient for each pound of pulp. Time, 20 minutes to boil the juice by itself; a few minutes to boil it with the sugar or till it jellies.

How to Clear Jelly.—The method of clearing the jelly is as follows: Let the jelly boil 5 minutes, take it off the fire, and allow it to stand till cool; stir in briskly the shells and whites of two eggs well beaten, and again allow the jelly to boil without stirring, then take it off the fire, and when it has stood two minutes strain through a thick flannel bag.

Claret Cup.—The recipe for claret cup is as follows: Two bottles claret, four bottles soda water, four bottles lemonade, one glass brandy, one glass maraschino, one glass cherry brandy, two oranges cut in thin transverse slices; rub ¼lb. lump sugar on the yellow rinds of two lemons until they have become yellow and well flavoured, then pound them in a mortar; into the bottom of a punch-bowl put the sugar and sliced orange, pour the brandy over it, and let it stand closely covered for two hours; then, just before required, add the claret and other ingredients, stir, and add some lumps of ice. A punch ladle should be used to fill the glasses; champagne tumblers are usually used for claret cup.

Cocoanut Ice.—Pare the cocoanut and throw it into cold water, then grate it, and boil it in clarified sugar, in the proportion of a pound to each pound of cocoanut, till quite thick; stir it frequently to prevent its burning, then pour it on a well buttered dish, and cut it into any form desired.

Butter Scotch.—Two cupfuls of light brown sugar, one cupful of butter, one tablespoonful of vinegar, and one of water. Mix all together and boil twenty minutes; add quarter teaspoonful of baking soda, drop a little in water. If it is crisp it is ready to take off; if not, cook longer. When done pour into a flat buttered tin.

Candy Rock.—Equal quantities of sugar and golden syrup, boil in a suitable pot till when you dip in a spoon in cold water and then in the candy and then back in cold water it crisps like glass. Pour it out on a greased dish, and as it gets cool throw up the edges and work it with the hand or use a hook until it glistens like gold. The hands should have a little flour on them occasionally. Draw it into sticks or leave it like rock if preferred.

Ginger Candy.—Mix together ¼lb. of sifted loaf sugar, ½oz of pounded ginger and one drachm each of pounded cloves and cinnamon, after which add half a wine-glassful of boiling water. Put this mixture on a fire, and boil slowly until it arrives at candy height. Pour it on a greased slab or tin, and as it hardens cut it into squares. After, put them before the fire to harden, and then away in a tin box.

Chocolate Creams.—Put 1lb. of loaf sugar in a stewpan, pour upon it as much milk or thin cream as the sugar will absorb, dissolve it over the fire, and boil slowly until it will candy when dropped into cold water. Neither stir it nor allow it to stick to the pan; take it off and stir it until you can cream with a spoon. Add a

42

tablespoonful of extract of vanilla, and beat it until cool enough to handle. Then fashion it into balls the size of a filbert, lay these aside on buttered paper. Put half a pound of unsweetened pure chocolate on a tin plate over a kettle of boiling water. When it is dissolved dip the balls into it and lay them out on buttered paper to cool. If the sugar grains like sand instead of creaming it has been boiled too long, and it will be necessary to begin anew with fresh sugar.

Everton Toffee.—Get 1lb. treacle, the same quantity of moist sugar and ½lb. butter. Put them into a saucepan large enough to allow of fast boiling over a clear fire. Put in the butter first, and rub it well over the bottom of the saucepan, and add the treacle and sugar, stirring together gently with a knife. After it has boiled for about 10 minutes ascertain if it is done in the following way: Have ready a basin of cold water and drop a little of the mixture into it from the point of a knife. If it is sufficiently done, when you take it from the water it will be quite crisp. Now prepare a large shallow tin pan, or dish, rubbed all over with butter to prevent it adhering, and into this pour the toffee from the saucepan to get cold, when it can easily be removed. To keep it good it should be excluded from the air.

Acid Drops.—Boil 1lb. of lump sugar with cupful of water and one spoonful of vinegar, until the sugar becomes thick and glossy, and brittle to the touch. Then pour it upon a stone, and add to it a quarter of an ounce of tartaric acid and two drops of essence of lemon; after well mixing, cut into the drop-like form, and round them well with thumb and finger.

HOUSEKEEPING HINTS.

If you wish to have a wall papered which has been previously whitewashed, it must be well brushed over with vinegar, or the paper will not stick.

If a clean cloth, wrung out of water to which half a teaspoonful of ammonia has been added, is used to wipe off a carpet recently swept, it will remove the dusky look and brighten the colours.

How to Select Oilcloth.—In buying an oilcloth, select one that has been manufactured for at least two years; the longer it has stood previous to use the better it will wear. It is reasonable to suppose that the paint will have become hard and durable.

A Stale Loaf.—If the loaf has become dry, but is still wholesome, dip it into a bowl of water for three minutes; let it stand for half an hour for the moisture to penetrate, then bake it in a steady oven. This is best eaten hot.

To Clean Gloves. Procure one pint of benzoline. Pour a little into a basin, into which put the gloves, and gently rub where specially soiled. Pour off benzoline, and repeat process till quite clean. Suitable for suede, kid, and any kind of leather, rendering them equal to new. Dry in open air.

To keep lemons fresh, put them in cold water, and change the water every other day.

Whenever salt becomes caked in its receptacles, put into them a pinch of ground arrowroot, and the salt will remain perfectly dry and fine, whatever the temperature may be.

Kerosene will soften boots and shoes that have been hardened by water, and render them as pliable as new.

One of the most convenient things to be found in a kitchen is a set of tin measures with small lips, measuring from a gallon down to half a gill. They fit one inside the other, and so require very little space.

A teaspoonful of borax put in the last water in which clothes are rinsed will whiten them surprisingly. Pound the borax so that it will dissolve easily. This is especially good to remove the yellow tinge that time gives to white garments that have been laid aside for two or three years.

Lamp-burners, to give a good light, should be cleaned at least once a month. To clean them, take a piece of soda the size of a walnut, put it into a quart of soft water, place the lamp-burner in it—an old tomato can is good enough—and set it on the stove: after boiling for five minutes remove the burner, and when put back on the lamp it will be as good as new.

A small quantity of liquid ammonia, or acetic acid, added to the bath thoroughly cleanses the pores of the skin and adds considerably to the enjoyment.

How to Wash Blankets.—Put 1 pint of household ammonia in the bottom of your tub, having had the blankets well beaten, to remove all clinging dust, before you get the tubs out. Then lay the blanket lightly on over the ammonia, and pour upon it a sufficient quantity of warm water to cover the blanket entirely. Then with a stick or the hand flop the blanket about in the solution, pressing all the water that will come out of it against the side of the tub, without wringing, as you remove it to the rinse water. You will be amazed to see the dissolved dirt coming out through the fibres, as no washing or rubbing with soapsuds will bring out. Rinse in the same way, in the same moderately warm water (not boiling water), and by simply pushing the blanket about in a tub. Press through the wringer and hang out to dry in a windy place, not in the sun. As the blanket hangs there drying, a little water will collect in the four corners, which it is rather an amusement to squeeze out, to help in the drying process. If you do not care to put a second blanket in the first ammonia water, which must be done promptly, as the ammonia evaporates quickly, divide the quantity, taking half a pint for each one of the two tubs, and wash two blankets at once.

To Avoid Smells in Cooking.—A pinch of soda on a hot stove drives away disagreeable odours of cooking.

Spots from Furniture. Spots can be cleaned from varnished furniture by rubbing with spirits of camphor.

Fruit Stains from the Hands.—Fruit stains may be removed from the hands by rubbing with dampened tartaric acid.

44

Crown Jams—The Best. VERNEYS, Makers.

Ironing Silk Handkerchiefs.—White silk handkerchiefs must not be dampened, but pressed with a moderate iron when dry.

Baking Pastry.—The most perfectly made pie-crust will not be light unless the pie is put into a very hot oven at first.

Scorched Linen.—Scorch marks may be removed with lemon juice and salt gently rubbed on the place and put in the sun.

For Hanging Brooms.—A screw eye inserted in the top of a broom or mop handle is far more convenient and lasting than a cord.

Polishing Irons.—Lacking beeswax, polish irons by dampening brown paper with kerosene and rubbing them over it when cold.

A Substitute for Cream.—When there is a scarcity of cream, the white of an egg well whipped is an excellent substitute for the real article.

Stuffing for Pincushions.—Dried coffee grounds answer well for filling a pincushion. They do not attract moths like wool, nor mice as bran does, and if well dried they do not smell.

Colouring for Frosting.—Lemon juice will whiten frosting, cranberry or strawberry juice will colour it pink, and the grated rind of an orange strained through a cloth will colour it yellow.

Clean Sponges.—To keep your sponge in good condition, you should occasionally wash it in warm water with a little tartaric acid or soda, afterwards rinsing it in clean warm water.

To Renovate Furs.—This is the Russian method. Place rye flour in a pot and heat, stirring it as long as the hand can bear the heat, then spread evenly over the fur and rub vigorously. When done, beat the skin to remove the flour.

To Remove Stains from Silver.—Medicine stains are taken off by rubbing with a cloth dipped in sulphuric acid, then washed in soapsuds.

Ink Stains.—When on a white surface, should be wet with milk and rubbed with salt, allowing it to remain on for some time. Two or three applications may be found necessary.

Varnish Stains.—To remove stains of varnish on the hands is sometimes very difficult. As soon as possible, rub with a little alcohol and wipe them with a soft rag, afterwards wash thoroughly in soap and water.

Cleaning Oil Paintings.—If the paintings are not very much soiled, they may be cleaned with spirits of turpentine; but as this is apt to render them rather dull, they should be rubbed afterwards with a little linseed oil or painting medium.

Bad Temper has an injurious physical effect on the digestion, as it tends to drive the blood to the brain, thus leaving the stomach unable to perform its functions properly.

To Clean Bronze. Wash well with stale beer, and dry with a soft cotton or linen cloth.

We Recommend SQUATTER WHISKY.

45

We ship Butter to all parts F.O.B. Brisbane. QUEENSLAND MODEL DAIRY.

Canned Fruits. VERNEYS, Preservers.

Wash for the Hands.—Twopennyworth of glycerine, twopennyworth of camphorated oil, the juice of two lemons, a little boracic acid (dissolved). Mix all well together, bottle, and use as required.

Cold Cream.—Half a pint of rose water; four ounces of oil of almonds; three drachms of white wax; three drachms of spermaceti. Melt the wax and spermaceti together with the oil of almonds. Then beat well, adding rose water slowly till cold. Put in a pot and pour some rose water on top.

Wash for the Hair.—Half an ounce of glycerine; half an ounce of spirit of rosemary; five ounces of water; to be well mixed together and shaken.

For Chapped Hands.—Use rain or boiled water with a handful of oatmeal; rub with glycerine after each washing, and wear soft leather gloves at night.

For Whitening the Hands.—Squeeze half a lemon into half a cup of milk, which at once curdles; rub the mixture well into the hands; when dry rinse in clear water and dry with a soft towel.

To Preserve the Teeth.—Brush night and morning with finely powdered charcoal; also rinse the mouth with lukewarm water after partaking of food.

To Remove the Oily Appearance of the Skin.—Use the following lotion once daily, that is just before drying the skin in the morning:—Half an ounce of fine borax powder, one quart of camphor water, and one ounce of pure glycerine well mixed together.

To Freshen the Face.—A very hot water bath to the face and back of the neck, followed by a cold spray, will entirely dissipate a tired and haggard appearance.

To Clean Brass.—Use a paste of rotten stone and sweet oil; rub on with a piece of cloth and polish with a leather.

To Remove Mildew from Linen.—Steep for ten or twelve hours in a mixture made by pouring a quart of boiling water on two ounces of chloride of lime, and adding three quarts of cold water.

To Remove Grease from Books.—Brush the spots over with turpentine, then wet with spirits of wine.

To Take out Wine Stains.—Drop melted tallow from a burning candle on the spot while wet. Allow it to remain for a few days, then scrape off the grease and wash.

To Clean Marble.—Mix in equal quantities bullock's gall and a jelly made by boiling yellow soap with a small quantity of water; add to this half the quantity of spirits of wine and mix the whole to the consistence of paste by adding dry pipeclay. Lay this mixture thickly on the marble, leave it for two or three days, then wash it off, applying a fresh coating if necessary till the colour is restored.

To Take Rust out of Steel.—Cover the steel with sweet oil well rubbed in, and in forty-eight hours use unslacked lime finely powdered, and rub until all the rust disappears.

We Recommend SQUATTER WHISKY.

ACCIDENTS AND COMMON AILMENTS.

Fainting.—Make the patient lie down with head very low, loosen the dress, give plenty of air. Apply smelling salts cautiously to nose, sprinkle face with cold water smartly. If faint continues long, or feet and hands are cold, apply hot bottles. When patient can swallow, give a little spirits in water.

* * *

Apoplexy is attended with insensibility; the patient generally falls, grows purple in the face and breathes in a snoring manner. Place patient in bed with head raised; if hot apply cold water to head and send for doctor. Stimulants should be avoided.

* * *

Epilepsy.—Patient usually gives a scream, becomes deadly pale, falls on his face, becomes convulsed and then profoundly insensible. Loosen articles of dress, keep patient quiet and beyond danger of hurting himself until consciousness returns. It is then a case for medical treatment.

* * *

Snake Bite.—1st. Tie a ligature immediately above the bite, between it and the heart.—2nd. Cut the bitten part out round the fang wounds, thus (:), a quarter of an inch deep. Let this wound be sucked freely by persons who have no wounds, sores or cracks in their mouth.—3rd. If ammonia is available, give it, mixed with water, every half-hour, as long as depression exists, in the following relative doses:—Two drops to an infant and fifteen drops to an adult, regulating the dose according to age in the above proportions. If ammonia is not available, give any other spirit; half a teaspoonful to a child, and a teaspoonful to an adult, mixed with three parts of water.

* * *

Sunstroke.—Sunstroke is caused by over-heating the blood. It is not necessary to be exposed to the direct rays of the sun to have sunstroke. An attack may come on during the night.—To prevent sunstroke, the body should be loosely clothed, and the head and back of the neck protected with some white material. The diet should be simple and too much animal food should not be eaten during the hot weather, and all alcoholic drinks should be avoided.—When sunstroke has occurred, lay the patient in the coolest place procurable, remove his clothing, and douche him all over, but especially over head and spine, with cold water. The bowels should be well moved with enema, if procurable.

NOTE.—This treatment must be continued until consciousness returns and fever abates.

* * *

Choking arises from food, fluids or other substances sticking in the throat or in the air passages. Where the patient turns dark in the face no time is to be lost. Push your two forefingers right down the throat and try to hook away or push aside the hindrance; it will assist the operation if another person grasps the tongue in the folds of a towel; if this does not succeed you may by pressing the hinder portion of the tongue bring on vomiting. Slap or thump between the shoulder blades. For children it is a good plan to take the child up by the heels and at the same time give it a shake or slap its back. For fish bones swallow a piece of bread. If these remedies fail, medical aid should at once be called in.

* * *

Suffocation by Gases or Bad Air.—Drag the patient as quick as possible into fresh air; loosen clothing, dash cold water on head, face and upper parts of chest; if the breathing is stopped artificial respiration must be resorted to.

47

G. A. BÜNZLI,

○

SURGICAL INSTRUMENT MAKER
AND CUTLER. . . .

ALBERT STREET,
TWO DOORS FROM ELIZABETH STREET.

Sir,—

I beg respectfully to call your attention to the following. Having had 26 years' experience in the trade I can guarantee any work intrusted to me.

I devote special attention to all classes of DEFORMITY INSTRUMENTS, ARTIFICIAL LIMBS, and TRUSSES, having been 18 years at this particular work in Brisbane.

CUTLERY of all descriptions made to order, including Spaying Knives; also, Surgical Instruments made to instruction at shortest notice. Having first-class machinery, I undertake all kinds of REPAIRS, namely, Survey Instruments, Sewing and Typewriting Machines, Musical Boxes, Etc.

Please note that Ladies will have the personal attendance of Mrs. Bünzli.

Trusting to be favoured with your esteemed patronage,

AWARDED . . .
GOLD MEDAL

QUEENSLAND INTERNATIONAL
EXHIBITION, 1897,

I remain, yours faithfully,

G. A. BÜNZLI.

Date Vinegar. VERNEYS, Agents.

Poisoning.—In case of poisoning by irritants, such as vitriol, carbolic acid, etc., which can be recognised by the burning sensation of the mouth, the terrible suffering of the stomach, retching and vomiting of blood, etc., emetics should not be given, but give the patient as much milk as possible. For non-irritant poisons, give a tablespoonful of mustard or salt with warm water, and do all you can to make the patient sick. If by narcotics, such as chloroform, etc., do not permit the patient to sleep, dash cold water on the head and face, walk the patient about, etc., until the effects of the poison have passed off.

* * *

Broken Limbs.—Keep the limb quiet and steady until the surgeon comes. Do not raise the patient from the ground until the nature of the injuries have been ascertained. If the patient has to be carried home let it be on a shutter or stretcher, on which he can lie flat instead of being doubled up in a vehicle.

* * *

Fire.—If your own dress, throw yourself at once on the ground so that the rising flames cannot catch the upper part of your clothes. Roll about (so putting the flames out by pressure), at the same time, if possible, wrap yourself up closely in a rug, tablecloth or any handy covering. If another person's dress, treat in a similar manner.

* * *

Burns, Treatment of.—White lead paint is used successfully at the Roosevelt Hospital, N.Z., mixed thick. (2). Olive oil and lime water on lint. (3). Carbonate of soda dissolved in tepid water. Freely bathe the injury, then quickly cover with the powdered soda.

* *

Bites and Stings.—Rub dilute carbolic acid 1 to 20, then cover with piece of lint soaked in same. (2). Make a poultice of bread and hot water, dilute carbolic acid and mixture of opium. (3). Dilute ammonia or acetic acid. (4). Rub in chalk or carbonate of soda.

* * *

Bruise.—Scrape an English potato very fine and apply as poultice. Bathe in cold water.

* * *

Toothache or Neuralgia.—If in hollow tooth, apply on a small piece of lint carbolic acid, being very careful that none of the acid touches any flesh. To prevent a burn from the acid apply olive or other oil. This ailment is well described as the outcry of an impoverished nerve; every attention should therefore be paid to the well being of the body.

INFANTILE NOTES.

Feeding, How Often.—For the first month about every one and a-half hours; for the second month every two hours; for the third month every three hours; gradually lengthening the space of time as baby advances in age, till three meals a day is arrived at.

* * *

Artificial Feeding.—Till six or seven months old the safest food is a mixture of cow's milk one part, and water two parts, with a little sugar and a pinch of salt, given in small quantities at a time.

QUEENSLAND MODEL DAIRY, Turbot Street. Telephone 379.

We Recommend SQUATTER WHISKY.

Exercise.—An infant may be taken into the open air a fortnight after birth in summer, or a month after in winter, and this should occur daily. At about three months old encourage an infant to muscular exertion by laying him on his back on a rug, or carpet when he will stretch and kick with glee.

* * *

Sleep.—Have a regular hour for putting a child to bed. Lay children down awake, and thus accustom them to falling asleep themselves. It is healthier for even a young infant to have his own cot or crib. Any extra warmth required besides the blanket, may be furnished by a hot water bottle. Should a child be wakeful and fractious, the bowels in almost every case require attention.

* * *

Weak Ankles.—Should a child have weak ankles, bathe them 5 minutes at a time, after his morning ablution, with baysalt and water (a small handful dissolved in a quart of rain water), then dry carefully, and rub in camphorated oil liniment. Do not put him on his feet early. Do not, without competent advice, use iron instruments or any mechanical support.

* * *

Scurf.—To remove scurf from a child's head. After the daily bath, rub glycerine well into the roots of the head, then gently brush but not comb the hair.

* * *

Clothing of Children.—The clothing of a child should reach up to the neck, be large and full about the chest, free from tight strings, and suited to the season of the year. The chest, bowels and feet should be kept comfortably warm, and the head cool. Let a child always wear flannel next his skin, that is a flannel shirt, having it new in winter time, and he will be much less liable to take cold. Give particular attention to the clothing of a child's feet. Let the sock or stocking fit comfortably and be wool; let the shoe be broad at the toe, have good thick soles, but uppers of soft pliable leather. The best kind of hat for a child in summer time is a broad-brimmed cotton one, as it is very light, shady, and allows a free escape of perspiration. For winter a knitted or crocheted hat or bonnet of wool is comfortable and warm. Do not leave off winter clothing too early—let the spring be well advanced.

* * *

The Nursery.—For a nursery, choose a room with a cheerful aspect, plenty of light, and with perfect ventilation. Throw the windows wide open every time the child leaves the room, if only for half an hour. For warming the room have an old-fashioned open fireplace with a good-sized chimney, and let it be protected by a fire-grating about three feet high. Do not use either a gas stove or a coal stove — the continued use of either will cause a child to grow up stunted, weak, and unhealthy. Let the room be kept at a moderate temperature in winter time not exceeding 60 degrees Fahr. The best light is oil, then candles; especially good are Price's patent candles. The size of the nursery should allow eight cubic feet of room for each child, the ceilings should be white and clean, the walls papered with a tasteful design of wall paper. Do not hang gaudy cheap prints about, but by a few good coloured pictures encourage a taste for drawing and painting. The most suitable bed is one with a wire mattress, horsehair or fibre mattress, mackintosh, blankets and pillows. It should be placed out of any draught, not facing the light, and if possible with the head either north or east. Let the child's nursery be the cheeriest room in the house, with an abundance of playthings, space and light to use them, and with a merry nurse to help in the games. However well chosen and fitted be the nursery, yet let the child have much outdoor exercise and amusement. Do not buy cheap painted toys, especially those painted green, but rather white-wood toys; also purchase according to age, sex and inclination of the child.

50

GOVERNMENT DEPARTMENTS.

Executive and Legislative.

GOVERNOR AND COMMANDER-IN-CHIEF—His Excellency The Right Honorable Baron Lamington, K.C.M.G.; £5,000 per annum, with £500 travelling expenses and £500 for forage, horse, &c. The English Government grant £800 each way to and from England.

Baron Lamington [Charles Wallace Alexander Napier Cochrane-Baillie] was born in 1860. He is the son of the first Baron Lamington, by Annabella Mary Elizabeth, daughter of Alexander Robert Drummond, of Cadlands, Hants. He took his B.A. degree at Oxford in 1894, and was M.P. for North St. Pancras until he succeeded to the Peerage in 1890. He was Assistant Private Secretary to the Marquis of Salisbury when Prime Minister, from 1885 till 1886. He holds a lieutenancy in the Yeomanry Brigade of the 11th Lanarkshire Regiment. He was married on June 13, 1895, to Miss May Hozier, daughter of Sir William Hozier, Bart.

PRIVATE SECRETARY.—P. W. G. Stuart, £400.

AIDE-DE-CAMP—Captain C. E. M. Pyne (Royal Warwickshire Regiment), £300. Two Orderlies—one at £140, and one at £120.

EXECUTIVE COUNCIL.

PRESIDENT—His Excellency the Governor.
VICE PRESIDENT—The Hon. T. J. Byrnes, £300.
PREMIER AND ATTORNEY-GENERAL—The Hon. T. J. Byrnes, £1000.
HOME SECRETARY—The Hon. J. R. Dickson, £1000.
POSTMASTER-GENERAL—Hon. W. Horatio Wilson, M.L.C., £1000.
SECRETARY FOR AGRICULTURE—Hon. J. V. Chataway, £1000.
SECRETARY FOR PUBLIC LANDS—Hon. J. F. G. Foxton, £1000.
SECRETARY FOR MINES—Hon. R. Philp, £1000.
SECRETARY FOR PUBLIC INSTRUCTION—Hon. D. H. Dalrymple, £1000.
SECRETARY FOR WORKS AND RAILWAYS—Hon. John Murray, £1000.
WITHOUT PORTFOLIO—Hon. A. H. Barlow.

AGENT-GENERAL FOR QUEENSLAND—

LONDON—Hon. Sir H. Tozer, K.C.M.G., £1,250.

————o————

Parliament.

LEGISLATIVE COUNCIL. (38 Members.)
PRESIDENT—Hon. Sir H. M. Nelson, P.C., K.C.M.G., LL D., £1000.

We Recommend SQUATTER WHISKY.

CHAIRMAN OF COMMITTEES —Hon. F. T. Brentnall, £500.

Hon. William Allan
" William Aplin
" John Archibald
" Andrew Henry Barlow
" William Draper Box
" Frederick Thomas Brentnall
" Robert Bulcock
" Chas. H. Buzacott
" Felix Clewett
" James Cowlishaw
" John Deane
" John Ferguson
" Edward Barrow Forrest
" William Forrest
" George Wilkie Gray
" A. C. Gregory, C.M.G.
" F. H. Hart
" John Christian Heussler
" Frederick Hurrell Holberton

Hon. James Lalor
" William Frederick Lambert
" Peter Macpherson
" Charles Ferdinand Marks, M.D.
" Boyd Dunlop Morehead
" Hugh Mosman
" Albert Norton
" Patrick Perkins
" William Grene Power
" Alexander Raff
" James Thornelee Smith
" Joseph Capel Smyth
" William Frederick Taylor, M.D.
" Andrew Joseph Thynne
" John Sargent Turner
" James Tyson
" Andrew Heron Wilson
" Walter Horatio Wilson
" Henry Conwell Wood

Clerk of the Council and of the Parliaments—Henry Wyat Radford.   Clerk Assistant and Usher of the Black Rod—Charles William Costin.   Principal Messenger —Joseph Kelly.   Messenger—R. Lane.

Clerk of the Assembly—Lewis A. Bernays, C.M.G., F.L.S., &c.   Clerk Assistant and Sergeant-at-Arms—Hon. C. G. Holmes a'Court.   Clerk—J. Doran.   Principal Messenger—T. J. Woosley.   Second Messenger—J. Doran.

JOINT ESTABLISHMENT—LEGISLATIVE COUNCIL AND LEGISLATIVE ASSEMBLY.
Librarian—Denis O'Donovan, C.M.G., F.R.S.L., F.R.G.S., &c.   Principal Shorthand Writer—John Gilligan.   Shorthand Writers—Henry Willoughby, R. Morris, W. F. O'Carroll, R. P. Earle, C. A. Bernays, S. Hodgen, J. Brennan. Caterer—C. Baldwin.

MEMBERS OF PARLIAMENT, THEIR ELECTORATES AND ADDRESSES
(72 Members.)

N.B.—When Parliament is in Session the invariable practice is to address letters to Parliament House.   Members of the Assembly receive £300, free railway pass, and travelling expenses.

SPEAKER—Hon. Alfred Sandlings Cowley, £500.

CHAIRMAN OF COMMITTEES—John Thomas Annear, £500.

Albert—Robert M. Collins, Pimpama

Aubigny—William Thorn, Goombungee

Balonne—G. W. B. Story, Cobb & Co., Petrie's Bight

Barcoo—George Kerr

Bowen Robert Harrison Smith, Bowen

Brisbane (North) T. Macdonald-Paterson, Edward-street; R. Fraser, Elizabeth-street

Brisbane (South) W. Stephens, Vulture-street; Henry Turley, Raymond Terrace, South Brisbane

Bulimba—Hon. Jas. R. Dickson, C.M.G., Toorak, Breakfast Creek

Bulloo—John Leahy, U. M. & A. Co., Eagle-street

Bundaberg—Thomas Glassey, Harcourt-street, Valley

Bundamba Lewis Thomas, Bundamba

Burke John Hoolan, Georgetown

Burnett W. J. Ryott Maughan, Brisbane

Barrow N. E. N. Tooth, Maryborough

Cairns—Isidore Lissner, Creek-street, Brisbane

53

QUEENSLAND MODEL DAIRY, Turbot Street. Telephone 379.

Cambooya—H. Daniels, Russell-street, South Brisbane

Carnarvon—Hon. J. F. G. Foxton, Albert-street, Brisbane

Carpentaria—George C. Sim. Croydon

Charters Towers—J. H. Dunsford, Charters Towers; Anderson Dawson, Charters Towers

Clermont—John M. Cross, South Brisbane

Cook—John Hamilton

Croydon—William H. Browne, Croydon

Cunningham—Thomas McGahan

Dalby—Joshua Thomas Bell, George-st., Brisbane

Drayton and Toowoomba — William H. Groom, Toowoomba; J. Fogarty, Toowoomba

Enoggera—James George Drake, George street, Brisbane

Fassifern—Hon. George Thorn, Ipswich

Fitzroy—A. J. Callan, Bowen Hills, Bris.

Flinders—Charles McDonald

Fortitude Valley—John McMaster, Valley; F. McDonnell, Taringa

Gregory—William H. Corfield. Winton

Gympie—William Smyth, Gympie; Jacob Stumm, Gympie

Herbert Hon. Alfred Sandlings Cowley, Terrace-street, Toowong

Ipswich T. B. Cribb, Ipswich; A. J. Stephenson, Ipswich

Kennedy George Jackson

Leichhardt Herbert Freemont Hardacre, North Quay, Brisbane

Lockyer William D. Armstrong, Gatton

Logan James Stodart, Mary-st., Brisbane

Maranoa Robert King, Roma

Mackay—Hon. David Hay Dalrymple, Wickham-terrace, Brisbane; Hon. J. V. Chataway, Cleveland

Maryborough—John Thomas Annear, Merivale-street, South Brisbane; John Bartholomew, Maryborough

Mitchell—C. B. Fitzgerald, Longreach

Moreton—Matthew Battersby, Caboolture

Murilla—J. Moore, Juandah, Chinchilla

Musgrave—Wm. Henry Bligh O'Connell, Bundaberg

Normanby Hon. John Murray, Rockhampton

Nundah T. Bridges, Nundah

Oxley — Samuel Grimes, Edmonstone-street. South Brisbane

Port Curtis Jason Boles, Gladstone

Rockhampton—W. Kidston, Rockha'pton; George S. Curtis, Rockhampton

Rockhampton (North) — J. C. Stewart, Rockhampton

Rosewood—D. T. Keogh. Ipswich

Stanley—Frederick Lord, Maida Hill Brisbane

Toombul Andrew L. Petrie, Queen-street, Brisbane

Toowong—T. Finney, Queen-st., Brisbane

Townsville Hon. R. Philp, Townsville; W. J. Castling, Townsville

Warrego James Crombie, c/o U.M. & A. Co., Eagle-street, Brisbane

Warwick Hon. T. J. Byrnes, Yeronga

Wide Bay C. M. Jenkinson, Gympie

Woolloongabba—Thos. Dibley, Woolloongabba

Woothakata—J. Newall, Herberton

Chief Secretary's Department.

Chief Secretary and Premier—Hon. T. J. Byrnes. £1000.

Under Secretary H. S. Dutton, £700.

Agent-General Hon. Sir Horace Tozer, K.C.M.G., Westminster Chambers, Victoria-street, London, E.C., £1,250.

Secretary—C. S. Dicken, C.M.G., £700.

We Recommend SQUATTER WHISKY.

54

PUBLIC SERVICE BOARD.

Chairman—Captain Townley, £1000 ; Thos. Mylne, £800 ; M. O'Malley, £800.
Secretary—J. O. Bichard, £200.

DEFENCE FORCE.

Governor and Commander-in-Chief—His Excellency the Right Honourable C. W. A. Napier, Baron Lamington, K.C.M.G.
Commandant—Col. H. Gunter, £700.
Lieut.-Col., Assist. Adj. Gen. and Chief Staff Officer—J. S. Lyster, £400.
Staff Officer Mounted Infantry, etc.—Lieut.-Col. P. R. Ricardo, £300.

MARINE DEFENCE.

Acting Naval Commandant—Walton Drake, R.N., £375.
Officer Instructor Naval Corps—E. F. de Chair, £300. Staff Paymaster—E. V. Pollock, £250.

IMMIGRATION.

Officer-in-charge and Inspector Pacific Islanders—J. O'N. Brenan, £250.

---o---

Home Secretary's Department.

OFFICE : TREASURY BUILDINGS.

Home Secretary—Hon. J. R. Dickson, C.M.G., £1000.
Under Home Secretary—W. H. Ryder, £700.
Chief Clerk—. F. Sloan, £500.
Registrar-General—Joseph Hughes, £700.
Compiler of Statistics—T. Weedon, £400.
Government Resident, Thursday Island—Hon. J. Douglas, £700.
Officer-in-charge Labour Bureau—J. O'N. Brenan, £200.
Chief Inspector Factories and Shops—C. McLay, £300.
Health Officer, Brisbane—C. J. H. Wray, L.R.C.P., Edin., £700.
Commissioner of Police—W. E. Parry-Okeden, £800.
Chief Clerk—R. H. Lawson, £500.
Government Printer—E. Gregory, £500.
Comptroller-General of Prisons—C. E. de F. Pennefather, £600.
Inspector Hospitals for Insane, &c.—(vacant) £100.

DEPARTMENT OF JUSTICE.

Attorney-General—Hon. T. J. Byrnes, £1000.
Under Secretary—William Cahill, £600.
Registrar of Titles—J. O. Bourne, £600.
Registrar of Patents, &c.—P. J. McDermott, £350.
Registrar of Friendly Societies—R. Rendle, £100.
First Deputy Registrar—G. M. Jones, £400.
Master of Titles—E. Gore Jones, £400.
Chief Commissioner of Stamps—Hugh M. Milman, £600.
Chief Clerk—E. J. Hennessey, £400.
Registrar, Supreme Court, Brisbane—William Bell, £700.
Crown Solicitor, Brisbane—J. H. Gill, £700.

We Recommend SQUATTER WHISKY.

SUPREME COURT.

Chief Justice—His Honor Sir Samuel W. Griffith, G.C.M.G., £3,500. Puisne Judges—His Honor Pope Alexander Cooper, His Honor Patrick Real, His Honor Virgil Power; Northern Judge—His Honor Chas. E. Chubb; each £2,000 per annum. Crown Prosecutors—Hon. A. Rutledge and Chas. Jameson, £500 each.

DISTRICT COURTS.

Judges—G. W. Paul, Granville Geo. Miller, Arthur Baptist Noel; each £1000 per annum. Crown Prosecutors—F. W. Dickson, Henry E. King, E. Mansfield; each £400 per annum and allowed private practice.

SHERIFF'S OFFICE.

Sheriff—(Vacant). Office—Supreme Court Buildings, Brisbane.

INTESTACY, INSANITY, AND INSOLVENCY OFFICE.

Official Trustee and Curator—J. B. Hall, £600. Office—Treasury Buildings.

DEPARTMENT OF RAILWAYS.

Secretary for Railways—Hon. John Murray, £1000. Commissioner—R. J. Gray, £1,500. Secretary to Commissioner—T. S. Pratten, £475. Chief Engineer—H. C. Stanley, M.I.C.E., £1000 and £400 allowance. Traffic Manager—J. F. Thallon, £1000. Locomotive Engineer—H. Horniblow, £650.

DEPARTMENT OF PUBLIC INSTRUCTION.

Secretary for Public Instruction—Hon. D. H. Dalrymple, £1000. Under Secretary—J. G. Anderson, M.A., £750.

TREASURER'S DEPARTMENT.

Treasurer—The Hon. Robert Philp, £1000. Under Secretary, T. M. King, £800. Marine Board—Chairman, Captain T. M. Almond, £100; as Portmaster, £600. Shipping Master—J. Mackay, £360. Collector of Customs—W. H. Irving, £650. Chief Clerk—J. C. Kent, £430. Manager, Government Savings Bank—T. W. Wells, £550.

DEPARTMENT OF PUBLIC LANDS.

Secretary for Lands—Hon. J. F. G. Foxton, £1000.
Under Secretary—F. X. Heeney, £800.
Chief Clerk—W. J. Scott, £500.
Land Board—Members: W. A. Tully, T. S. Sword, E. Mansfield, £1000 each. Secretary—P. W. Shannon, £300.
Division of Runs—Commissioners: W. Gibson, H. B. Rogers-Harrison, £700 each; A. Warde, W. S. Paul, T. W. Palmer, £430 each. Travelling allowance, £200 each.
Survey Branch—Surveyor-General—Archibald McDowall, £750. Chief Draftsman—H. Macintosh, £370.

CROWN LAND COMMISSIONERS AND LAND AGENTS.

There are Commissioners and Land Agents at the following places; as changes occur frequently, it is best to address them as "Commissioners for Crown Lands" or "Land Agents" as at the respective places:—Aramac Banana, Barcaldine, Birdsville, Blackall, Bowen, Brisbane, Bundaberg, Burketown, Cairns, Charleville, Charters Towers, Clermont, Cloncurry, Cooktown, Croydon, Cunnamulla, Dalby, Eidsvold, Gayndah, Georgetown, Gladstone, Goondiwindi, Gympie, Herberton, Hughenden, Hungerford, Ingham, Inglewood, Ipswich, Isisford, Longreach, Mackay, Maryborough,

Mourilyan, Nanango, Normanton, Pentland, Port Douglas, Ravenswood, Rockhampton, Roma, St. George, St. Lawrence, Springsure, Stanthorpe, Surat, Tenningering, Tambo, Taroom, Thargomindah, Thornborough, Thursday Island, Toowoomba, Townsville, Warwick, Winton, Windorah.

PASTORAL OCCUPATION BRANCH.

Officer-in-charge—J. E. Burstall, £400.

DEPARTMENT OF AGRICULTURE.

Secretary for Agriculture—Hon. J. V. Chataway, M.L.A., £1000. Under Secretary— Peter McLean, £500 and £100 travelling allowance. Chief Clerk—E. G. E. Scriven, £300. Colonial Botanist—F. M. Bailey, £300. Fruit Expert—A. H. Benson, £600. Tobacco Expert—R. S. Nevill, £500. Entomologist, Hy. Tryon, £300. Agricultural Chemist—J. C. Brunnich, £300. Principal, Gatton Agricultural College ————————— Curator Botanic Gardens—P. McMahon, £300. Overseers: State Nursery, Mackay—D. Buchanan, £156 and quarters; State Nursery, Kamerunga, Cairns—E. Cowley, £156 and quarters; State Nursery, Westbrook—H. A. Tardent, £156 and quarters; State Farm, Hermitage—C. Ross, £156 and quarters. Director Stock Institute—C. J. Pound, £500.

INSPECTOR OF BRANDS—CATTLE AND SHEEP.

Chief Inspector—P. R. Gordon, Brisbane, £500.

DEPARTMENT OF MINES.

Secretary for Mines—Hon. Robert Philp, £1000.
Under Secretary—P. F. Sellheim, £750.
Government Geologist—R. L. Jack, £1000.
Government Analyst—J. B. Henderson, £340.

DEPARTMENT OF PUBLIC WORKS.

Secretary—Hon. John Murray, £1000. Under Secretary—R. Robertson, £600. Government Architect and Engineer for Bridges—A. B. Brady, £750.

MEDICAL BOARD.

President—Dr. John Thomson, M.B. Secretary—C. A. J. Woodcock. Office—George-street, Brisbane.

POSTMASTER-GENERAL'S DEPARTMENT.

Postmaster-General—Hon. W. H. Wilson, £1000. Under Secretary and Superintendent of Telegraphs—John McDonnell, £800. Superintendent Mail Branch—R. T. Scott, £500. Accountant—Jno. Lawry, £550. Electrical Engineer—John Hesketh, £600.

AUDITOR-GENERAL'S DEPARTMENT.

Auditor-General—Edward Deshon, £1000
Accountant—R. H. Mills. £550

ADDRESSES OF GOVERNMENT DEPARTMENTS.

MANY persons, not only outside but also within the Colony, are frequently at a loss to know to whom to address on business matters connected with the various Government Departments. To such persons the following may prove of assistance:—

MINISTERIAL DEPARTMENT—THE CHIEF SECRETARY.

Persons in Europe desiring information respecting the Colony – Secretary, Agent-General, No. 1 Westminster Chambers, Victoria-street, London.
Defence Force (Land)—Colonel Commandant, Q.D.F., Brisbane, Queensland.
Defence Force (Marine)—Naval Commandant, Brisbane, Queensland.
Immigration, Pacific Island Labour, Government Labour Bureau, Government Relief—Immigration Agent, Brisbane, Queensland.

MINISTERIAL DEPARTMENT.—THE HOME SECRETARY.

The health of the community—Secretary, Central Board of Health, Brisbane, Qld.
(1) Registration of Births, Marriages, and Deaths ; Ministers of Religion authorised to marry ; and of Treasurers of Hospitals; (2) Statistics of Queensland—The Registrar-General, Brisbane, Queensland.
Executive Police—Commissioner of Police, Brisbane, Queensland.
The printing and publishing of Government Reports, Documents, &c.—Government Printer, Brisbane, Queensland.
The custody and control of insane persons—Inspector of Hospitals for the Insane, Goodna, Queensland.
The custody and control of criminals—Comptroller-General of Prisons, Brisbane, Queensland.
Benches, Police Magistrates, Clerks of Petty Sessions, Electoral Registrars, Benevolent Asylums, Government Steamers, Government Medical Officers—Under Secretary, Home Secretary's Department, Brisbane, Queensland.

MINISTERIAL DEPARTMENT JUSTICE.

Judicial administration of the Superior Courts—Under Secretary, Department of Justice, Brisbane, Queensland.
Relating to Accounts and Estates of Insolvent persons – Principal Trustee in Insolvency, Brisbane, Queensland.
The Estates of persons dying Intestate—Curator in Intestacy, Brisbane, Queensland.
The Estates of Insane Persons and their maintenance —Curator in Insanity, Brisbane, Queensland.
Friendly Societies, Building Societies, Trade Unions —Registrar of Friendly Societies, Brisbane, Queensland.
Patents, Designs, Trade Marks, Copyright—Registrar of Patents, Brisbane, Qld.
Titles to Land, Mortgages, Transfers, &c.—Registrar of Titles, Brisbane, Queensland.
Stamps, Stamp Duties, Probate and Administration Duties — Chief Commissioner for Stamps, Brisbane, Queensland.

MINISTERIAL DEPARTMENT.—PUBLIC INSTRUCTION.

State Schools, Provisional Schools—Under Secretary Public Instruction, Brisbane, Queensland.
Orphan Asylums, State Children boarded-out Inspector of Orphanages, Brisbane, Queensland.
Museum—Curator, The Museum, Brisbane, Queensland.

MINISTERIAL DEPARTMENT—THE TREASURER.

The Public Account, Government Stocks and Debentures, Public Revenue, Public Expenditure—Under Secretary, Treasury, Brisbane, Queensland.

The purchase, supply, &c., of stores for the use of the Government—Colonial Storekeeper, Brisbane, Queensland.

Customs, Distilleries, Excise—Collector of Customs, Brisbane, Queensland.

Inspection and Survey of Shipping, Mariners' Certificates, Inspection of Fisheries—Chairman, Marine Board, Brisbane, Queensland.

Harbours, Lighthouses, Pilots, Magazines, Dredges—Portma-ter, Brisbane, Qld.

Government Savings Bank—Manager, Government Savings Bank, Brisbane, Qld.

Artesian Bores, Waterworks for Local Bodies—Hydraulic Engineer, Brisbane, Qld.

MINISTERIAL DEPARTMENT—PUBLIC LANDS.

Sale of Crown Lands, Leases of Crown Lands, Leases of Squatting Runs, Opening of Roads through Crown Lands—Under Secretary for Public Lands, Brisbane, Qld.

Survey of Crown Lands, Trigonometrical Survey—Surveyor-General, Brisbane, Qld.

MINISTERIAL DEPARTMENT—AGRICULTURE.

Agriculture, State Nurseries, Botanic Gardens, Forest Nurseries, Meat and Dairy Produce Encouragement Act—Under Secretary for Agriculture, Brisbane, Qld.

Diseases in Live Stock, Brands, Stock Institute, Live Stock and Meat Export—Chief Inspector of Stock, Brisbane, Queensland.

MINISTERIAL DEPARTMENT—MINES.

Goldfields, Mineral Lands—Under Secretary for Mines, Brisbane, Queensland.

Geological Survey—Government Geologist, Brisbane, Queensland.

The Chemical Analysis of matters having a public interest—Government Analyst, Brisbane, Queensland.

MINISTERIAL DEPARTMENT—PUBLIC WORKS.

Public Works generally, Inspection and Valuation of Sugar Lands, Inspection of Guaranteed Sugar Works—Under Secretary for Public Works, Brisbane, Qld.

Public Buildings, Public Bridges—Government Architect, Brisbane, Queensland.

MINISTERIAL DEPARTMENT—RAILWAYS.

General Railway Business—Commissioner for Railways, Brisbane, Queensland.

Railway Construction, Railway Surveys, Railway Maintenance—Chief Engineer for Railways, Brisbane, Queensland.

Traffic, Railways—General Traffic Manager, Brisbane, Queensland.

Rolling Stock, Railways—Locomotive Engineer, Brisbane, Queensland.

Railway Stores—General Railway Storekeeper, Brisbane, Queensland.

MINISTERIAL DEPARTMENT—POSTMASTER-GENERAL.

Postal matters, Telegraph matters, Telephone matters—Under Secretary, Post and Telegraph Department, Brisbane, Queensland.

Meteorology—Government Meteorological Observer, Brisbane, Queensland.

DAIRY NOTES.

To Keep a Small Dairy Cool.—Close the gable ends of the building with battens nailed three inches apart. Nail canvas over the battens, and on a small platform above place a kerosene tin full of water. Over the edge of the tin hang a bunch of woollen rags, reaching to the bottom of the water, and falling over the canvas to a greater length than the ends lying in the water. The rags act as a syphon. The water is drawn up from the tin by what is known as capillary attraction, and constantly drips on the canvas, keeping it always moist. As a breeze blows through the wet canvas, the temperature inside the building is reduced by many degrees.

*　　　*　　　*

Good Butter.—The essential things for making good butter are cleanliness, cool temperature and careful manufacture.

*　　　*　　　*

Butter cannot help being tainted if the dairy is a receptacle for every kind of produce, and the store for meat, onions, and general lumber.

*　　　*　　　*

Milking.—The cow should be milked at a regular hour each day, and always milked out, as the last of the milk is much richer in fat than the first. The cow should not be beaten or excited during the operation of bailing or milking. If the calf be allowed to run with the mother, she can no longer be considered suitable for dairying as the milking vessels become destroyed, owing to the calf being unable to consume all the milk the cow is capable of.

*　　　*　　　*

Improving the Milk Yield.—Give your cows three times a day, an ordinary pailful of water slightly warmed and salted, in which about one and a-half quarts of bran has been stirred; your cow will give twenty per cent. more milk.

*　　　*　　　*

The Herd.—The best breed of cows to have for a dairy herd is Shorthorn cows crossed with Jersey or Ayrshire bulls.

*　　　*　　　*

Lucerne will communicate its flavour to the cream and butter only if the cows are fed with it immediately before milking. Lucerne, green maize, imphee, sorghum, and Cape barley are the best fodder crops.

*　　　*　　　*

Calves for the Dairy or Butcher.—The theory that the young calf reveals the future cow is based on the form and heredity of the calf's ancestors. If the calf has the beefy form, and her ancestors were noted for their beefy qualities, it is safe to say that such a calf will not make a profitable butter cow; but if the three days' calf has the marked dairy form and is descended from a line of butter cows and sires, she can be developed into a good butter cow. The theory is based on the principle of breeding that like begets like.

*　　　*　　　*

Be Gentle with your cows. A gentle man gets more milk from a cow than a harsh man.

Separate the Weaker Animals; they need extra feed, whereas with the stronger they get scant feed.

* * *

A Simple Remedy for bad tempered cows that horn their mates is to screw a ¾-inch round or octagon nut on the tip of their horn. A new nut will cut its own thread on to the horn.

* * *

The Duration of Pregnancy in a cow is 285 days.

* * *

Salt.—Place around your yards or fields in proper receptacles plenty of rock salt, covered from the rain. Few farmers are aware that in addition to its being an essential for the building up of the animal salt is useful in facilitating the passage of the albumenoids of the food from the digestive canal into the blood and the circulation generally; thus increasing the energy of the vital processes.

* * *

Put a thoroughbred bull at the head of your herd and breed up.

* * *

Don't be too officious when the cow is calving. Nature generally does her business in the proper way.

* * *

One of the important items in making the most out of feed is to feed and milk at regular intervals.

* * *

Cream should never be allowed to stand long enough to show a watery appearance between the cream and the milk.

* * *

Don't leave the cows with cracked or sore teats day after day, and then beat them because they kick while being milked.

* * *

Flavour depends very largely upon the sweetness and the flavour of the food given, and the surroundings of the milk and cream before it is turned into butter.

* * *

Don't attempt to be a dairyman if you feel like kicking a cow every time you see her. They feel it often before you kick, and can never do their best.

* * *

The treatment a cow gets the first forty-eight hours after calving will usually determine her productiveness for the year. Better starve than overfeed her at this time.

* * *

Don't be in a hurry to get the cows out of the paddock at night, nor go after them with a dog, unless it is a well-trained sheep dog that knows his business, knows the cows, and the cows know him.

* * *

One hundred pounds of good milk contains 87 pounds of water, 4 of fat, 5 of milk sugar, 3.3 of caseine and albumen, and 7 of mineral matter or salts.

* * *

"Testing Cows" means making their milk for one day, seven days, or thirty days, into butter. "Testing milk" means a different thing entirely. It means to ascertain how much fat there is in a given amount of milk.

* * *

The Dutch not only know a good cow when they see it, but they know the relative value of milk, butter and cheese. They realise the fact that butter sells for so much a pound in the market; while cheese, though much cheaper, furnishes the consumer more nutrition per pound. Cheese contains more of the flesh-forming elements, while butter can only be converted into heat or fat.

We Recommend SQUATTER WHISKY.

FARM NOTES.

Fodder should be stored under shelter if possible. A cheap tarpaulin is good for this purpose, and the waste of a good deal of nutrition is avoided.

All Receipted Bills should be kept on a file, or in a clean, safe place. They are handy things to have in the house when you are billed for a debt already paid. Take receipts and carefully preserve them; don't trust too much to memory in business affairs.

Do not attempt to cover a big field with a little bit of manure.

The Life of a tradesman averages only about two-thirds that of a farmer.

If You are pushed for money, try and sell a portion of the farm. Don't borrow money these times, except as a last resource.

A Fence Post that is well seasoned before being set will last five times as long as the one set when unseasoned. Fence posts should be cut two years before being used.

Paint the posts well before placing them in the ground with boiled linseed oil, thickened to the consistency of paint by stirring in it pulverised charcoal.

Ringbarking.—The best time for ringbarking is from January to March, and even a month later if there be little rainfall at the time. The same time of year should be chosen for cutting suckers, which, however, should have two years' growth before being dealt with, otherwise your labour may be wasted, as they will probably sprout again the following season.

The Value of Salt.—An enthusiastic British Journal in a recent article, says "that a thousand or two pounds of salt sown to the acre will check the rust in cereals, protect oats against the grub and wire worm, prevent potato diseases, dissipate fungoid growth in pastures, stop the growth of mosses, will make rougher grasses more palatable, and sweeten herbage generally.

When to Sow Lucerne.—The best time to sow lucerne is as soon as all danger of frost is past. Work the ground well to get rid of weeds, and sow from 3lb. to 5lb. of seed per acre. Harrow very lightly; a bush harrow is regarded as the best by some lucerne-growers.

The Potato. This year witnesses the 301st anniversary of the planting of the potato in England. It was Sir Walter Raleigh, as everybody knows, who is responsible for the favour with which the gentle "spud" is regarded as an article of diet, and it was in 1597 that the seed, taken from America by the greatest courtier of his time, was planted in the garden of the famous botanist, Gerrard.

We Recommend SQUATTER WHISKY.

WARWICK

Lime and Its Effects.—Lime is a much used, and, very often, a much abused material on the farm. It has a very important role to play, and, if handled in a proper manner, is a valuable aid to the farmer. There are many who use this material again and again with a mistaken notion as to its true functions in the soil. In time, however, their experience teaches them the true place of lime in agriculture, but often their lands have been almost exhausted before they gain their wisdom. While lime has a value as a plant food, yet its greatest worth on the farm is due to its physical effect on the soil itself. It is very seldom that a soil does not contain a sufficient quantity of lime to furnish this ingredient as plant food pure and simple. Briefly described, the actions of lime are as follow: If applied on a sandy soil it fills up the openings, makes the particles adhere closer, causes them to retain moisture better, to absorb less heat during the day and retain more at night. On clay soils it separates the particles, making the soil more porous, thus easier for the passage of water and air, and, therefore, makes the soil warmer and easier to work. Lime also hastens the decay of vegetable matter in the soil, which, of course, renders the nitrogen more available. If a soil is sour, an application of lime will sweeten it. If a green crop is ploughed under, an application of lime will prevent the soil from becoming acid.

• • •

System on the Farm.—In every department of labour the essential to success is a systematic method. System is especially needed in farm work, because thrift of so many living things is in the power of the farmer. There should be a regular hour for feeding stock. Animals soon learn the hour for their meals when given regularly, and are impatient of delay. Bawling, bleating, or squealing for an hour before each meal does not hasten the development of fat in calves, lambs, or pigs. At other times the food is given too soon, the animal not being hungry, and not prepared to make the best use of it. There should be a certain time to begin feeding in the morning, and a time to quit feeding in the evening. The family meals should not vary ten minutes from the specified time; neither should the men ever keep meals waiting. Children should be off to school on time, neither too late nor too early. They will be more apt to have their lessons on time if everything is regular at home. The work is much easier to do when every one knows his time and place; life is more pleasant, and happy times come oftener. System preserves health, for we know that worry kills more people than disease. The man who plans his work carefully usually gets through it without worry. The man whose work worries him cannot do a good day's work. Better sit down and plan half a day than work and worry for a month.

• • •

Value of Cream Separators.—It is purely natural in its operation. It simply adds the natural revolving centrifugal force to the natural force of gravity, which latter causes cream to rise in the natural way, and thus effects its immediate as well as its complete separation, neither of which is otherwise possible. In separating it will save from 10 per cent. to 50 per cent. in quantity of the product for you, according to the system you may now be using, and the climatic conditions under which you work. In churning it will save from 5 per cent. to 10 per cent. in quantity, and fully one-half the time now required. In quality it will improve the selling value of product from a penny to threepence per pound, according to the system now used and the care now given it. It will give fresh, sweet skim-milk, still retaining the animal warmth, worth three times as much as such milk in the old way, and prevent the "scours" with the calves. It will do away with tuberculosis and other disease germs in the dairy products, thoroughly cleanse the milk and cream, lessen taints and odours, and enhance keeping qualities. It will save much time and labour all round. There is no endless washing of pans; no flies to fight, no warming of milk nor keeping of fires to do so; nothing but the cream to handle and care for. It will save in actual cash results alone £2 per cow per year and make dairy work a source of both profit and satisfaction. Where the separators are run four or five hours every day, they should be cleaned out every

We Recommend SQUATTER WHISKY.

two days or oftener. By this the boxes will never heat, and your separators will run more smoothly and do closer skimming. You cannot expect to do close skimming unless the separators run smoothly and at a high rate of speed, and keeping the bearings clean and well supplied with oil is the main point in running them properly. The separator may run all right at night, and very badly in the morning; or it may run even very badly for a part of the separation, and suddenly settle down and run smoothly for the rest of the time, owing to some slight change in the position of the rubber ring, or to the swelling equalising it. The only thing to do is to put in a new ring, and keep it as free from oil as possible. It may last for months, or it may swell unequally and cause trouble again almost immediately.

* * *

Churning.—If you want the butter to come in the granular state, stop churning when it reaches this point; draw off the butter; use the sieve to catch any particles of butter that are likely to flow out with the milk. These sieves can be procured cheaply. After the milk has been drawn off, wash with pure, clear, cold water. This is done by pouring the water in the churn and gently rocking the churn for a few minutes. Then draw off the water and repeat the operation until the water comes from the churn clear and uncoloured by milk. If done well, your butter ought to be entirely free of milk. Now spread the butter on the butter worker, and spread evenly over it a good grade of dairy salt—one ounce to the pound of butter. Distribute with the worker as evenly and as thoroughly as possible, but take care and not work the butter too much. If you prefer, you can distribute the salt before the butter is taken out of the churn. Let the butter stand several hours and then work lightly. If any water stands on the butter and does not seem to work out well, take up the moisture with a sponge kept for the purpose. Use a concussion box churn or one operated on that principle—discard any churn that has any dasher arrangement. Paddles and dashers inside the churn injure and destroy the grain of the butter.

FOWLS.

Feed for Hens.—If your pullets have been properly cared for they will begin to lay within five or six months old and when the cold weather comes they will keep on laying, providing they are properly fed and have wholesome water to drink. We should remember that the eggs in the ovary must have a period of growth and development and all that we are required to do is to furnish such food and otherwise make their surroundings such as will enable the hens to produce eggs. Watch the laying hens in the summer, when they are at liberty to forage where they please, and you will notice what a variety of food they consume. Different kinds of grain, insects, weed seeds, clover and other green food, with now and then a sharp gravel or other gritty substances as grinding material. As a substitute for insects, which they cannot find in winter, furnish animal food in the form of crushed bone or animal meal, not as quack medicine to "make them lay," but as a part of their regular food to supply the nutriment they require. Loose cabbage heads that have no market value, chopped onions, also clover hay cut fine and scalded or steamed, will be relished by fowls in want of green food.

Grit is as essential to fowls as teeth are to us. Another important item is charcoal. Charcoal helps to sweeten the system, so to speak. It prevents indigestion and bowel trouble, and is excellent for either fowls or chicks.

It does no harm whatever to hens to scratch and pick among horse manure.

LINSEED meal brightens the plumage, regulates the bowels, and promotes digestion.

To PREVENT DISEASE —Disease and lice are the great obstacles to be overcome in poultry raising. The house may be kept free from lice by a liberal use of kerosene emulsion and by lime-washing. Lime-wash serves a double purpose, that of ridding the house of lice and making the interior much lighter.

To CURE GAPES.—A very simple method of curing gapes in chicks, and one that is successful in the hands of some, is to pinch the windpipe. With the left hand hold the head of the bird up and the neck straight, and with the thumb and finger of the right hand pinch the windpipe smartly, slightly rolling it. Begin as low down as possible and follow it upwards to the mouth. Be careful to release it frequently to give the bird a chance to cough up the parasites.

LANGSHANS, as a rule, are very hardy.

A FIERY red comb is a sure sign of good layers.

CAREFULLY save all the meat scraps for the fowls.

REMEMBER that lice thrive amazingly during hot weather. Sifted wood ashes are best for removing lice in fowls.

LICE will not attack fowls in a good condition, as readily as they will those that are impoverished.

STALE bread soaked in milk is a good feed for young poultry.

OBSERVE which hens are the best layers and breed from them ; eat or sell the rest.

SUNSHINE should enter the chicken coop from the front not the top.

NOTHING will increase egg production quicker than green bone freshly cut. Machines for cutting cost 20s. to 35s.

IF you want plenty of eggs next winter, hatch plenty of pullets this spring.

THE cross of White Leghorn on White Cochin makes a good general purpose fowl.

THE fowl's heartiest meal should be its supper. It's a long time from supper to breakfast.

KEEP everything about the poultry house clean, with plenty of fresh air, sunlight and whitewash.

ONE variety of chickens on the farm is sufficient ; the same is true fo ducks, geese and turkeys.

COLDS, roup, and other ills, come in through the cracks in the fowlhouse. Stop them up at once.

SOFT-SHELLED eggs are due to one or two causes—an overfat condition, or lack of sufficient lime in food ; give them plenty of crushed oyster shells.

SHADE is necessary both for the fowls and chicks. If the stock cannot get under natural shade, such as trees, then build some sort of protection from the sun.

A MIXTURE of two parts lard to one of kerosene oil, thoroughly applied, will remove the rough, scabby formation on the legs of fowls.

AIR-SLAKED lime should be strewn about the places where the fowls and young stock roost, so as to keep down all odours.

THERE are many persons who think Sunday is a sponge with which to wipe out the sins of the previous week. H. W. Beecher

67

HORSES.

COUGHS AND HEAVES.—For coughs and heaves in horses give in ordinary cases a teaspoonful of oil of tar every other night. In bad cases give larger doses. Feed less hay or corn. Heavy horses are always greedy eaters and are sure to eat all they can find room for.

TENDER FEET.—For tender feet use linseed oil, one-half pint ; turpentine, four ounces; oil of tar, six ounces; origanum, three ounces. Shake well. Apply every other day all round the top of the hoof down one inch from the hair and down on the heel. The horse need not lose a day's work.

LAMPAS IN HORSES.—Lampas is not a disease. It is a term applied to a swelling of the mucous membrane of the hard palate immediately behind the upper incisors of the horse. It usually occurs in connection with teething in young animals and occasionally interferes with mastication. The old barbarous practice of scarifying deeply with a sharp horseshoe nail and burning with a hot iron is cruel and unnecessary. Swabbing the mouth twice daily with half an ounce of alum in a quart of water and allowing a few ears of old, hard corn for the colt to gnaw at will usually prove sufficient as remedial measures.

To PREVENT a horse kicking or pawing in the stall, fasten with a strap, over the hoof just below the fetlock, a small linked chain, say a foot long, leaving the other end loose. He soon tires of whipping his shins.

LINSEED FOR HORSES.—A horse doing very hard work, and receiving a full daily allowance of oats, is much better for about two ounces of linseed oil added to his food. This makes just about a wineglassful. The animals grow extremely fond of it, relish their food, and thrive in consequence.

POTATOES are one of the best things to keep a horse in good condition. They stimulate the digestion and free them from worms.

To CURE KICKING.—If you have a horse that is in the habit of kicking, put him in a narrow stall that has both sides thickly padded. Suspend a sack filled with hay or straw so that it will strike his heels, and let the horse and sack fight it out. Be sure to have things arranged so that the horse cannot hurt himself. The sack will be victorious every time, and in the end the horse will absolutely refuse to kick the sack or anything else.

THE CARE OF THE FOAL.—No foal should be allowed to have the milk of any mare while she is feverish or seriously ill. Her milk should then be drawn away twice daily, or oftener, if needful, and the foal meanwhile should be fed three or four times daily with new cow's milk—at any rate, for the first two or three weeks—diluted with one-third of water, and sweetened with a little sugar or treacle. If this disagrees with it, condensed milk, judiciously diluted, often answers satisfactorily. When from the death of the mare, or her proving, as sometimes occurs, a hopelessly bad nurse, the foal has to be brought up entirely by hand, cow's milk is used in the manner advised for the first fortnight. Thereafter into one of the meals of milk there should be introduced a little well-boiled gruel, which is best made of a mixture of wheat flour and finely-ground oatmeal. The amount of this farinaceous food should gradually be increased. If the bowels be constipated treacle should be given with the milk. Their undue relaxation usually results from the cow's milk being given in too concentrated a state, when the caseine forms a tough refractory curd in the foal's stomach. This evil may be remedied by uniformly using the milk of a young, recently-calved cow, and diluting it, as recommended, with one-third of water.

SIMPLY giving an injection of warm water with a syringe has saved the life of many a foal. Every horse breeder ought to know enough to keep a close eye upon the regularity of the bowels in the very young stock.

IN BREAKING the colt do not think you have to break his heart, and in this way let him know you are master. You must gain his confidence by kind but firm treatment.

THE COLT that is kept fat will make the easy-keeping horse.

WITH MODERATE CARE and good usage a horse's life may be prolonged to twenty-five, thirty-five, or forty years.

NEVER stop a horse going up hill unless you have a brake on the waggon. When going at full speed never stop your horse suddenly. It is a great strain on his shoulders and knees.

PIGS.

KEEP only quiet, gentle sows for mothers. Be kind to your pigs, be patient and quiet in handling them, and don't abuse them. Never allow a sow to get chilled in farrowing; it may kill her and the litter too. Give the pigs all the milk, bran, oats, vegetables and grass that you can get for them, with some corn, until you want to fatten them; then you may fatten almost entirely on corn. Do not starve your pigs nor overfeed them, nor compel them to pick their food out of the mud. Provide warm, dry quarters in winter. Divide them up, so that those of the same class, or which require the same treatment, shall be together. Give them good pasture in summer; it will take less grain and they will do better. Give plenty of water and shelter, and when fat and large enough for market sell, and don't exhaust your resources in the hope of receiving better prices.

BE CAREFUL and not overfeed while the sow is sucking.

Do NOT allow weaned pigs to run with those that are sucking.

WITH good clover or lucerne pasture pigs can be made to fatten very rapidly and at low cost.

THE MISTAKE of keeping and using crossbred males is the main cause of the degeneration of the pigs on many farms.

A PIG should make a pound in weight for every day of its life. If it does this it is ready for market at any time after it is six months old.

As soon as the pigs are two weeks old, begin to feed them in a side trough. This will push them along nicely and save the sow.

FEED AND EXERCISE.—There is encouragement in the more common practice of giving pigs a wide run—plenty of grass and clover, and less of the everlasting corn diet. We no longer aim at masses of living lard.

FEED FOR THE BOAR.—Boars that are doing service need careful attention and good feeding. Do not feed any great quantity of corn; try a few peas, ground oats, and a handful of oil meal, and exercise them as much as possible.

A GRAIN of prudence is worth a pound of craft.

BOASTERS are cousins to liars.

BEES.

SET the hives close to the ground and not up on high benches or against a fence or building.

ANYONE can handle bees in safety if armed with a good bee-smoker. The best fuel to use in a smoker is dry spongy rotten wood.

You can keep down swarming by taking out the queen cells that the bees are building preparatory to swarming, if you get all of them.

IF you have not time to watch your bees, and are afraid of loosing swarms, clip the wings of all queens and no swarms will take leave of absence from the apiary.

ITALIANS THE BEST.—The Italian bees are the best. A number of other varieties have been brought to this country and thoroughly tested, but very few of them are ever heard of at all, and all unite on the superiority of the Italians.

WHEN TO HANDLE BEES.—Bees will not object to being handled during the middle of the day, but will resent being disturbed early in the morning or late in the evening, hence it is proper to take advantage of this. By many this is considered the most dangerous time to go about them, but intimate acquaintance with them proves this mistake.

SWARMING.—During the swarming season there is always danger of losses unless the bees are constantly watched, and we can be on the ground just when they begin to issue from the hive, so that we can discover the queen and see if she takes wing properly. If the queen cannot fly, she is likely to get lost, as she will travel quite a distance from the hive. Unless the queen is able to take wing with the swarm, the bees will invariably return to the hive again; but if she is discovered and secured, the swarm can be hived by removing the hive they issued from and placing a new hive on the old stand, and as they return liberate the queen with them.

IT is not good policy to allow a colony of bees to swarm more than once. Second swarms are not profitable, and they cripple the old parent stock so that it will do but little good all the season.

THE QUEEN.—It is a well-known fact that a colony of bees cannot long exist without a queen, and she must be such an one as has met a drone and become fertilized, in order to lay eggs that will produce worker bees. These are essential to the welfare of the whole colony.

THREE THOUSAND EGGS DAILY.—The queen, if prolific, is capable of laying two to three thousand eggs daily during a season. And just in the same ratio as the eggs are deposited in the cells by the queen, so they will hatch out and become full-grown bees in twenty-one days.

THE BEST REMEDY for a queenless colony is to insert a frame of brood in the hive, and if it is not over three days old, the colony will raise a queen from it.

THE WORKER BEES.—All worker bees have a business end, provided with a sting for proper defence, and never become active workers outside of the hive *until they are fourteen days old*. The young worker bees are not idlers in the hive. But to them belong the duties of cleaning the cells, as well as to build queen cells and rear your young queens when it becomes necessary, which they always do, and fully understand all the necessities and wants when they are under fourteen days old. Feeding the young larvæ, also, belongs to their labours, while they remain in their vicinity.

70

MODERN HIVES.—Of course you cannot expect to raise good, saleable honey and plenty of it in the old-fashioned box hives. If you cannot make or buy improved hives (and they can be had cheap enough now) you should let bees alone and let other people have the benefits which you might have enjoyed very easily yourself. Hive your young swarm in one of the modern hives, and you can put on the surplus cases at any time when you think they are needed. If care is exercised no one need be afraid of being stung. Modern hives of course, have movable frames. These are calculated to give to the beekeeper a chance to examine the combs, the general condition of the colony, and, perhaps, to change queens, cut out queen cells, extract honey and so forth. It is not to be expected that an ordinary farmer, who is not also a professional beekeeper, will undertake to engage in any such jobs. Nor is there need of it. The frames can be wedged in so as to be tight and stationary, yet in proper position for taking apart for the purposes of examination and manipulation, should such ever be desired.

LAWS IN BRIEF.

A NOTE given by a minor is void.

A NOTE drawn on Sunday is void.

IGNORANCE of the law is no excuse.

IT IS a fraud to conceal a fraud.

THE LAW compels no one to do impossibilities.

AN AGREEMENT without a consideration is void.

SIGNATURES made with lead pencil are good in law.

A RECEIPT for money paid is not legally conclusive.

CONTRACTS made on Sunday cannot be enforced.

A CONTRACT made with a minor in invalid.

A CONTRACT made with a lunatic is void.

CONTRACTS for advertising in Sunday newspapers are invalid.

EACH INDIVIDUAL in a partnership is responsible for the whole amount of the debts of the firm.

PRINCIPALS are responsible for the acts of their agents.

AGENTS are responsible to the principals for errors.

IT IS NOT legally necessary to say on a note, "for value received."

A NOTE obtained by fraud, or from a person in a state of intoxication, cannot be collected.

IF A NOTE be lost or stolen, it does not release the maker; he must pay.

THE ENDORSER of a note is exempt from liability if not served with notice of its dishonor within twenty-four hours of its non-payment.

A MAN who is his own lawyer has a fool for a client.

To Remove Old Paint.—For removing old paint and varnish from woodwork, apply an emulsion formed of two parts ammonia shaken up with one part of turpentine. This so softens the paint that after a few moments it can be scraped or rubbed off.

We Recommend SQUATTER WHISKY.

71

GARDENING AND FARMING CALENDAR.

———o———

Written for the Colony of Queensland, and embracing the range of Field, Plantation, Kitchen, Flower, and Fruit Garden; also the Bush House.

———————

Revised by Mr. WILLIAM SOUTTER, *Brisbane.*

———————

As seasons alter considerably from time to time, a little common sense will be needed to apply the directions herein given; also localities, latitudes, and situations must be duly considered, or the very best of advice will prove misleading. To say that one month here agrees with another in Great Britain is pure fiction. Queensland winters, in many parts of the colony, much resemble English summers; and especially is this true of the North of the colony. Some portions of Southern Queensland, notably the higher portions of the Darling Downs district, very closely resemble—both in climate and productions—the more southern latitudes. In the warmer districts of the North where the progress of vegetation is much more rapid and the summer at least a month earlier than in the southern portions of the colony, nearly all garden and field operations may be performed considerably sooner. In the tropical North it has been proved useless to attempt many of the ordinary spring and summer crops owing to the unmitigated heat of summer both by day and night. Even maize is more a failure than a success generally as a summer crop, and the vegetables found to be profitable require to be mostly of a tropical character. In a more temperate climate, such as that of the Darling Downs, it may be necessary to defer these somewhat; and in still colder and later districts, such as the neighbourhood of Stanthorpe, further allowance will require to be made.

- - - - - - - - - -

JANUARY.

Kitchen Garden.—Do all sowing and transplanting immediately after rain, and whilst the ground is in a mellow state   Small sowings may be made of carrots, celery, cauliflowers, Brussels sprouts, cabbage, etc., in the cool districts of the colony. Should the weather prove favourable, plant out savoys, cabbages, cauliflowers, etc., selecting only the strongest plants, as the slender and weakly ones will not repay the trouble. Plant out celery in trenches which should be made about twelve or sixteen inches wide, twelve inches in depth, and four feet apart; the top spit should be turned alternately on either side, as this will be required in the after culture of the plant for earthing up. Six or seven inches of good rotten dung should be laid in the bottom of the trench and dug in; or, if the subsoil is bad, lay a few inches of rich vegetable compost over the dung. Lift the plants carefully, preserving a ball of earth at the root of each, and cut off the straggling leaves and side offsets. Plant in a row along the centre of each trench seven or eight inches apart. Planting is best performed in the evening, and a plentiful watering supplied; this should be frequently repeated if the weather prove dry.   The seed should be sown in boxes, and when the plants are large

QUEENSLAND MODEL DAIRY. We ship Butter to all parts F.O.B. Brisbane.

enough to handle transfer them to the prepared trenches. Look over cucumbers, melons, etc., for the purpose of stopping and thinning out shoots. Hoe, stir, and water advancing crops ; liquid manure will be found serviceable. Herbs should be cut for drying when at full growth and coming into flower—and some when in full flower, as lavender, marigold, and camomile, for their flowers only. Cut in dry weather, and spread or hang up in a dry airy place, out of the reach of the sun, that they may dry gently.

Fruit Garden.—Loosen the surface among fruit-bearing trees, mulch heavily to protect the surface roots from the sun. Examine vines, and regulate and remove all useless shoots, and gather the fruit as it ripens ; thin superabundant fruit upon orange trees. Some of the superfluous and ill-placed shoots may still be removed from peaches, plums, etc. Oranges, lemons, peaches and all kinds of fruit trees may now be budded

Flower Garden.—Continue to regulate carefully the growth of climbers, but avoid tying them too close, and allow them to grow according to their natural habit as much as circumstances will admit. Examine dahlias, etc., and see that the early ties do not pinch ; loosen them if they do, or the wind will easily break them at that point. Stake and tie all tall-growing plants, and cut back pelargoniums that have done flowering. Beds of verbenas, petunias, and pelargoniums should be kept free from weeds, and, if freely supplied with water in dry weather, will flower much better. Sow Amaranthus, Celosia, Centaurea, Browallia, etc, for autumn decoration in vacant places. Propagate carnations and pinks by layering. Those who require large blooms must now attend to disbudding, leaving one, two, or three, according to the strength of the plant. Roses may now be budded, and cut off all decaying flowers and flower stems, and destroy insects.

Bush-house.—Where any attempt is made to cultivate pot plants a bush-house is absolutely necessary, and is one of the most enjoyable appendages to a good garden. At this season it should be in perfection. Palms, ferns, and lycopods should be at their best ; also Caladiums, Gloxinias, Begonias, Achimenes and Fuchsias—all of which should be given a little manure-water twice a week. In applying manure-water, "weak and often," is the principle of success. It is not the best season for making additions or alterations to these structures, but there is no portion of the year when additions in the shape of ferns or orchids may not be made. In North Queensland, particularly, some very choice and rare retreats, with good collections of valuable plants, should, in course of time, become common. Pot-plants are not absolutely necessary to make an attractive bush-house ; the most satisfying one possible can be had by growing everything naturally, either in the borders or according to nature.

Field.—Break up land for wheat in the Southern district ; sow barley for green crop ; plant maize not later than the middle of the month for a winter crop, in rows four to five feet apart according to the nature of the soil, and three feet distant in the row. Make a sowing of Imphee or Farmer's Friend, pearl millet *(Penicillaria spicata)*, Sorghum halapense, Teosinte *(Euchlæna luxurians)*, Guinea grass, and Italian rye-grass ; these are most useful fodder plants, which cows are very fond of, and they will give twice the milk and butter on this feed. Sow millet and maize for green feed—these furnish fodder in enormous quantity ; to be sown thinly broadcast ; one seed produces several stalks. Dig up the early crop of potatoes if not already done, and those intended for seed should be exposed to the atmosphere a few days before being stowed away. In the North, English potatoes only succeed during the winter, and must not be put in before March or much later than June. Sweet potatoes may, however, be planted at any season of the year within the tropics when moisture favours. Persevere in keeping down weeds on cotton and sugar plantations, and for this purpose the cultivators should be kept going as long as the crop will admit of it. Ginger may be taken up when young for preserving purposes only. Tobacco will now ripen and should be gathered.

We Recommend SQUATTER WHISKY.

FEBRUARY.

Kitchen Garden.—The practice of keeping the ground loose and open about growing crops is very advantageous to them, more especially in stiff soils, as it materially assists the absorption of moisture. Larger sowings of a few vegetables may be made now than last month, such as cabbage, brocoli, turnips, carrots, onions, leeks and salads. Thin out turnips, sown last month, to about twelve inches apart. Plant out Brussels sprouts. Do not forget to earth up advancing crops of celery, and plant out for succession. Continue to gather cucumbers and various articles for pickling. Eschalots should now be taken up as soon as the leaves begin to decay. Prepare all spare ground for future crops, always bearing in mind that upon next month's operations the winter supply of vegetables depends. Dig in all failing crops as they become unprofitable, as all vegetable refuse will help to enrich the soil. The practice of burning superfluous vegetable matter is a sinful waste, entirely out of harmony with nature; nature's method is slowly to decompose it and return it again to the earth as plant food. Cucumbers and melons must be frequently thinned and stopped. In earthing up celery let it be done in dry weather, and when the plants are also dry; lay the earth lightly to the plants, taking care not to break down the leaves, and also not to bury the hearts of the plants.

Fruit Garden.—Oranges, peaches, etc., which were too tender to be budded last month, may now be subjected to that operation, but it should not be deferred later than this month. Any trees that have been previously budded and failed may be worked again. Go over the stocks that were budded last month, and let all the ties be loosed. During dry weather gather grapes, etc., and store away as desired. Plant out strawberries in well-trenched and manured ground. Take the strongest runners up with a trowel; trim away a few of the under leaves; plant in rows two feet apart and twelve to fifteen inches in the row, keeping them well-watered until rooted. The best strawberry growers always contrive to make the bed as hard as possible, only leaving a small space close around each plant at all loose. The strawberry likes a strong soil bordering on clay, which must, however, be well drained. Anywhere within the tropics bananas and pineapples may still be planted, and also all manner of tender tropical fruits if in pots; but in putting them out a good protection from the scorching rays of the sun should be furnished until they are well established in their new quarters.

Flower Garden.—The beauty of a flower garden may be greatly enhanced by a judicious arrangement of plants and contrast of colours; and the trouble of occasionally noting any improvements that may be made in contrasting the colours of the dahlias, verbenas, etc., so as to produce a better effect another season, will be well repaid. Many of the finest plants are now in perfection, and by observing them in different situations an idea may be formed of how they may be placed to the best advantage. Caladiums, Coleus, Amaranthus, etc., may be planted out either in beds or vacant places among shrubs in the borders; the beautifully-coloured foliage, when well arranged, produces a fine effect during the autumn months. Tie up chrysanthemums and other tall-growing plants; remove all decaying flowering stems, and keep walks and borders neat. Where strong-growing annuals produce rambling shoots near the ground, they should be trimmed. This will cause them to form handsome and regular heads, and to show themselves to greater advantage than if the branches were permitted to spread near the ground. Sow Brompton and Ten-week Stocks, Phlox Drummondii —one of the most beautiful annuals cultivated—Dianthus, Myosotis and Forget-me-not, Pyrethrum, Pansies, Sturt's Desert Pea (*Clianthus Dampieri*), and all kinds of annuals for spring flowering. Layer roses, camellias, carnations, and picotees—in fact all plants that it is desired to increase by this means. In the warmer districts of the colony it is necessary to make some artificial shade to grow many of the choicest annuals, but enthusiastic lovers of these pets will be amply repaid for the trouble by the result. The shade, however, must not be a living one. This month and the next are the best for the work, for if left later the heat of

We Recommend SQUATTER WHISKY.

75

summer overtakes them before they have reached their prime and then they are done. Bulbs that have flowered may be taken up and stored in a suitable place till the proper season for planting them.

Bush-house.—If the usual moist heat of this month is experienced, plants in the bush-house will be making luxurious growth. Towards the end of the month, gradually withhold manure water; as all kinds of bulbous plants show signs of going to rest, give them less water. Put in first batch of fuchsia cuttings, which will form good bushy plants, and flower early in spring. Put in coleus cuttings for stock, and as the old plants become shabby throw them away, for they are never worth keeping over one season. Gloxinias, Achimenes, and Tydeas now flowering will be the better of an occasional watering with weak liquid manure. The shade furnished in the bush-house affords an opportunity for sowing many things in seed pans or boxes, but they must be watched so that the plants do not become weakly and drawn.

Field.—The different kinds of sorghum should be cut as they arrive at maturity, and the seed preserved in an airy building. Green provender for winter use is to be provided by sowing broadcast the various Sorghums, Imphees, and Millets; also the well-known *Setaria Germanica*, or, as some call it, Panicum; also Cape barley, lucerne, oats, etc. Tares and vetches may, in cool weather, be sown for the same purpose, and in order to support the weak stems of the vetches, they may be mixed with a bushel of rye seed to every two bushels of tares; these will only succeed on the Downs. The following variety of turnips may be sown :—Skirving's purple-top swede, Sutton's champion purple-top swede, long white French and green-top yellow. The potato seed prepared last month should now be planted, and this is the best time for planting a main crop. Most of the American varieties thrive well in Queensland, especially Early Rose, Late Rose, Brownell's Beauty, Beauty of Hebron, Snowflake, Early Vermont. Districts are known to suit one variety better than others, so the common sense and observations of cultivators must be thoroughly utilised to make the most of what they have. North of Mackay, potato-planting is not to be recommended for a month or two from this.

MARCH.

Kitchen Garden.—This is the best season to ensure a good supply of vegetables for winter use by sowing onions, leeks, peas, turnips, Early Horn carrots, parsnips, beet root, cabbages, cauliflowers, savoys, etc. The January sown cabbages will now be ready for transplanting. Prick out these as soon as they are large enough, and earth up those advancing. Thin out the plants regularly from the seed bed, observing to take the strongest first; the smallest may be left in the seed bed longer to increase in strength. Continue to sow in succession several sorts of small salad seeds, such as mustard, cress, radish, etc. When a constant supply of these are wanted, there should be some seed sown once every week or fortnight. Draw flat shallow drills, sow the seeds pretty thick, and cover them about a quarter of an inch; in dry weather they must be watered. Cauliflowers and Brussels sprouts may also be planted out. Reject such whose stems are crooked. Earth up crops of celery which are planted in trenches, as they advance in growth, that they may be blanched to a proper length. Trench, manure, and prepare any vacant ground for future use, leaving the surface in a rough state. Plant asparagus and rhubarb beds; both require a rich, deep, and fairly moist soil. In warm situations the rhubarb is better for shading.

Fruit Garden.—Trench and prepare ground, either by the spade or with plough and subsoiler, at least eighteen inches in depth for planting fruit trees, so that the soil may be in a fit state when required. Gather fruit as it becomes ready, and frequently examine any already stored. In the fruit rooms see that the shelves show no symptoms of decay or mould about them, otherwise the odour will be communicated to the fruit. If the weather be dry, it will be necessary to water plentifully the strawberry beds planted last month. The buds should again be looked to ; young shoots tied and suckers removed.

We Recommend SQUATTER WHISKY.

Flower Garden.—Now is the best time for planting most kinds of bulbs, such as Narcissus, Gladioli, Tritonia, Watsonia, Sparaxis, Ixia, Anemones, Ranunculus, Hyacinths, Amaryllis, Liliums, etc. Soil and manure for bulbs; procure some one or two year's old cow-dung—say, to three barrows of cow-dung add one barrow of good sharp sand, well mix together; draw a drill four inches deep and four wide for the smaller bulbs, and twelve for the larger ones; fill the drill with the dung and sand, mix it up lightly with the soil, make it firm by pressing down, and plant the bulbs—the small ones two inches deep and the larger ones three inches—covering the whole of the bulb or tuber. Plant Ranunculus twelve inches apart, and the larger growing ones eighteen inches. Patches of showy annuals should now be sown in vacant places which exist about the edges of borders. The following are some of the best:—Various species of Calliopsis, Gaillardia, Lupinus, Phlox Drummondii, Zinnia, Aster, Candytuft, Larkspur, Schizanthus, Scabiosa, Stocks, Marigolds; and herbaceous perennials, such as Phlox, Dianthus, Alternanthera, Iberis, Pyrethrum, Statice Halfordi, Tritonia uvaria, Myosotis, Salvia, Pæonies, etc., may be increased by dividing the roots. Roses may now be pruned and the suckers removed. Within the tropics leave pruning until June. In pruning roses cut back to two or three inches above the origin of the young wood; robust growing kinds should not be pruned so severely as the weaker ones. Strong shoots of many roses, if pegged down on the surface to nearly their full length, will throw out numerous flowering shoots. Carnations and pinks that have struck from pipings or layers may be planted out as soon as they have rooted. Cool shady borders are best for these everywhere in Queensland.

Bush-house.—Caladiums and Gloxinias require special care in watering; and as the various kinds go to rest, turn the pots on their sides in some dry corner of the house. Early in the month sow Calceolaria, Primula, and Cineraria seed. Farther north than Mackay success with these florist's flowers is dubious, especially the first two. Calceolaria seed is very small, and consequently often difficult to raise. It should be sown in pots, well drained with any kind of rubble, and filled to within an inch of the rim with light sandy soil, which should be well watered half an hour before sowing. The seed may then be sprinkled thinly on the surface, and will require no covering with soil. The pots should then be placed on coal ashes in a shady spot, and the top of the pots covered with a piece of glass. No water must be given until the young plants appear, when the glass should be gradually tilted on one side so as to admit air, and water through a very fine rose when required. This method applies to the raising of all small and delicate seeds.

Field.—Lucerne, Italian rye-grass, and other artificial grasses may be sown for pasture or hay. The soil must be well prepared; harrow the seed in with a light harrow, and if rolled so much the better. Wheat and oats may now be sown. This is an excellent time to plant a crop of potatoes. Maize should be gathered when ripe, and stored in a perfectly dry and well-ventilated building. Gather cotton as it comes to maturity, and gather and house tobacco when ready. This is the best month to sow artificial grasses and renew pastures; but the indigenous grasses are best sown in August. The following is a list of imported grasses that have done well in Queensland, more especially on the Darling Downs:—Perennial rye-grass, cock's-foot grass, prairie grass, Timothy grass, sweet-scented vernal grass, meadow grass, Kentucky blue grass, foxtail meadow, crested dogtail grass, fescue meadow, fescue sheep, fescue—red or creeping. The following fodder and pasture plants have also been successfully grown in this colony:—Clover: White, alsike, and scarlet. The quantity required of these is from two to two and a-half pounds per acre. Also clover—red perennial, lucerne, sainfoin grass, common bent grass, Italian rye-grass, woolly soft grass, pearl millet, Phillips' panic grass, buffalo grass, Guinea grass, prickly comfrey, Texas blue grass, sheep Burnett, the good scaroo bush of Africa, and panicum miliare. Prairie grass is specially valuable in the winter and spring months, when other green feed is scarce.

APRIL.

Kitchen Garden.—Make sowings of peas, broad beans, cabbages, saluding, etc. Be careful to thin crops of turnips, carrots, spinach, lettuce, etc., before they become weakly and drawn through standing too closely together. Celery should be earthed up as it advances in height. Before earthing, for which take advantage of dry weather, the ground should be well watered the day previously, and the soil should be broken up fine, and care taken not to allow any soil to get into the heart of the plant. Stir the surface of the soil deeply among growing crops, to admit air to the roots, and keep down weeds. Any spaces of kitchen garden ground which are now vacant should, when required, be manured and trenched for the reception of future crops. Gather pumpkins and store in a dry place. Where rhubarb and asparagus are desired, now is the time to make ready for them by deep trenching and manuring, and then sow seed of good varieties where they are to remain, thinning them out as necessary afterwards. Asparagus may be grown even farther north than Mackay, but rhubarb is not thrifty even at Rockhampton, and seldom survives the summer.

Fruit Garden.—New plantations of oranges, loquats, bananas, pineapples, etc., may now be made, in order that the roots may take hold of the soil before winter, care being taken to mulch the surface around the young trees with boughs; freely water should the weather prove dry after planting. Strawberries may still be planted; the old beds should now be cleared of all runners, the surface soil stirred about them, and receive a top-dressing of well-rotted manure, which will prove beneficial in promoting strength; and if in dressing these plants the main plants are not allowed to stand singly, nor permitted to straggle all over the bed, the quality of the fruit would be much improved. Oranges may now be planted; avoid planting those grafted on the Lemon stock. The soil best suited for the successful growth of the orange is a rich chocolate on a dry substratum, and if upon hilly slopes of volcanic origin, so much the better. The success of the orange depends as much upon situation and soil as upon latitude, and hence the difference in productiveness and quality of the fruit of the same variety. The neglect of these conditions, for example, will convert the St. Michael orange, one of the finest flavoured, into a bitter and nauseous fruit. Although there is no difficulty in finding soil in sheltered situations in nearly all parts of Queensland, still as a general rule it would be better in selecting sites for plantations to choose easterly aspects, that being the surest protection from the cold westerly winds. The land should be well turned up, trenched, and left in ridges a few months prior to planting. If the subsoil is cold and wet, the trenches should be from two to two and a-half feet deep; but where the bottom is gravelly or hard, eighteen inches will be sufficient; and if the soil is of an inferior quality a compost should be prepared of virgin soil, mixed with manure and a good dressing of bone dust for the purpose of filling up the beds. The trees should be planted from twenty-five to thirty feet apart, according to the quality and situation of the soil; and during the following summer, when the dry weather sets in, mulch round them to a distance of at least three feet radius; keep the ground loosened on the surface all the year round, and water thoroughly before the young trees begin to suffer from drought. In pruning, care should be observed not to remove the young fruit-bearing shoots of the previous year's growth which will bear during the present. All varieties of the orange thrive well in Queensland—the Bahia or Navel, Blood, Siletta, St. Michael's, Thorny Mandarin, Canton Mandarin, Emperor of China Mandarin, Parramatta, Queen, and Washington Navel. One of the finest mandarins in the colony is the Beauty of Glen Retreat. Lemons, unless grafted on the Orange stock do not succeed in Queensland; the best sorts are the Lisbon and Malta. The West India lime and the Persian or sweet lime also thrive admirably and should be largely cultivated. All deciduous fruit trees that have shed their leaves may be pruned. Look carefully over fruit which has been gathered, as it will require considerable attention the first few weeks; in gathering, care must be taken to pick every variety at the proper time. Car

should be exercised in gathering not to shake it from the tree, but to take every fruit singly, handling it as if it were an egg. If these precautions are observed the fruit will be much improved for keeping. There would be a much better market for fruit if the growers bestowed more care on the gathering. Fruit will not keep that has been bruised, and one damaged fruit in a box will tend to destroy the whole lot.

Flower Garden.—The present month is a favourable time for transplanting large sized evergreens, shrubs, trees and also herbaceous plants, as they will now make fresh roots, and be better able to resist the cold, dry winds of winter. Plant and clip hedges. Plants removed this month will require much less attention than if transplanted late in winter. Continue to plant bulbs of various kinds. Proceed with the propagation of favourite kinds of roses, either by cuttings or layers, and remove suckers from budded plants. Take up dahlias that have done flowering, when they have died down; dry the tubers, and stow them away amongst dry earth or sand in a dry and airy place. In showery weather plant out annuals of all kinds for winter and spring flowering, and divide perennials as in last month. Carnations, picotees, etc., may be propagated from pipings or cuttings. Borders and beds may be made, and every part of the garden should be kept as clean as possible. The annuals recommended to be sown last month may still be tried if not already in.

Bush-house.—If sown as previously advised, primulas and cinerarias will will now be ready for picking out into well-drained beds of light soil with plenty of manure. Rotten heaps are excellent for this purpose, covered with about half an inch of soil, into which prick out the seedlings. The roots will then penetrate into the hops and will lift, when required for potting, with good balls, and with little or no injury if done with care. Look after caladium bulbs and store them when ripe in some dry place. The best plan for keeping them through the winter is to stack the pots on their sides.

Field.—This is generally the busiest time for cotton gathering; it should be picked immediately after the pods burst, and before being wetted by rain; any damp cotton should be carefully sun-dried before storing. Great loss is frequently sustained by allowing the cotton to remain too long on the plant. Maize and different kinds of sorghum should be gathered as they ripen, and stored in a dry place. Potatoes will require to be earthed up and kept free from weeds. Full crops of maize and English potatoes may be put in anywhere North now. Sow flax fodder plants and grasses, if required. Sow wheat, oats, barley, vetches, rape, buckwheat, field peas, and onions in the colder parts of the colony; plough land for Spring crops in the early districts.

MAY.

Kitchen Garden.—Earth up celery; attend to keeping up a succession of turnips, carrots, beet, parsnips, and a supply of salading. Plant out cabbages; hoe and loosen the ground between the rows of cabbages, etc., already planted, which will kill weeds and vermin, and greatly assist the growth of plants. Transplant cardoons, onions, leeks, etc. Strawberry beds may still be made. Peas and beans may be sown for early crops. Asparagus beds should be cleaned and dressed; clear off all weeds, and cover the beds with a good coat of rotten horse-dung. Rhubarb beds require a good dressing of manure. Rhubarb should be planted in deeply-trenched and well-manured ground; it succeeds best in rich deep soil, rather light than otherwise; it may be raised from seed, but the mode of propagation generally adopted is by division of the roots. Plant three feet apart in rows from three to four feet asunder. The cutting and drying of herbs as they mature should be attended to. Continue to prepare all vacant ground by digging and trenching, especially that intended for root crops.

Fruit Garden.—Look over pineapples frequently, and gather them as they ripen. Plant orange, peach, and other varieties of fruit trees, and the planting

73

should be completed by the end of this month. The sooner the trees are planted the better. Be careful that the soil is neither wet nor retentive of water- no soil intended for fruit trees should be. In such cases it should be thoroughly drained before planting. Without this it is useless to look for success in fruit-growing. In planting be careful to keep the roots near the surface; they are sure to find their way deep enough, and by way of steadying them in the soil drive a good stout stake. A good rule is to plant them just as deep as they had previously been in the nurseries, which is easily ascertained by observing the collar where the portion that had been under the soil exhibits the bark much smoother and paler than that which was above it; but allowance should be made for the soil subsiding, which it will invariably do. See that the surface is well mulched all round newly-planted t ees, in order to protect the roots from atmospheric conditions which at times are too powerful. Orange trees should be thinned. Pineapples require a loose rich soil, and should be planted in rows, 6 to 8 feet apart and 18 inches from plant to plant in the row. Plantations should always be in sheltered localities, that is to say, protected from the cold westerly winds, but still open to the early and continuous sunshine. In the dry weather they require a liberal supply of water, and occasionally a considerable dressing of manure. When an overgrowth of suckers takes place, the smaller and inferior ones should be removed. Generally the Queen is the most prolific producer, well flavoured, hardier, and quicker in coming to maturity than the others; but for winter months the Smooth-leaved Cayenne is the next in rank, being a liberal producer during the cold winter months of the year, and having a very large and well flavoured fruit. Fruit trees, vines etc,, that have shed their leaves may be pruned. Look carefully over fruit that has been stowed away, as it will require more attention the first few weeks after being gathered than afterwards.

Flower Garden.—Camellias are now beginning to flower, and during the next two months will stand unrivalled amongst shrubs for beauty. The following twelve varieties that are deserving of cultivation, are:—Alba-pleno (white), Fimbriata (white), Isabella (white), Incarnata, Lady Hume (blush), Leda (delicate blush), Lady St. Clair (pink), Charles Albert (pink), Edith (rose pink), Emma (deep rose), Queen of Denmark (crimson), Countess of Belmore (crimson), Miniata (crimson). The best soil for the camellia is a strong well-drained loam, with a good mixture of decayed vegetable matter. When the camellia is showing for flower, it must be supplied with an abundance of water. Any roots of dahlias that still remain in the ground should be taken up. See that chrysanthemums and other tall plants now in flower are well staked and tied. Bulbs may now be planted. Shrubbery and flower borders may receive a fresh dressing of soil and manure where necessary. Attend to roses. Good deep soil, well trenched and manured, is required for the rose, either in garden beds or roseries. Those in pots should be planted out, and the knife should be freely used in pruning. Remove superfluous flower buds and thin shoots, when these should be thinned out so that the head of the tree is not at all crowded, and then be shortened to within twelve buds of the base; a crop of fine flowers will be the result.

Bush-house.—Gradually withhold water from the plants as the weather becomes colder. Examine the drainage of all large-growing ferns, palms, &c. Give camellias in pots manure-water, especially those that do not readily open their flowers. Make sure the drainage is all right.

Field.—Cotton gathering must be diligently attended to throughout the month; the third crop of tobacco should now be ready, and the cutting, housing and curing of this are subjects of considerable importance. In the North tobacco planting is regularly done during this month or the next. Ginger and arrowroot will be ready to be taken up in early situations. Sow broad beans, field peas, cabbage, chicory, and gram. Oats, wheat, and barley may still be sown in the late districts. Potatoes will require to be earthed up and kept free from weeds. Artificial grasses may still be sown for permanent pasture and succession of other crops.

We Recommend SQUATTER WHISKY.

JUNE.

Kitchen Garden.—Wherever drainage is necessary, the work of cutting drains and trenches should be vigorously proceeded with, when the ground is in a fit state for doing so. In stiff and retentive soils a thorough and efficient system of drainage is of the greatest importance; in very light or sandy soils it is not so necessary. Sow peas, beans, carrots, parsnips, spinach, onions, leeks, beet, cabbage, Swede and white Pomeranian globe turnips, cauliflower, and lettuce; also parsley and other herbs. Thin and transplant onions sown last month. Plant strawberries, rhubarb, sea-kale, etc., always taking care that the ground has been well worked and manured. Plant a few early potatoes. Earth up celery, when the soil is not too wet; this crop will require the ground to be well trenched, manured, and well supplied with water. Trench and manure all spare ground, and hoe between growing crops of vegetables, a free use of the hoe at this season being beneficial to the plants.

Fruit Garden.—Pruning the apricot, peach, nectarine, pear, apple, mulberry, cherry, plum, etc., should be proceeded with. The peach, nectarine, and apricot require a different pruning to the apple, pear, plum, and cherry. The former produce their fruit upon one-year-old wood. The apple, pear, plum, and cherry bear principally on wood of one or two-years'-old spurs, and when a proper head is formed of branches they require but little pruning. The apple, pear, plum, etc., do best in a well-drained, compact loam, which should be thoroughly sweetened by working in dry weather before planting. The varieties recommended are those which have shown themselves most adapted for cultivation in this colony, viz.:—*Plums* for colder parts of the colony, especially the Downs, near the Main Range, from Stanthorpe northwards—Angelina Burdett, Black Damson, Brynstone Gage, Denison's Superb, Greengage, Yellowgage, Magnum Bonum, Early Orleans, Imperiale de Milan, Coe's Golden Drop, Jefferson, Kirk's Golden Yellow. *Plums* for the coast districts—Wildgoose, Huling's Superb, Washington, Newman, Kelsey, Blood, Red Heart, and most of the Japan Plums. *Apricots:* Moore Park, Turkey, Large Early, Breda, Man-field Seedling, etc., are only of service on the Downs. *Nectarines:* Red Roman, Stanwick, Albert Victor, Newington, Victoria. *Peaches* for the Downs—Alexandra Noblesse, Alexander, Amelia, Briggs' May, Chinese Cling, Columbia, Crawford's Early, Early Beatrice, Fleita's St. John, Heath Dr. Hogg, Grosse Mignonne, George the Fourth, Hale's Early, Morris' White, Royal George (true), Rivers' Early, Stump-the-world, Piquet's Late, President Church Pineapple. *Peaches* for the coast districts—Chinese Cling, Common China, Flat China, Fairholme, Honey, Chinese Free, Coxen's China, Mowbray's China, Newington, and many seedlings from the Flat China and Early China, which are more or less distributed through the coast country, and many of which are really good. *Quinces:* China, Orange, Rea's Seedling, Common. *Pears* for the Downs: Pears of almost every variety can be grown on the Southern Downs at Stanthorpe. *Pears* for the coast district: China, Le Conte, Kieffer's Hybrid. The two latter are hybrids between the old China and some good European kinds, and are as handsome, healthy, and productive as the China, with fruit of greatly improved quality. Some of the European pears, when worked on the quince, bear a few fruit in the coast districts. The apricot, almond, and nectarine, and also many plums, pears, and apples, give very little satisfaction in the colony except on the Darling Downs.

Flower Garden.—Cold nights may now be expected; any choice tender plants liable to injury from frosts or low temperature should be carefully protected when there is the least appearance of danger. Soft-wooded plants, for bedding out purposes, such as Verbenas, Petunias, Heliotropes, etc., may be propagated, so as to secure a good stock for spring use; also Fuchsias, and other florist's plants intended for culture. Choose young tender shoots of all these, about two inches in length, as they will make better plants than larger cuttings. Cuttings of Pelargoniums must be taken from well-ripened wood. Also put in cuttings of Spiræas, Poinsettias, Roses, Ligustrums, and shrubs and trees of all kinds that it is

V. & S. Tomato Sauce Leads. VERNEYS, Makers.

desired to multiply. It is a good plan to make a shady cutting bed for cuttings of all kinds, as it insures them rec-iving more regular attention and watering; and let the shade be dead, not the shade of living trees or climbing plants. The worst place for striking cuttings in any garden is under living shade. As a rule, cuttings of Pelargoniums, Geraniums, and Petunias fare best when put out at this season of the year where they are wanted to grow, so as not to be again disturbed. Double Petunias may be regularly propagated that way, but if struck in a cutting bed and then transplanted, they bear the removal. Dahlia roots should be taken up and stored in a dry cool place, where no damp can reach them. Reverse the roots to allow the moisture to run out of the hollow stem. Grass lawns may now be formed, and hedges and border edgings planted and any alterations with a view to general improvement undertaken.

Bush-house.—One of the first duties of the gardener is to anticipate any probable atmospheric changes that might prove detrimental to his stock, by removing all tender plants, from the bush-house to more sheltered positions, such as glass-house or frame, for their better protection. Many of the choicer ferns stand in need of such protection.

Field.—All artificial grasses for permanent pasture may still be sown. Lucerne, which upon suitable ground is a very profitable crop, and one which no farmer should be without, may be sown in deep and well cultivated soil; it will succeed best in rich moist land that is occasionally inundated. The White Clover thrives well everywhere south, but not much farther north than Brisbane. Crimson clover, Bretagne clover, cow grass, and Alsike clover are all advisable for cultivation in suitable localities. Low Lang's Swede, Imperial Swede, and Imperial green-top turnip. Prepare ground for mangel-wurzel. Onions may be sown, and the earlier sowings transplanted. Land intended for potatoes should now be ploughed, and in warm situations a few may be planted. Sweet potatoes are now ripe, and should be taken up as wanted; yams may be lifted and stored. Great care is necessary in digging up the tubers of yams, as they often penetrate the soil to the depth of three feet, and are consequently liable to be injured by being cut or broken during the operation. Ginger and arrowroot may now be taken up.

JULY.

Kitchen Garden.—Trenching and preparing the ground may be proceeded with as in the last month and the necessity for the liberal use of manures cannot be too strongly urged where really first-class vegetables and fruits are desired. Sow cabbage, tomatoes, French beans, parsnips; also mustard and cress for salading. Cauliflower and lettuce may be sown and transplanted as required. Sow spinach for successional crops; former sowings of this may be thinned. Onions of previous sowings may be thinned and transplanted. For onions select a piece of ground in good condition; if the surface is not firm, render it so before sowing by treading or rolling. Sow largely of peas and broad beans, especially if you can give them water; of the former Sangster No. 1, Yorkshire Hero, Bedman's Blue Imperial; of the latter the Mazagan is the most moderate grower, and requires the least room; the Broad Windsor excels for flavour, and the Long Pod for quantity. Sea-kale and rhubarb may be planted in beds that have been deeply trenched and well manured. Asparagus beds may still be made and old beds lightly forked over. Plant Globe and Jerusalem artichokes; the latter prefer a rather strong soil, and, being very prolific, a small piece of ground will produce a sufficient quantity.

Fruit Garden.—The general pruning and thinning of the peach, nectarine, apple, pear, fig, mulberry, orange and vine, should be finished. Grafing the orange, lime, lemon, citron, shaddock, etc., may be proceeded with towards the end of the month and during the next. Plant fruit trees as soon as possible. The present month may be regarded as the best for making new plantations of vines. Experience has proved that the vine will succeed in our poorest soils; but the best, however, is any soil composed, in part or whole, of granitic soil with an

(left margin) QUEENSLAND MODEL DAIRY, Turbot Street. Telephone 379.

We Recommend SQUATTER WHISKY.

admixture of clay, gravel or sand, and a small proportion of vegetable mould resting on a porous substratum. Bone-dust is accounted a very good manure during the first year or two of the vine's growth—wood ashes are almost as good. In planting the vines, success in striking vine cuttings depends more upon the character of the season than upon the manner of preparing the cuttings. This will be understood when it is said that prunings carelessly dug into the ground often grow as well as cuttings carefully planted. An important condition is that the base of the cutting be in close contact with the soil, and that the soil be closed around the cuttings generally. In gardens where water can be given on the occurrence of dry weather not a single failure need occur. Twelve to fifteen inches is a convenient space of well-ripened wood, two to three inches at the surface of the ground. The base is prepared by cutting the wood smoothly across below the joint. In the warmer parts of France shoots of the previous year's wood, from thirty to thirty-six inches long, are employed. The lower portions of these are laid horizontally in the ground, from twelve to fifteen inches deep, the top being brought up to the surface and a little above it. In dry seasons such cuttings would obviously stand a better chance of growing than others having only a few inches below the ground. Shoots intended for cuttings should be collected as they are cut, and at once laid into the ground and planted. The careful vigneron will study not to overtax the ground's capabilities by overcrowding, such as planting 2500 vines to an acre instead of 680 or 120.). This evil, especially in our climate, prevents the roots from spreading, and eventually causes the plant to die back until it loses all its productive vitality. There are various methods adopted in training the grape vines ; some prefer the trellises ; others the single stake and the gooseberry principle. For trellises procure sawn or split hardwood posts, three or four inches square by five feet long ; place these eighteen inches in the ground, in rows, twelve to sixteen inches apart ; bore half-inch holes for two wires—one in the top, the other midway to the ground—and use No. 12 or 14 galvanised wire. The single stake method is to procure hardwood stakes six feet in length and three inches square, placed six feet apart each way in straight lines. In the first year each plant should be cut down to the lowest, second or third, bud ; the second year these shoots should be allowed to grow, one upright and the others horizontal for trellis, the latter being reduced to twelve or fourteen inches. The same principle of close pruning should be observed every succeeding year, care being taken, however, to give prominence to the main shoots or future stems. When the bunches of fruit just begin to show they should be thinned by nipping off with the finger and the thumb, to correspond with the age and strength of the vines, and all other shoots on the stems not required for fruit-bearing should be removed until the vines are in bloom. In the winter following, the fruit-bearing shoots should be pruned to one bud, and the summer growth stopped. For the production of good table grapes the long rod principle is to be preferred to the usual method of pruning. By the long rod is meant allowing the vines to grow to a much greater height than other methods admit ; in this case the trellis should be at least nine feet high and the branches trained regularly to the top; the bunches of fruit should also be thinned to admit of the berries having plenty of room to develop. The following are a few varieties that thrive best in the colony :—

Table Varieties.

Black Barbarosa	Muscat Canon Hall	Snow's Muscat Hamburg
Buckland Sweet Water	Muscat of Salomon	Mill Hill, Hamburg
Black Hamburg	Muscat Gordo Blanco	Morocco Prince
Black St. Peter's	Muscat Madresfield	Golden Champion
Calabrian Raisin	Muscat Mrs. Prince's Black	Golden Hamburg
Muscat of Alexandria	Muscat Tynningham's	Duchess of Buccleuch
Muscat Bowood	Royal Ascot	Frankenthall
Muscat Champion		

We Recommend SQUATTER WHISKY.

Wine Grapes.

Verdeilho	Mollar Negro	Chasselas Noir
Mataro	Roussette	Chasselas Vibert
Grenache	Oporto	Carbenet
Black Cluster	Verdot	Bolas Blanco
Reisling	Red Hermitage	White Sherry
Black Hermitage	Rulander	
Espedlone	Carignan	

The following are a few of the best kinds of American grapes, most of which are suited for coastal cultivation :—

Adrionduc, black	Goethe, pale pink	Ontario, black
Catawba, red	Iona, red (very superior)	Othello, black
Concord, black	Irving, white	Pocklington, white
Crevelling, black	Israella, black	Rebecca, white
Delaware, red	Ives (wine), black	Regna, purple
Devereaux (wine). black	Massasoit, red	Rogers' No. 12, purple
Diana, red	Maxatawney, white	Rulander (wine), black
Eva, white	Merrimac, black	Salem, purple
Flowers (wine), black	Noah (wine), white	Senasqua, black

Flower Garden.—Flower borders and beds may be lightly dug or forked and receive a top dressing, after which see that they are properly stocked with suitable flowering shrubs and perennial herbaceous plants, so that they may present an attractive and gay appearance in the coming spring. Plant roses and prune such as have not been done previously. Annuals and biennials of various kinds may be sown, as French and African Marigolds, Globe and other Amaranthus, Balsams, Coreopsis, Gillardia, Convolvulus, etc. Bulbs, such as Amaryllis and Gladiolus, may still be planted. Fuchsias, Verbenas, etc., may still be increased from cuttings, and last year's plants may be repotted and the growth encouraged; a compost of about equal parts of turf loam, thoroughly decomposed stable manure, and a fine white sand will suit. Cuttings should be under shade and kept moist—not saturated.

Bush-house.—This is one of the most trying months of the whole year for bush-house plants; the cold winds usually prevalent penetrate every crevice, and the more tender vegetation suffers from low temperature. If the previous directions have been carried out, little will need to be done in this department beyond attending to its general cleanliness and appearance. All plants of a succulent nature, as Begonias, should have water sparingly applied during the cold months of the year; too much wet will destroy the lot.

Field.—Silk culture, which forms a profitable industry in all countries where it can be successfully produced, should be perseveringly tried here, as there can be no doubt from the experience we have already obtained, that its establishment among us is only a question of time. The suitability of the climate of many parts of the colony cannot be disputed. The different varieties of the White Mulberry (*Morus alba*), the leaves of which are the best food for the silkworm, may be planted, and will succeed on poor soil. The trees should be planted far enough apart to allow light and air to circulate freely—about twenty feet will be sufficient. Mulberries are readily propagated from cuttings of the previous year's growth. Continue to prepare ground for tobacco, maize, and other field crops, and as no plant exhausts the soil more than tobacco, it should not be grown, except on very rich soil, more than two or three years without being enriched with very strong manure. The best varieties of maize for field culture are Yellow Flint, White Flint, Tuscarora, Washington Market, Mammoth Dent, Canada Yellow, etc.; for garden, Darling's Early Sugar, Evergreen Sweet, Black Mexican, Boston Market, Sweet Mammoth, and Dolly Dutton. Continue to plant and transplant onions, and sow a few pumpkins and Swede turnips, mangold, sugar beet, and early potatoes. Barley and oats may be sown in late districts.

AUGUST.

Kitchen Garden. In making sowings of vegetables, small and frequent sowings answer best, as by this means a constant succession is provided, and in many cases the loss consequent upon large quantities of vegetables coming to maturity at

the same time avoided. The following may be sown:—Cucumbers, melons (rook or musk), melons (water), vegetable marrows, pumpkins (these will require protection from frost and cold till well established), carrots and parsnips for main crops; the last should be sown in shallow drills, fifteen inches apart, and be thinned out when large enough to pull. This vegetable succeeds best in a rich deep soil, not too stiff, and open situation; a fine, sandy loam is well adapted for its growth. The ground should have been trenched (and manured, if necessary) some time previously, as the addition of fresh manure just before sowing causes the roots to fork. Scorzonera, red and silver beet, cress, endive, peas. and broad beans may also be sown, but more sparingly than before; loosen the soil between growing crops and keep it free from weeds by the frequent use of the hoe. On the Darling Downs this month is especially suitable for planting a general crop.

Fruit Garden.—All operations connected with planting fruit trees, as apples, pears, quinces, peach, orange, mulberries, figs, etc., should be finished. If delayed after this month, much attention will be required in watering, especially if large plants should be removed. The most suitable figs for this colony are Black Genoa, Black Italian, Blue Provence, Brown Turkey, Castle Kennedy, Early Violet, Smyrna, White Genoa, White Provence, and White Adriatic. Every means should be resorted to during the winter to destroy the eggs and larva of insects that are injurious to the trees during the period when vegetation is most active, and as these always harbour in the bark and in the ground near the tree, there is no season of the year when their haunts can be so easily invaded and the enemy dislodged as now. For this purpose remove all filth and excrescences from the surface of the bark, such as old scales, moss, lichen. with a blunt scraper, such as an old knife or a piece of hoop iron, then wash the stem and branches well with a mixture of brine and soft soap, or other insecticide, applying it with a brush and rubbing it well into the crevices; the ground should also be turned over and a sprinkling of lime or soot applied. Grafting should be proceeded with according to the order in which the buds break. Manure orange trees if the soil is not naturally rich; if it is, they do not require it. Night soil or good rotten stable manure suits best. In applying fertilizers, fork them lightly in, leaving the surface soil rough. Orange trees may now be pruned of all the superfluous branches and shoots in the centre so as to admit of air and light. Propagate persimmons by grafting; this excellent fruit tree deserves a place in every garden; there are quite a number of varieties in cultivation, all good.

Flower Garden.—Herbaceous plants may now be divided and planted in permanent quarters; continue to plant Amaryllis, Crinums, Gladioli, and other bulbs. Balbous plants in general require a light, rich, rather sandy soil, well reduced and made fine by turning. For gladiolus, a mixture of sandy loam and leaf mould is the most suitable, and a portion of thoroughly decomposed cow-dung may be advantageously incorporated with the soil when it is of a poor nature. Flowering shrubs of all sorts may be transplanted. of which the following are some of the best:—Poinsetia, Weigelia, Tecoma velutina, Escallonia, Poinciana, Erythrina, Lagerstraemia, Clerodendron, Bouvardia, Datura, Gardenia, Tabernemontanum, Cestrum, and many species of Hibiscus, etc.; in the tropical north crotons are especially suitable. In sheltered borders the croton will thrive well on the coast from Brisbane northward.

Bush-house.—Plants in pots will require special attention in shifting, watering and keeping free from insect pests of all sorts, as future success will greatly depend on their proper management at this season. The Fuchsia when well cultivated is one of the loveliest plants, and possesses the advantage of retaining its blossom for a great length of time. Old plants of these repotted last month must be attended to, and a vigorous growth encouraged by frequent shifting into larger pots as required; care must be taken that the plant never becomes too dry. Cuttings may be potted when they are rooted. Begonias, Achimenes, Gesnerās, Gloxinias, etc., may be repotted or replanted for early flowering. Repot palms and ferns. Pot off stock plants of all kinds that were struck in early autumn, also all seedling plants from store pots. Plants that have been well established in pots can be planted out at any time when required.

Field.—Plant potatoes and select for the seed the best formed tubers of medium size and cut them lengthways, leaving two or three eyes ; a better crop will be obtained from these than from the small whole potatoes which are frequently used for planting ; reject tubers with deep eyes. This applies only to South Queensland and more particularly to the Darling Downs. Sow *Sorghum saccharatum* in seed beds for planting out; transplant when six inches high, leaving the plants about one foot apart. This is an excellent fodder, either green or dried, and will produce five or six cuttings in the season. Maize may be planted, and will also make a good summer crop as fodder, for which purpose it may be planted closer than if intended for grain. Sow pearl millet and teosinte. Rice may be sown in low-lying moist lands in the warmer districts. Hemp and linseed for fibre and oil. which will always command a ready market. Tobacco seed should be sown this month. Plant cassava. The plant is propagated by cuttings from the stem, a foot in length, which may be planted at distances six feet apart in rows, and generally comes to sufficient maturity in ten or eleven months to allow of the tuberous roots being used, which are the only parts converted into food ; the juice is deadly poison, but rendered innocuous by heat, and the bread which is obtained is estimated to yield more nourishment to human beings in the proportion of one acre of cassava to five acres of wheat. The climate is admirably suited to the cultivation of this plant ; it flourishes best in a dry alluvial soil; excessive moisture will rot the roots; a little moisture, however, in the earlier stages is necessary. Pumpkins for feeding cattle may be sown. Complete the manufacture of arrowroot, and, if the season is favourable, commence planting.

SEPTEMBER.

Kitchen Garden.—Keep this department thoroughly clean and in good order by taking every opportunity of eradicating weeds, either by hand-pulling or frequent hoeings. Weeds help materially to exhaust the soil, and they are much more easily kept under by never being allowed to ripen and shed their seeds. The sowing of onions, leeks, parsnips, carrots, beets, and other roots for main crops should be completed this month. Sow pumpkins, vegetable marrow, cucumbers and melons ; also tomatoes, capsicums, etc. White maize will form a vegetable which, when eaten green, will be found equal to peas. Rosellas can be sown this month. A succession of radishes may be obtained by sowing a few at intervals of a fortnight. French beans may be set in rows three feet apart. Transplant cabbage upon favourable occasions, but only in the southern districts. Asparagus and rhubarb should now be ready for use ; in cutting the former allow the heads to grow six inches above the ground before they are cut, and then cut level with the surface. In gathering the rhubarb for use, the leaf stalks should be bent down and pulled, not cut off. The flower stems, if seed is not required, should be cut off soon after they make their appearance.

Fruit Garden.—Be specially careful to destroy caterpillars among vines at this season. Stakes and trellising, if not already attended to, should be done at once. As the vines break, rub off the superfluous shoots and tie in young fruiting shoots. See that recently transplanted fruit trees do not suffer from want of water, and keep the surface of the soil well mulched. Pears and apples may still be grafted, but all grafting should be completed this month. Give support to early peach trees. In warm situations, loquats and mulberries ripen this month. Both these very desirable fruits may be cultivated to perfection in this climate. Strawberry beds should be well watered in dry weather twice a week, and mulched with short grass, in order to prevent the fruit from lying on the ground, and also for the purpose of retaining moisture. Young mango plants will now be making vigorous growth; keep an eye upon these and regulate the shape of the trees by removal of the young shoots. The Mango thrives so well in Queensland that it cannot be too largely planted, care being taken to give them an easterly aspect. and shelter from westerly winds. This is a good month for planting all sorts of tropical and sub-tropical fruits.

Flower Garden.—With the advancing season the flower garden will assume a gayer and more attractive aspect. Azaleas and Verbenas will now produce their beautiful flowers in profusion. Flowering shrubs may still be transplanted, but great care should be taken to remove as much earth as possible with the plant. Layers of Camellias, Azaleas, Magnolias, etc., may be made. Sow Balsams, Cock'scombs, Phloxes, Zinnias, Solanums. Plant Dahlias, but it will be advisable to reserve some to plant in November for late autumn flowering. To cultivate the Dahlia to perfection, the soil must be enriched by a plentiful supply of the strongest manure. The various kinds of Gladiolus, Amaryllis, etc., now begin to bloom, and should be sheltered from boisterous weather.

Bush-house.—Finish repotting palms, ferns, and all kinds of bush-house plants. Pot caladium bulbs. Plants will now require copious waterings, but by no means use manure water until there is active root action. Make sure that the shading of the bush-house is in good order, neither too dense or too thin. Allow no living creepers to overgrow the house nor act as a shade.

Field.—Plant Purple Arrowroot (*Canna edulis*) in rows four feet apart and two feet between the plants. Cuttings of sweet potatoes may be planted; take them six inches or more in length, and plant on ridges three feet apart, and two feet between the plants. Yams may also be planted. The West Indian variety is the strongest growing kind, and should be planted in rows three feet apart, leaving the same distance between the plants; the other kinds may be planted closer. The West Indian variety is by far the most favourable, both on account of its flavour and size; its roots are frequently three feet in length, and weigh about thirty pounds. It is extensively cultivated in the tropical parts of the continents of Asia, Africa and America, and is an excellent substitute for the English potato. When dug out of the earth, the roots are put for some time to dry in an airy place, and may afterwards be kept in casks of sand for a long time. The yams are raised from the cuttings of the roots. They require a light and deeply-worked alluvial soil, with a moderate degree of moisture, and generally come to maturity in six or seven months. The Okra (*Hibiscus esculentus*), the young pods of which are much used in tropical countries as a vegetable for soups, etc., may be grown by sowing in drills, three feet apart, and afterwards thinning the plant to two feet apart in the drill. The Rosella (*Hibiscus sabdariffa*), from the calyx of which excellent jam is made, may be grown by sowing at a distance of from five to eight feet apart each way. An excellent fibre is obtained from it, combining softness, strength and durability. Plant maize for summer crop and green fodder; it is a fine fodder plant for cattle, horses and pigs. Plant white arrowroot and sow tobacco. Sow sunflower—the seeds of which are used for making oil and for fattening fowls. Continue planting and hill potatoes, and finish cotton pruning. If the season be favourable, sugar cane may be planted towards the end of the month, but next month is the most general time in the southern portion of Queensland. Plant Coffee, Cocoa, Allspice, Cinnamon, etc., in the northern districts.

OCTOBER.

Kitchen Garden.—As vegetation is now making rapid progress it will be necessary to keep the hoe in constant use for earthing up or thinning the crops and loosening the soil between them. Carrots, parsnips, beet and all root crops should be thinned as soon as they are sufficiently forward. Melons, cucumbers, vegetable marrows, pumpkins, squashes and gourds may be sown and planted out; also capsicums and tomatoes. Of this last-named vegetable the large American varieties, such as Allington's, Hathaway's Excelsior and Trophy, and many newer varieties, are the best—some of which exceed a pound in weight, and are much more fleshy than the old kinds. Continue to sow lettuce, radishes, endive, etc., for salads. These should be watered plentifully in dry weather, as they will otherwise lose their crispness and flavour. The Egg plant may also be sown. It is cultivated for its fruit, which, when properly prepared, is excellent.

We Recommend SQUATTER WHISKY.

Fruit Garden.—Vines should be frequently looked over for the purpose of regulating their growth, by thinning and taking out the superfluous shoots, and stopping and shortening others that they may require it ; the permanent shoots should be tied up as soon as they are long enough. Upon the slightest appearance or suspicion of disease (*Oidium Tuckerii*) apply sulphur, either by itself or mixed with finely sifted lime. In most instances, if preventive measures are taken in time, the disease will be effectually checked. Newly-planted trees will now begin to require mulching. The operation of disbudding, which merely consists in rubbing off the superfluous and badly-placed young shoots and buds, may be advantageously performed on peach and other trees when practicable. The result will be a marked improvement in the fruit and prevents the necessity for much wasteful pruning in the winter. In peach trees very gross shoots may be pruned away. If scale appears on the orange trees, use some approved insecticide. Plant bananas and pineapples ; amongst the former the following varieties will be found well adapted for profitable cultivation :—Cavendish, Sugar, Dacca, and Lady's Finger. This is the best season for planting Custard Apple, Jack Fruit, Rose Apple, Mango, Alligator Pear, Chinese Date Plum, Sapodilla Plum, Bread Fruit, Durian, Papaw, Litchi, Longan, and other fine tropical and sub-tropical fruits. These delicious fruits may be as easily cultivated in many parts of the colony as the peach ; the chief point is to plant them in good soil that has been well trenched and manured, and, if necessary, drained. The Strawberry, Mulberry, Loquat, Cape Gooseberry, etc., may be gathered as they ripen.

Flower Garden.—Roses will now be in perfection, and may be regarded as one of the chief attractions of the garden ; they should be frequently looked over for the purpose of destroying the leaf-rolling caterpillar, aphis and other pests, and removing decaying flowers which, if allowed to remain, have an untidy appearance. As a rule, hybrid perpetuals flower well only in Southern Queensland ; the Noisettes, Teas, and Bourbons succeed better in higher temperatures. Plant out and stake Dahlias, tie up climbers and other plants where requisite, and water in dry weather anything newly planted. Continue to plant Verbenas, Pelargoniums, etc. Sow showy annuals, as in last month. Take up bulbs as soon as the leaves are withered, and store them in a dry place to prevent their rotting or making unseasonable growth.

Bush-house.—Fuchsias and all pot plants must be well attended to and kept clear from insect pests, many of which will make their appearance this month. A frequent use of the syringe will be of great service for this purpose, and will also assist the growth of the plants. Re-pot Caladiums in rich, light compost, also Achimenes, Gloxinias, Begonias, and Eucharis amazonica. Fuchsias will be making rapid growth. To produce sturdy bushy plants, they should be frequently topped, and, if required for show purposes, they should receive the last topping about six weeks before they are wanted to flower. As soon as they show flower-buds freely, give them a little weak manure water ; use the syringe to keep down thrip. A little sulphate of ammonia dissolved in the water—about an ounce to six gallons—would be very beneficial for the purpose.

Field.—This, with the latter part of the preceding month, is the best season for planting sugar cane ; any portion of the cane having perfect eyes will do. The holes should be eighteen inches square and eight or ten inches deep, and in the rows five feet apart, and two or three feet from each other, according to the soil and situation. One or more cuttings may be laid longitudinally in each hole, special care being taken to keep the eyes uppermost. Cover the canes at first not more than an inch, and when the shoots are a few inches in length draw a little earth about them, and continue to do so at intervals, as required, until the holes are filled up. The soil should be very loose, in order to allow the roots to spread with facility, which in their turn collect abundance of moisture. This is the best season for sowing cotton, coffee, China grass, and other fibrous plants, more particularly jute. Of cotton, three or four seeds should be dropped into holes from three to five feet apart, according to the nature of the soil ; afterwards thin

to a stand of one plant. Where the seed is not an object, it is preferable to open a furrow with the plough; strew the seed pretty thickly, and harrow. When the young plants appear, cut them out with a hoe or pull to stand three or four each. When the plants have gained a little more strength, select the strongest plant in each stand, and draw the rest by the hand, leaving only a single plant. The seed is better for being damped before planting. The New Orleans variety has proved to be the best adapted for cultivation on the more exposed or distant lands from the coast. The Sea Island is a more valuable kind, but the crop cannot be depended upon. It produces well on the more sheltered lands of the seaboard, the principal drawback to its cultivation being its extreme liability to damage from rain, which upon the New Orleans variety does not exert such a prejudicial effect. In some localities, after very wet seasons, during which the cotton plant has run to wood at the expense of fibre, it will be found more profitable to sow fresh seeds than to prune the old plants. Sow rice for a general crop. Coffee is usually raised from seed, and afterwards planted out at regular distances varying according to climate and the nature of the soil, but generally eight feet apart; in soils where they attain the height of ten or twelve feet, the intervals between should be from nine to twelve feet. The berries grown upon low, rich, moist soils are the largest, but those grown in drier and more elevated localities are the best flavoured. Generally, however, the trees require considerable moisture, and plenty of warmth, tempered by shade when the sun is most powerful. They frequently commence bearing when about two years old, and the berries are fit to gather when they assume a dark red hue. Arrowroot, sweet potatoes and yams may also be planted. The Ground Nut (*Arachis hypogea*) may be planted in rows about two feet apart, and a foot between the plants in rows; it thrives best on light sandy soils and is very prolific, and if cultivated upon a large scale would no doubt prove remunerative. Continue to transplant tobacco, leaving the plants about four feet each way. Hay will soon be ready to cut in the early districts. Any potatoes not earthed up attend to at once, in order to protect them from heat. If the season is favourable, maize may be sown for fodder, and some for grain. Turmeric and ginger should now be planted in well prepared soil, and after planting should be mulched with cow-dung; a sandy soil suits them best.

NOVEMBER.

Kitchen Garden.—A few vegetables of various kinds may still be sown as required; but should the weather prove dry, the seed beds must be well and regularly watered. The branches of tomatoes should be supported to prevent the fruit from lying on the ground, and the shoots thinned and stopped occasionally. Sow French beans, lettuce, radish, cucumbers, melons, etc., as in last month; a rich soil and plenty of moisture is essential to secure good crops of these. Sweet corn should be sown all through the summer at intervals of a fortnight or three weeks. The cutting of asparagus should now cease, and the beds may receive a top-dressing of salt with beneficial effect. Keep the surface soil between the crops well stirred, and let more than common care be taken to destroy weeds of all kinds. There is no work that requires more attention than this, for weeds are at no time more detrimental than at present, especially among all close-growing crops of young plants. It is therefore of the utmost importance to destroy them before they grow so large as to overrun advancing young crops. By never allowing weeds to gain any strength they can be as nearly as possible mastered with a minimum of labour and outlay.

Fruit Garden.—When there is a superabundance of fruit on fruit trees, it should be thinned, care being taken to leave the largest and best fruit. As a general rule, the branches ought not to be allowed to become so overladen with fruit as to require propping. Complete pineapple and banana planting in order that they may have the full benefit of the summer. Loosen the soil among vines and keep them free from weeds and caterpillars; renew the stakes where required, and look over them frequently to thin and stop the shoots so as to

Canned Fruits. VERNEYS, Preservers.

throw all the strength of the plant into the fruit as it swells. It is a very common mistake to leave too much young wood on vines, as it only serves to crowd the fruit and also prevents it from ripening thoroughly. Another mistake is to remove leaves away from shading the fruit, causing a tendency to black spot and to prevent the full growth and maturing of the fruit. Remove suckers, and all barren shoots that will not be wanted next season. If the weather is warm and moist, *Oidium* may make its appearance ; if so, sulphuring will be required immediately.

Flower Garden.—There will now be an abundance of work for the scythe, hoe, and digging fork. Flower beds and borders should be kept perfectly clean and neat. Tie up climbers and all tall-growing plants that need support, and cut down all herbaceous plants when they have done flowering ; and continue to take up and store bulbs as in last month. Plant out dahlias for late flowering, and transplant annuals, Coleus, Caladiums, and other tender foliage plants, in showery weather, and shade them from the hot sun for a few days. Edgings of Alternanthera may be planted at any time during summer when moisture is sufficient. Water newly-planted shrubs and trees, and see to the mulching and attend to the watering in dry weather, especially of plants newly removed.

Bush-house.—If previously well attended to, Caladiums, Alocasias, and Marantas will now be making a good show, and if in a healthy state, will be benefitted by the application of weak manure water twice a week. Syringe ferns freely to keep down thrip and red spider, and should mildew make its appearance on any plant give an application of flowers of sulphur. A flour dredge is useful for applying this. Gloxinias will now be opening their first flowers, and when syringing be careful not to wet the blossoms.

Field.—Plantations of Cotton, Indigo, Arrowroot, Ginger, Turmeric, etc., must be made, and all weeds destroyed when young. Use the horse-hoe for this purpose, when practicable, or as soon as the crops will admit of the operation. Sugar cane planted last month should have a little more earth drawn about it ; this must be continued for the next three or four months. When tobacco has reached its full height, and is coming into flower, it must be topped, and frequently looked over and pinched, the weak leaves thinned out, leaving only the larger and more fleshy ; all the strength of the plant will thus be given to those which are retained. From eight to ten leaves is enough for each plant. Wheat, Barley, and Oats will now be ready for harvesting, and will demand the farmer's careful attention to get the operation properly performed. Haymaking should be finished this month, and if it is desired to save the seeds of any of the grasses, it should be remembered that seeds ripen after being cut, and if care be not taken the seed will fall out. As the annato plant flourishes in this climate, it would probably pay to cultivate it for the sake of the dye called annato, which is obtained from the red pulp covering the seeds. It is better not to plant maize this month, but defer it to the end of December, as the November crop but very rarely succeeds.

DECEMBER.

Kitchen Garden.—Hoeing and surface stirring between crops will still be of the greatest importance ; these operations are not only destructive to weeds, but they check rapid evaporation and pulverise the ground. In dry weather, celery, cucumbers, melons and pumpkins should be watered. In watering any kind of plant, it is much better to give a copious supply once daily ; and, where practicable, it is both economical and beneficial to get the water well down in the soil rather than upon the surface. Surface watering is very deceptive ; plants are often starved for want of water when watered inadequately from the surface. A dibber or pointed stick will serve to make a hole ; the water should be gradually poured in and then covered with dry soil. If the supply of vegetables for the summer is running short, cabbage (St. John's Day), and French beans may be sown in the cooler districts of the colony ; also sow pumpkins and custard marrows for a late crop.

Fruit Garden.—Proceed with thinning the shoots of vines and also the fruit where it is too abundant. If mildew (*Oidium Tuckerii*) appears, dust the vines with sulphur and fresh slaked lime. Most kinds of fruit trees, as peaches, etc., may now be budded, and all fruit should be gathered as it ripens.

Flower Garden.—Everything in this department should now be kept in the neatest possible order, by clearing away weeds and all rubbish. Edgings should be trimmed and climbers tied; all tall-growing plants neatly staked and tied up where necessary. Roses may be budded when the bark upon the stock separates freely from the wood. Carnations, pinks, etc., may be propagated from pipings or layers. Pot plants will require constant attention in watering, shading, keeping free from insects, etc.; most of these would be better plunged in ashes or gravel at this season. Flower seeds may be gathered, taking care to select none but the best varieties. Look over bulbs that have been stored, and see that they are perfectly dry and not attacked by mice or insects.

Bush-house.—Plants in the bush-house will now be at their best, and if properly looked after will be in luxuriant growth. Propagate gloxinias and foliage begonias, by inserting the leaves as cuttings in light sandy soil in a shady spot. Propagate crotons and dracænas by cuttings.

Field.—The operations for the month will consist chiefly in hoeing and keeping free from weeds sugar, cotton, and all other crops. Look frequently over tobacco; top any that has not been previously done, and pinch off all side shoots as soon as they make their appearance; the first crop will be ready to cut; this will be shown by the leaf turning partially yellow at the tip. Cotton should also be topped, and have the superfluous shoots thinned out. Draw a little earth occasionally to newly planted sugar cane. Potatoes planted in Spring should now be ripe, and must be taken up as soon as they are ready, as they will rot if left long in the ground. Seed from this crop must be saved for the March planting, as at that time of the year imported potatoes fit for seed purposes cannot be obtained. Yams should be staked for the purpose of supporting their vines, and to prevent their trailing upon the ground. Maize should be planted for winter crop; pumpkins and cabbage for winter feed for cattle. Too much attention cannot be given at this season to keeping the weeds under, as, if they now get the upper hand, it will be almost impossible to overcome them during the season, and where the land is suitable to their operations, no better investment presents itself to the cultivator than labour-saving implements for this description of work.

ORCHARD.

KEEP ON SPRAYING.—Any farmer who has a dozen or more apple or pear trees, should have a spraying apparatus and familiarize himself with the use of fungicides and insecticides. The difference in value between a good and a poor crop will more than pay for the outfit, and it often comes handy for spraying other crops, such as potatoes, tomatoes, &c.

MANURING FRUIT TREES.—Orchardists, as a rule, fail in feeding their trees, by merely dumping a little heap of manure around the base of each, when it should be scattered evenly over the entire surface as far as the branches extend. The roots usually extend at least twice as far as the branches; and if the branches of a large tree extend 20 feet from the centre, the roots have pushed out at least 40 feet.

PEARS flourish better if in proximity to stone.

KEEP the cultivator going in the orchard.

THE fruit that falls without shaking is too mellow.

WHERE the ground is very rich there will be but little, if any, blight.

TREES that are permitted to grow haphazard in their growth are rarely satisfactory.

EVERY tree should be trained to a symmetrical form. An ill-shaped tree looks like a deformity.

ALL wounds on trees are the better for being painted or covered with something to keep out water.

GIVE quinces a rich soil, good cultivation and careful pruning, and the fruit nearly always proves profitable.

SOME growers claim that the close planting of pear trees is an advantage, as they help to protect each other.

Do not set a tree as you would a fence post. If you expect it to grow and give good results, give it plenty of room.

No home is beautiful, however magnificent the dwelling itself may be, without its quota of trees, shrubbery and flowers.

An orchard will not thrive in a flat, wet soil. Underdraining will put the soil in a good condition and cause the trees to thrive.

THE presence of any kind of diseased material in an orchard or vineyard increases the chances of the appearance of the disease another year.

RUBBISH of any sort should never be left in the orchard. It harbors insects, and later on they multiply and come forth to wage destruction.

STIMULATING the vine by animal manure makes it grow until late in the autumn, and the wood will not ripen as well and the fruit buds do not thoroughly develop.

TREES, under good cultivation, in a good, congenial soil, will make a vigorous growth if they are of a strong, vigorous growing kind, and it is in this case that pruning, when the tree is dormant, promotes the growth of the wood.

THINGS TO BE REMEMBERED.

Clean all garden tools when put by. Never leave tools outside when not in use. Keep the barrow, lawn mower, and roller well lubricated. The pruning knife should be kept sharp. Keep a box of labels ready for naming plants, a hank of soft twine for tying up, a supply of stakes, and a book for making notes in.

We Recommend SQUATTER WHISKY.

GARDEN REQUISITES.

A well equipped garden should be supplied with a steel spade, digging fork, shovel, mattock, pick, steel bar, edging iron, hoes and rakes of various sizes, axe, hammer, hand saw, trowel, garden line, barrow, watering pots, buckets, riddles of several sizes, shears, knives, and above all a place to keep them in.

TABLE showing the Number of Plants required to plant an acre of land, from 1 foot to 30 feet, from plant to plant.

Distance Apart.	Number per Acre.	Distance Apart.	Number per Acre.
Feet.	Number.	Feet.	Number.
30 x 30	48	9 x 9	537
28 x 28	55	8 x 8	680
26 x 26	64	7 x 7	889
24 x 24	75	6½ x 6½	1,031
22 x 22	90	6 x 6	1,201
20 x 20	100	5½ x 5½	1,440
19 x 19	120	5 x 5	1,742
18 x 18	134	4½ x 4½	2,151
17 x 17	150	4 x 4	2,722
16 x 16	169	3½ x 3½	3,556
15 x 15	193	3 x 3	4,840
14 x 14	222	2½ x 2½	6,970
13 x 13	257	2 x 2	10,890
12 x 12	202	1½ x 1½	19,360
11 x 11	360	1 x 1	43,560
10 x 10	435		

TABLE showing the Number of Plants required to plant a mile in length, from 1 foot to 100 feet apart.

Distance Apart.	Number per Mile.	Distance Apart.	Number per Mile.
Feet.	Number.	Feet.	Number.
100	52	30	176
95	55	25	211
90	58	20	264
85	62	15	352
80	66	10	528
75	70	9	586
70	75	8	660
65	81	7	754
60	84	6	880
55	96	5	1,056
50	105	4	1,320
45	117	3	1,760
40	132	2	2,640
35	151	1	5,280

We Recommend SQUATTER WHISKY.

The A.M.P.

ALL are familiar with the popular designation of the Australian Mutual Provident Society; the great Australian society which, founded but forty-nine years ago, has in that comparatively limited period, increased its business by such gigantic strides as to occupy at the present time the proud and enviable position of the leading " Mutual " Life Office in the British Empire.

The year 1849 marks the inception of the society. Its operations for the first twelve months were by no means encouraging, only thirty life policies, assuring £9,450, and twelve policies for endowments and annuities, being written during that time—a result not calculated to inspire the founders with very sanguine anticipations for the future, and which none dreamt was to form the foundation of the immense business now on the books. There is a tendency to smile upon noting the almost apologetic tone of the first annual report, and contrasting the statement of affairs therein contained with the masses of figures, running into tens of millions, which the members of the society are now accustomed to have placed before them. " Heavy preliminary expenses " are mentioned, although "the strictest economy has been observed." A sum of £226 represents the total expenditure for the first year, and against this there was on hand a stock of books and stationery valued at £136, leaving the actual cost of the year's business at £90. The receipts totalled £268, so that there was an available cash balance of £42. That in forty-nine years the business should have increased to its present magnitude cannot but strike us as little short of marvellous, and affords incontestable evidence of the thoroughly efficient and economical management which has always been a ruling characteristic of the institution, and which has enabled the Australian Mutual Provident to pay a rate of bonus unequalled by any other kindred company in the world. A striking illustration as well of the financial resources as of the provident habits of the Australian people is also presented when it is remembered that the business has hitherto been strictly confined to the Australasian colonies, although a recent modification of the by-laws admits of further policies being granted to members who, since first assuring, have removed to other countries a concession which will doubtless be considerably availed of.

We Recommend SQUATTER WHISKY.

94

To the society's liberal regulations must be attributed a large measure of its success. The policies now contain absolutely no restriction as to residence, occupation, &c., and beyond a clause prohibiting suicide within 13 months of the date of issue the only condition of the contract on the part of the assured is payment of the premium. The non-forfeiture system, by which unpaid premiums are advanced from the surrender value, and the policy thus sustained in force as long as there is sufficient margin of value to meet a single instalment, is one for which many have had cause to be grateful, and instances are on record of substantial sums having been paid to widows under policies believed to have long since lapsed, but which, on chance application to the office, were found to be still current, although for years no premium payments had been made.

At 31st December, 1897, the amount of insurances on the society's books totalled £41,726,041, providing an annual premium income of £1,364,120, the total annual income (including interest) at the date named being £2,091.706. The surplus for the year available for distribution amongst the policy-holders reached the large sum of £445,235, which provided reversionary bonuses of about £835,000,. The funds at the close of 1897 stood at £14,479,578. That the society has a large interest in this colony is apparent from the fact that Queensland securities represent nearly two and a-half millions of the invested funds.

The Australian Mutual Provident Society to-day stands pre-eminently before the world a monument to Australian finance, and as an office whose career and whose success have been without check. Amongst the whole of the British Mutual Life Insurance offices it ranks foremost, an institution born of the soil, and one of which Australia and Australians are justly proud.

POPULATION

OF THE

CHIEF TOWNS OF QUEENSLAND, WITH DISTANCE FROM BRISBANE AND DIRECTION.

CENSUS, 1891.

Brisbane—Population, 100,913; Area, 50,266.

Town	Population	Approximate Distance	Direction	Town	Population	Approximate Distance	Direction
Adavale ..	192	620	West	Herberton ..	1,175	1,000	N.
Allora ..			WSW	Hughenden ..	1,516	1 200	N W.
Aramac ..	388	750	N.W.	Ipswich..	7.625	24	W.
Barcaldine ..	2,480	700	N.W.	Longreach ..	2,000	730	N.W.
Beaudesert ..	450	47	S.	Mackay ..	3,597	521	N.
Beenleigh ..	536	22	S.	Maryborough ..	9,700	177	N.
Blackall ..	777	622	N.W.	Mitchell ..	376	368	W.
Bowen ..	1,082	725	N.	Mount Morgan ..	3,514	400	N.
Brisbane ..	100,913	---	—	Mount Perry ..	351	220	N.W.
Bundaberg ..	5,000	222	N.	Normanton ..	580	1,382	N.W.
Burketown ..	164	1,500	N.W.	Port Douglas ..	494	1,000	N.W.
Caboolture ..	248	31	N.	Ravenswood ..	1,000	800	N.W.
Cairns ..	2,460	990	N.	Rockhampton ..	11,629	420	N.
Charleville ..	1,456	480	W.	Roma ..	1,691	317	W.
Charters Towers	4,597	820	N.	Sandgate ..	1,756	13	N.E.
Clermont ..	1,812	575	N.W.	Southport ..	895	46	S.
Cooktown ..	2,620	1,050	N.	Springsure ..	264	485	N.W.
Croydon ..	1,231	1,287	N.W.	Stanthorpe ..	735	207	S.W.
Cunnamulla ..	658	560	W.	St. George ..	900	380	WSW
Dalby ..	1,378	152	W.	Thursday Island	2,400	1,430	N.
Eidsvold ..	1,258	230	N.W.	Toowoomba ..	7,007	100	W.
Gayndah..	513	230	N.W.	Townsville ..	8,564	870	N.
Geraldton ..	353	920	N.	Warwick ..	3,400	166	S.W.
Gladstone ..	932	354	N.	Winton ..	625	1,150	N.W.
Gympie ..	8,000	116	N.				

To File a Cross-cut Saw. —Procure two saplings about five inches in diameter standing about two feet apart. Saw them off about four feet from the ground, then split the tops of the two standing trunks of the saplings and insert the back of the saw in the splits, leaving the teeth projecting upward.

ROMA

SHIPPING OF VARIOUS COUNTRIES OF THE WORLD.

MARITIME INFORMATION.

It is estimated that there are 30,020 Sailing Vessels, and 13,822 Steamers employed in the trade of the World. Of these, 8,766 Sailing Vessels and 7,326 Steamers fly the British Ensign.

STATISTICS OF STEAMERS AND SAILING VESSELS ACCORDING TO THEIR FLAG.

Country.	Steamers.		Sailing.		Recorded as Lost.	
	No.	Tonnage.	No.	Tonnage.	Steamers.	Ships.
English	7326	10,511,640	8766	3,269,456	182	396
German	1009	1,386,439	1271	573,407	15	95
French..	691	957,430	1662	261,223	14	117
American	504	766,847	3904	1,359,506	6	171
Spanish	441	531,439	1147	168,573	9	42
Norwegian	630	505,620	2818	1,176,957	12	233
Italian ..	240	346,455	1699	472,311	12	98
Dutch ..	215	323,300	645	189,779	4	55
Japanese	368	327,834	252	33,020	10	44
Russian	365	285,992	1759	363,302	3	38
Austrian	178	257,142	213	68,631	5	10
Danish..	288	251,757	883	153,369	3	45
Swedish	526	246,963	1470	286,876	5	74
Grecian	123	117,244	1060	246,243	3	16
Brazilian	331	141,739	320	78,519	Nil.	6
Belgian	119	135,043	12	2,308	4	Nil.
Turkish	94	71,631	1246	241,190	2	7
Portuguese	51	57,798	204	46,916	2	3
Chinese	45	54,793	13	1,318	Nil.	Nil.
Chilian	42	46,269	142	73,162	1	6
Other Nations	372	194,029	527	150,832	11	8

Confession of a fault makes half amends.
Denying a fault doubles it.
Envy shooteth at things and woundeth herself.
Foolish fear doubles danger.
God reaches us good things by our own hand.
He has hard work who has nothing to do.
It costs more to revenge wrongs than to bear them.
Knavery is the most laborious trade.

We Recommend SQUATTER WHISKY.

QUEENSLAND STATISTICS

(WEEDON'S *Queensland, Past and Present.*)

FOR YEAR ENDED 31ST DECEMBER, 1897.

Area, 668,497 square miles (427,838,080 acres)

Population, 484,700 (271,372 males and 213,328 females)

Births, 14,313; Marriages, 2894; Deaths, 5,428

Revenue, £3,602,457

Expenditure, £3,676,695

Public Debt, 31st Dec., 1897, £33,498,414

Interest on Public Debt, £1,297,139

Revenue, 1859 to 1896-7, £69,301,438

Expenditure do. £70,689,462

Imports, £5,429,191; Exports, £9,091,55,

Mineral Production, £2,784,501 (total to end of 1897, £51,228,578)

Railways open for traffic, 2,609 miles

Cost of construction, £18,016,150

Manufactories, 1,888; hands employed, 22,785

Value of machinery and plant, £3,694,801

Value of output, £6,332,484.

Chief Minerals produced, 1897—Gold, £2,558,141; Silver, £25,118; Lead, £4,117; Tin, £37,509; Copper, £12,645; Coal, £189,889; Opal, £10,850; Bismuth, £134; Wolfram, £195; Manganese, £1,506.

VALUE OF CURRENT COINS.

	ENGLISH VALUE.	
	s.	d.
Sovereign	20	0
20 Franc Piece	15	11
20 Mark Piece	19	6
Friederich D'Or (German)	17	0
Half Imperial	16	5
20 Kronor	21	8
Crown Union (German)	7	3
Shilling	1	0
Franc	0	9½
Mark (German)	0	11¾
Florin (German)	1	8
Florin (Dutch)	1	7¾
Kroner	1	1½
Dollar (American)	4	1
Dollar (Spanish Silver)	3	4
Peseta	0	9
Sechser	0	2
10 Pfennigs	0	1

We Recommend SQUATTER WHISKY.

MEN AND WOMEN OF THE DAY.

ALBANI, MADAME (*née* Marie Emma Lajeunesse), prima donna; born near Montreal; educated in Canada. Famous opera singer. Visited Brisbane April, 1898.

ALLEN, GRANT; born Kingston, Ontario, February, 1848; son of Church of England clergyman; educated Canada, U.S.A., and Birmingham, England. Author of a large number of novels and historical guides. Address, Savile Club, London.

AUSTIN, ALFRED, Poet Laureate; born Leeds, May, 1835; educated Stonyhurst and Oscott Colleges, Barrester. Address, Ashford, Kent.

BARLOW, HON. A. H., M.L.C.; born at Wanstead, Essex, near London in 1837. Arrived in Sydney in 1848. Member for Ipswich from 1888 to 1896. Appointed to Legislative Council 1896, and is a Minister without portfolio. Address, Ipswich.

BARLOW, Rt. Rev. C. G., D.D., Bishop of North Queensland since 1891; ordained 1881. Address, Townsville, N.Q.

BARING-GOULD, S., M.A., J.P., Rector of Lew-Trenchard. Author of numerous works, covering almost the whole domain of literature, his latest being "Guavas the Tinner," "A Study of St. Paul," "The Broom Squire," "Napoleon Bonaparte," etc.; born 1834. Address, Rectory, North Devon.

BECKE, G. LOUIS; born Sydney; son of F. Becke, of Northampton, England. Trader, etc., in South Seas from 1870 to 1892; also on the Californian coast. Author of numerous novels on the South Sea Islands. Address, Morley's Hotel, Trafalgar Square, London, W.

BERESFORD, LORD CHARLES W. DE LA POER, C.B., M.P. for York, Captain Royal Navy; born February, 1846; second son of the Marquis of Waterford. Served with conspicuous gallantry in many naval

engagements. Author of numerous publications on naval and Egyptian matters. Address, Portman Square, London.

BOLDREWOOD, ROLF (Thos. Alexr. Brown), novelist; born London, 6th August, 1826; educated Sydney College, New South Wales, Australia. Pioneer squatter in Victoria; also Magistrate and Warden, goldfields, New South Wales, until 1895. Author of Australian novels and other publications. Address, Melbourne Club, Melbourne, Victoria.

BOOTHBY, GUY NEWELL, novelist; born Adelaide, October, 1867; educated at Salisbury. Author of "Dr. Nikola," "The Marriage of Esther," and other works; also a great traveller. Address, Alveston, Thames Ditton.

BOOTH, REV. WM., General of Salvation Army; born 10th April, 1829; educated at Nottingham. Founded Salvation Army in 1878. Has visited almost every country in the world. Address, 101 Queen Victoria Street, London.

BOWEN, RT. HON. SIR GEO. FERGUSON, created, 1856, G.C.M.G., D.C.L., LL.D.; born 1821; educated at Charterhouse and Trinity College. Secretary of Government, Ionian Islands, 1854-9; first Governor of Queensland, 1859-68; New Zealand, 1868-73; Victoria, 1873-79; Mauritius, 1879-83; Hong Kong, 1883-87; Royal Commissioner to Malta, 1888.

BYRNES, HON. T. J., M.L.A. for Warwick, Attorney-General and Premier; born Brisbane, November, 1860; educated at Bowen, and Sydney and Melbourne Universities. B.A. and LL.B., M.L.C. and Solicitor-General 1890; Attorney-General 1893. Returned for Cairns in 1893. Defeated at North Brisbane election 1896. Returned for Warwick by substantial majority at same election. Address, Yeronga, near Brisbane.

We Recommend SQUATTER WHISKY.

CAINE, Thos. Henry Hall, novelist; born May, 1853; educated Isle of Man. Author of "The Deemster," "The Bondman," "The Manxman," and "The Christian." Address, Greeba, Isle of Man.

CARNEGIE, And., American Manufacturer and Author; born Dunfermline, Scotland, November, 1837. Address, Pittsburgh, U.S.A.

CHAMBERLAIN, Rt. Hon. Jos., M.P. for Birmingham since 1876. Secretary of State for Colonies. Thrice Mayor of Birmingham. Address, Highbury, Birmingham.

CORELLI, Marie, novelist; Italian and Scotch parentage; educated in French convent. Commenced writing when barely 14 years of age. Unmarried. Author of "A Romance of Two Worlds," "Sorrows of Satan," "Mighty Atom," "Ziska," etc., etc. Address, Longridge Road, London.

CRAWFORD, F. M.; born Italy, August, 1854; educated United States, and Trinity College, Cambridge. Editor and Author. Address, Fifth Avenue, New York.

CHATAWAY, Hon. J. V.; born Sept., 1852. Minister for Agriculture. Educated at Winchester College. Member for Mackay since 1893. Address, Cleveland, Moreton Bay.

COWLEY, Hon. A. S., Speaker of Legislative Assembly; born Gloucestershire, April, 1848. Arrived in New South Wales from South Africa in 1871, Maryborough, Queensland, 1873, Lower Herbert 1875. Member for the Herbert since 1888. Minister for Lands 1890. Address, Parliamentary Buildings, Brisbane.

CROCKETT, Rev. S. R., novelist; born Galloway, Sept., 1860. Author of numerous popular works in Scotch dialect, including "The Stickit Minister," "Lad's Love," "Bog Myrtle and Peat," etc. Address, Norfolk Street, London.

CROOKES, Professor W., F.R.S., Vice-President Royal Society. Author of many valuable chemical treatises and original inventor of Röntgen Rays. Address, Kensington Park Gardens, London.

DALRYMPLE, Hon. D. H.; born Newbury, England, December, 1840; educated Independent College, Taunton.

Arrived in Melbourne 1852, Rockhampton 1868, Mackay 1864. Member for Mackay since 1888. Minister for Public Instruction since 1895. Address, Treasury, Brisbane.

DICKSON, Hon. J. R., C.M.G.; born Plymouth, England, 1832; educated at High School, Glasgow. Arrived in Victoria 1854, Queensland 1862. Represented Enoggera from 1873-88. Defeated for Toombul same year. On his return from a trip to Europe in 1892 he was elected as member for Bulimba, which seat he still occupies. Secretary for Public Works and Mines 1876, Colonial Treasurer same year, Leader of Opposition 1881, Colonial Treasurer 1883, Acting Premier 1887, represented Queensland at Federal Council 1886-7 and 1896, present Home Secretary. Address, Toorak, Brisbane.

DUFFY, Sir C. Gavan; born Ireland, April, 1816; educated Monaghan and Belfast. Founded Nation Newspaper, Irish Confederation, and the Irish Tenant League. Minister for Public Works, Vic., 1857, and Prime Minister 1871, Speaker 1877. Author of numerous works on Ireland. Address, Nice.

EDISON, T. A.; born 1847, U.S.A. Inventor of the Phonograph and numerous other remarkable inventions in science; fully 470 patents have been registered by him. Address, Hartford, U.S.A.

FOXTON, Hon. J. F. G., M.L.A., Major; born near Melbourne, September 24, 1849; educated Melbourne Grammar School. Arrived Queensland 1864. Admitted as a solicitor 1871. Made discovery of tin in Carnarvon 1872. Member for Carnarvon since 1883. Minister for Lands since 1896. Holds Royal Humane Society's bronze medal. Address, Toowong, Brisbane.

GRIFFITH, Sir S. W., G.C.M.G., C.J. of Queensland; born 1845. Premier of Queensland 1883-88. President of Federal Council of Australasia 1888-93. Address, Merthyr, Brisbane.

HAGGARD. H. Ryder, novelist. Author of numerous novels on South Africa, including "Dawn," "King Solomon's Mines," "Allan Quartermaine," "John Haste," "The World's Desire," etc. Address, Ditchingham House, Norfolk.

HOOKING, Rev. Silas R., Methodist; born Cornwall, March, 1850. Author of "Her Benny," "Sea Waif," "Alick Green," "The Heart of Man," etc. Address, Highgate, London.

KANE, Capt. H. C., R.N.; born 1843. Commander of H.M.S. *Calliope* during the great hurricane at Samoa, 1889, when three German and three American men-of-war were wrecked. Address, Summer Place, S.W., London.

KIPLING, Rudyard; born Bombay, 1864; educated North Devon. Prominent author, editor, and traveller. Author of "Barrack Room Ballads," "The Light that Failed," "Seven Seas," and other works on Indian life. Address, Savile Club, London.

KRUGER, S. T. Paul, President of the Transvaal Republic; born at Rustenburg in 1825. In 1872 he became a member of the Executive Council of the South African Republic under President Burgess, and in 1882 he became President for the first time. In 1883 he was re-elected President for five years, and in 1888 was for the third time elected President.

LAMINGTON, Lord, His Ex. Baron (C. W. A. N. Cochrane-Baillie), K.C.M.G., B.A.; born 1860; educated Oxford (B.A.). M.P. for North St. Pancras 1890. Assist. Private Secretary to Marquis of Salisbury, Prime Minister, 1885-6. Married June, 1895, Miss May Hozier, daughter of Sir W. Hozier, Bart. Address, Government House, Brisbane.

MacGREGOR, Sir W., K.C.M.G., M.D., L.R.C.P. Ed., M.B., Administrator of British New Guinea; born 1846. Brought up to medical profession. Has successively held Government appointments at Seychelles, Mauritius, and Fiji. Represented Fiji at Federal Australasian Council 1886, and several times been Acting Governor of Fiji and High Commissioner of the Western Pacific. His administration and exploration in New Guinea has received high praise. Address, Port Moresby.

MELBA, Madame (Mrs. Armstrong). prima donna; born Melbourne. Spent early portion of her life at Kelvin Grove, Mackay. Address, Paris.

MURRAY, Hon. John; born Ayrshire, Scotland, July, 1841. Member for Normanby since 1888. Arrived in Victoria

1852, Brisbane 1864. Three times Chairman of Gogango Divisional Board. Present Minister for Railways and Works. Address, Rockhampton.

NANSEN, Fridyof, LL.D., D.Sc., Ph.D., Arctic explorer and author; born Christiania, October, 1860; educated at Christiania. Was commander of the North Pole expedition 1893-6, in which he reached the highest latitude yet obtained (86 deg. 13·6 min.) Author of "Across Greenland," "Farthest North," etc., etc. Address, Christiania, Norway.

NELSON, Hon. Sir H. M., K.C.M.G., P.C., LL.D., etc.; born 1835. President Legislative Council. Premier of Queensland 1894-98. Address, Middle Ridge, Toowoomba.

PHILP, Hon. Robt. Arrived in Queensland at ten years of age. Attended Normal School. Eleven years with firm of Bright Bros. & Co.; afterwards joined Mr. James Burns and established present extensive mercantile firm of Burns, Philp & Co. Was elected member for Musgrave in 1886, and has represented Townsville since 1888. Is now Minister for Mines and Colonial Treasurer. Address, Mary Street, Brisbane.

PRAED, Mrs. Campbell, authoress; born Beaudesert, Queensland, March, 1851. Author of many Australian and other novels, including "An Australian Heroine," "Moloch," "The Head Station," "Outlaw and Lawmaker," etc., etc. Address, Elm Park Gardens, London.

RHODES, Rt. Hon. Cecil J., Privy Councillor. The foremost South African statesman. Member of Executive Council since 1889. Born 1853. Educated Oriel College. Premier of Cape Colony 1890-91. Treasurer-General of Cape Colony at 31 years of age. Formed British South Africa Co. when 36. Address, Capetown.

ROBERTS, Gen. Sir F. S.; born Cawnpore, India, September, 1832; educated Eton, Sandhurst, etc. Fought throughout the Indian Mutiny. Commander Afghan War 1880. Commander-in-Chief in India 1893. Has been thanked by both Houses of Parliament and Government of India on numerous occasions for superior ability and gallantry before the enemy. Author of several works on war matters. Address, Dublin.

We Recommend SQUATTER WHISKY.

SALISBURY, Marquis of; born 1830; Privy Councillor. K.G., D.C.L., etc. Premier of United Kingdom 1885-92, and since 1895. Has been special Ambassador and Commissioner to Foreign Powers on several occasions. Address, Hatfield House, Hertford.

STONE-WIGG, Rt. Rev. M. J., B.A., M.A., first Bishop of New Guinea; born Kent, England, 1861; educated Winchester and University Colleges. Has served in St. Andrew's and Holy Innocents, London; Assistant Curate St. John's Pro-Cathedral, Brisbane, 1889; Vicar 1891; Canon Residentiary and Sub-Dean 1891; first Anglican Bishop New Guinea 1898. Address, Port Moresby.

STRETCH, Rt. Rev. J. F., LL.D., Bishop Coadjutor of Brisbane; educated Trinity College, Melbourne (B.A.); ordained 1878. Has been Dean of Ballarat and Vicar of Christ Church Pro-Cathedral. Address, Toowong.

WEBBER, Rt. Rev. W. T. T., D.D; third Bishop of Brisbane; since 1885, born 1837; educated Pembroke College, Oxford (M.A.). Vicar of St. John the Evangelist, Holborn, 1864-85. Took prominent interest in school board matters,

and in ameliorating the condition of the poor of London. Address, Bishopsbourne, Milton, Queensland.

WOLSELEY, Gen. Sir Garnet J. W., K.P., Privy Councillor, G.C.M.G., etc. Commander-in-Chief since 1895. Born June, 1833. Entered the army in 1852. Lieutenant-General and Governor of Cyprus 1878. Received thanks of Parliament and grant of £25,000 for his conduct of the Ashantee War. Author of several books on war tactics, etc. Address, Grosvenor Gardens, London.

WILSON, Hon. Walter Horatio, M.L.C.; born North Wales, July, 1839; educated Shropshire. Arrived in Victoria 1853, Queensland 1865. M.L.C. 1885. Postmaster-General same year. Minister without portfolio 1890-93. Postmaster and Secretary Public Instruction 1893-4. Attorney-General 1897-8, during the absence of the Hon. T. J. Byrnes from the colony. Present Postmaster-General. Address, Toowong.

WOOD, Sir Evelyn, V.C.; born Essex, February, 1838. Served in Army and Navy. In Indian Campaigns, Crimean, Ashantee, Kaffir, Zulu, and Transvaal wars. Address, Devonshire Place, London.

PENSIONS AND RETIRING ALLOWANCES,

WITH DATES WHEN FIRST PAID.

Ball, J., late Letter-carrier, Ipswich, £61; Dec. 8, 1887

Beal, J. C., late Government Printer, £347; December 18, 1898

Bennett, E. J., late Chief Draftsman, Survey Department, £345; August 1, 1889

Birrell, Henry, late Pilot, Keppel Bay, £115; July 31, 1886

Blair, Gordon, late Sub-Collector of Customs, Ipswich, £140; November 1, 1898

Bousfield, W. H., late Pilot, Moreton Bay, £98; July 1, 1885

Bree, John, late Turnkey, Rockhampton Gaol, £39; April 13, 1877

Brown, J., late Inspector of Distilleries, £113; July 1, 1890

Browne, D., late Postmaster, Bowen, £137; September 9, 1887

Burkitt, Horace, late Sub-Collector, Mackay, £205; March 2, 1896

Cardew, P., late Police Magistrate, Stanthorpe, £203; April 9, 1890

Carter, C. C., late Officer-in-charge, P.O. Branch, Lands Department, £257; Nov. 9, 1897

Chancellor, W. G., late Chief Inspector of Distilleries, £325; August 1, 1888

Clifford, J., late Attendant, Goodna Asylum, £75; March 31, 1895

Cox, Henry, late Turnkey, Brisbane Gaol, £70; October 1, 1882

Cracknell, W. J., late Superintendent of Telegraphs, £288; October 16, 1880

Curnow, Francis, late Commissioner for Railways, £507; August 1, 1889

Davidson, W. M., late Surveyor-General, £438; February 13, 1891

Day, George, late Officer in Charge of Stamps, £219; March 1, 1891

Day, D. A., late Postmaster, Bowen, £154; January 1, 1888

Day, W. H., late Police Magistrate, South Brisbane, £886; July 1, 1890

Dear, J. W., late Postmaster, Gin Gin, £175; March 20, 1897

Evans, J., late Letter-carrier, Ipswich, £70; February 1, 1886

Gallway, D., late P.M., Normanton, £269; October 1, 1893

Gill, R., late Postmaster, Ipswich, £266; November 1, 1888

Gilmore, S., late Turnkey, Brisbane Gaol, £64; August 1, 1889

Gorman, H., late Sheriff's Bailiff, Toowoomba, £82; April 4, 1889

Gordon, J., late Sub-Collector of Customs, £148; May 23, 1875

Granville, G. W., late Postmaster, Toowoomba, £246; March 10, 1896

Gregory, A. C., C.M.G., late Surveyor-General, £289; September 1, 1879

Grose, E. G., late Postmaster, Townsville, £189; September 29, 1887

Hamilton, J., late Superintendent, Dunwich, £104; January 1, 1887

Hardie, Peter, late Light-keeper, Woody Island, £114; November 1, 1897

Haseler, L. F., late Telegraph Manager, Dalrymple, £87; June 23, 1887

Haynes, C., late Assistant Pilot, Rockhampton, £177; November 1, 1895

Heath, G. P., late Portmaster and Chairman Marine Board, £473; July 11, 1890

Hill, W., late Director Botanic Gardens, £246; March 1, 1881

Hinton, F., late Clerk, General Post Office, £70; April 1, 1874

Johnstone, R. A., late P.M., Howard, £198; January 1, 1891

Lone, R., late Light-keeper, Gatcombe Head, £60; July 20, 1888

Lukin, G. L. late P.M., Maryborough, £467; March 18, 1898

Manning, A. W., late Under Colonial Sec., £600; June 30, 1869

Manton, J., late Officer-in-charge Border Customs, £118; July 1, 1888

Menihen, T. late Pilot, Dungeness, £124; February 1, 1898

O'Connell, Lady E. E., Widow late President Legislative Council, £250; March 24, 1879

Partridge, W., late Light-keeper, Pile Lighthouse, £94; July 1, 1888

Power, J., late Manager, Post and Telegraph, Beenleigh, £103; December 1, 1895

Prolinski, G., late Light-keeper, Brown's Crossing, £54; January 1, 1889

Rawlins, F., late Under Colonial Secretary, £334; January 1, 1880

Roberts, A., late Pilot, Rockhampton, £160; September 9, 1896

Roberts, T., late Coxswain, Pilot Service, £84; June, 1895

Robertson, J., late Engineer, tug "Mary," £64; June 23, 1887

Rogers, W. C., late Inspector of Distilleries, £177; July 1, 1893

Roughan, D., late Storeman, Colonial Stores, £74; March 1, 1887

Rundle, M. S., late Harbour Master, Rockhampton, £105; February 16, 1880

Sandrock, G. F., late Sub-Collector of Customs, Bowen, £158; November 4, 1895

We Recommend SQUATTER WHISKY.

PENSIONS--*Continued.*

Soarr. W., late Draftsman, Survey Office, £247; July 1, 1893

Shechy, E., late Superintendent Prison, Rockhampton, £159; November 12, 1895

Southwood, F. F., late Pilot, Cleveland Bay, £77; June 5, 1884

Thomas, J. S., late Officer-in-charge Selection Branch, Lands Department, £202; March 1, 1889

Tofft, J. P., late Coxswain, Customs, Townsville, £52; October 1, 1882

Towell, T., late Telegraph Manager, Ipswich, £283; September 1, 1896

Trimble, J. H., late Landing Waiter, Customs, £191; August 6, 1893

Walker, Susanna, late Office-keeper, Colonial Secretary's Office, £12; August 1, 1873

Watson, J., late Keeper of Quarantine Station, Hervey's Bay, £46; April 22, 1886

Westaway, E., late Chief Clerk, General Post Office, £188; July 1, 1893

Wight, G., late Officer-in-charge of Securities, £182; January 7, 1886

Wray, T., late Letter-carrier, £68; August 1, 1889

Wyborn, H., late Harbour Master, Moreton Bay, £225; November 1, 1889

POLICE PENSIONS.

Armstrong, Maxwell, 1st class inspector, £288 15s
Armstrong, William, senior-sergeant, £113 6s 8d
Atkinson, Thomas, sergeant, £115 10s

Barry, J. E., senior-sergeant, £157 10s
Bergin, Thomas, sergeant, £115 10s
Bliss, William, acting sergeant, £94 13s. 4d.
Brinkley, George, senior-constable, £71
Britton, William, 2nd class inspector, £880
Brown, Leonard, senior-sergeant, £170
Byrne, Michael, sergeant, £77
Byrne, Terence, sergeant, £102 18s 4d
Burke, Thomas, sergeant, £77

Cahill, Andrew, sergeant, £115 10s
Cahill, M., sergeant, £115 10s
Campbell, Alexander, sergeant, £102 13s 4d
Canning, John Hervey, sergeant, £102 13s 4d
Canning, Owen, constable, £66
Carey, Jeremiah, sergeant, £154
Carey, John, senior-sergeant, £170
Carney, B., senior-sergeant, £127 10s
Carr, E. H., 1st class sub-inspector, £195
Carson, William, sergeant, £102 13s 4d
Clancy, Patrick, senior-constable, £94 13s 4d
Colclough, Edward, sergeant, £115 10s
Cosgrove, Michael, constable, £66

Dawson, James, senior-constable, £94 13s 4d
Delamer, Michael, constable, £66
Devine, George, senior-sergeant, £113 6s 8d
Downie, James, senior-constable, £106 10s
Downie, William, senior-constable, £94 13s 4d
Dunne, Patrick, sergeant, £115 10s
Dunne, Patrick, sergeant, £77

Ferry, Manes, sergeant, £154

Graham, Daniel, constable, £88
Graham, David, senior-constable, £94 13s 4d
Graham, Edward, water police constable, £53

Hagarty, Andrew, senior-constable, £94 13s 4d
Halligan, Patrick, constable, £132
Halloran, T., senior-sergeant, £113 6s 8d
Hardy, John, senior-constable, £94 13s 4d
Harris, Henry, sergeant, £102 18s 4d
Healy, John, senior-constable, £106 10s
Higgins, P., 2nd class sub-inspector, £200
Hutchinson, Thomas, constable, £99
Isley, J. B., 2nd class inspector, £880

Johnson, Edward, senior-constable, £71
Johnson, Ralph, water police cons., £70 13s 4d
Joyce, Edward, sergeant, £102 18s 4d

Keane, Patrick, senior-sergeant, £113 6s 8d
Kelly, John, sergeant, £154
Kenny, Peter, constable, £99
Kilfeder, Robert, 2nd class sub-inspector, £90
Kilkeary, Thomas, constable, £66
Kinsella, Thomas, sergeant, £154

Lewis, John, 1st class inspector, £485
Linehan, Michael, constable, £66
Lloyd, S. J., 1st class inspector, £450
Lonergan, Matthew, senior-sergeant, £170
Lonergan, Thomas, constable, £71
Long, Alexander, constable, £66
Love, Paul, senior-sergeant, £170
Luttrell, Patrick, sergeant, £77

Mannion, John, constable, £? 4s. 1d.
Manton, Thomas, constable, £88
Mathers, William, 1st class sub-inspector, £260
Matthews, Peter, constable, £88

McCaffrey, Michael, constable, £99
*McCarthy, M., sergeant, £102 13s 4d
McCluskey, P., sergeant, £102 13s 4d
McCormack, James, constable, £66
McCosker, H., sergeant, £102 13s 4d
McDonagh, Peter, senior-constable, £94 13s 4d
McDonald, J., senior-constable, £50
McDermott, M. C., senior-constable, £71
McGrath, Patrick, constable, £71
McKiernan, Michael, 2nd class sub-inspector, £94
McManus, Bernard, constable, £71

Minogue, Thomas, constable, £66
Moore, John, 2nd class sub-inspector, £90
Morisset, A. L., 1st class inspector, £345
Murphy, Richard, constable, £99
Murray, F. J., 2nd class inspector, £880

Nutting, John Bligh, 1st class inspector, £102 10s.

O'Flaherty, M., constable, £66
O'Shea, William, constable, £60

Poingdestre, Lyndon J. A., first-class sub-inspector, £175

Power, F., constable, £88

* Pension suspended during the receipt of a salary as Inspector of Brands.

POLICE PENSIONS—Continued.

Quinlan, Martin, sergeant, £77
Quinn, E., 1st class sub-inspector, £123 10s
Roe, John M., sergeant, £151
Soullen, P., sergeant, £102 13s 4d
Sealy, Francis, constable, £71
Seymour, D. T., commissioner, £700
Sheridan, Michael, constable, £88
Size, John, constable, £66
Slattery, Robert, sergeant, £115 10s.

Splaine, John, constable, £99
Stephenson, J., 1st class sub-inspector, £120
Swords, Richard, constable, £132
Tompson, F. M., 2nd class inspector, £220
Walker, John, sergeant, £77
Walsh, John, senior-sergeant, £113 6s 6d
Walsh, P., constable, £132
Ware, Richard R., senior-sergeant, £127 10s
Woodcraft, R. F., sergeant, £102 18s 4d

CONSULS AND CONSULAR AGENTS.

RESIDING IN QUEENSLAND.

CONSULS.

Netherlands—The Hon. Johann Christian Heussler, M.L.C., Eagle Street, Brisbane
German Empire—The Hon. Johann Christian Heussler, M.L.C., Eagle Street, Brisbane
    "   "   Vice-Consul at Cooktown, Dr. A. H. F. B. Kortüm, Cooktown
Belgium—J. M. Mauson, Merchant, Eagle Street, Brisbane
Sweden and Norway—A. J. Carter, Eagle Street, Brisbane
Denmark—Poul Christensen Poulsen, Photographer, Queen Street, Brisbane
Switzerland—Jacob Leutenegger, Merchant, Elizabeth Street, Brisbane
Hawaii—Alexander Brand Webster, Webster & Co., Mary Street, Brisbane
Japan—Tsunejiro Nakagau, Townsville

CONSULAR AGENTS.

Portugal—The Hon. Frederic Hamilton Hart, M.L.C., Alice Street, Brisbane
France—The Hon. Edward Barrow Forrest, M.L.C., Parbury, Lamb & Co., Eagle Street, Brisbane
Italy—Barron L. Barnett, Eagle Street, Brisbane
United States of America—Brisbane : W. J. Weatherill, Queen Street, Brisbane
    "   "   "   John Henry Rogers, Townsville

CONSULS-GENERAL RESIDING IN AUSTRALIA AND HAVING JURIS-
DICTION IN QUEENSLAND.

SYDNEY.

Austro-Hungarian Empire—Julius Mergell
Chili—William H any Eldred
German Empire—A. L. R. Pelldram

Hawaii—W. E. Dixon
Portugal—Ernest Octavius Smith
France—Georges Biard d'Aunet

MELBOURNE.

Columbia—Thomas B. Fallon
Italy—C. B. Brenchi
Japan—A. Marks
Netherlands—J. A. De Vicq

Nicaragua—J. H. Amora
Liberia—Robert T. Litton
Russia—Baron D Ungern Sternberg
Belgium—T. Vollet

105

QUEENSLAND POSTAL INFORMATION.

LETTER POST.

Town.	Inland and Intercolonial.	Foreign.
Not exceeding—	Not exceeding—	Not exceeding—
½oz. .. .. 1d.	½oz. .. .. 2d.	½oz. .. .. 2½d.
1oz. .. .. 2d.	1oz. .. .. 4d.	1oz. .. .. 5d.
1½oz. .. .. 3d.	1½oz. .. .. 6d.	1½oz. .. .. 7½d.
2oz. .. .. 4d.	2oz. .. .. 8d.	2oz. .. .. 10d.
And so on at the rate of 1d. for every additional ½oz.	And so on at the rate of 2d. for every additional ½oz.	And so on at the rate of 2½d. for every additional ½oz.

PARCEL POST.

Inland.		Intercolonial.		United Kingdom.	
	s. d.		s. d.		s. d.
Not exceeding—		Not exceeding—		Not exceeding—	
1lb. ..	0 6	1lb. ..	0 8	2lb. ..	1 6
2lb. ..	0 9	2lb. ..	1 2	3lb. ..	2 3
3lb. ..	1 0	3lb. ..	1 8	4lb. ..	3 0
4lb. ..	1 3	4lb. ..	2 2	5lb. ..	3 9
And so on at the rate of 3d. per lb. up to 11lb.		And so on at the rate of 6d. per lb. up to 11lb.		And so on at the rate of 9d. per lb. up to 11lb.	

Size of Parcel not to exceed 3ft. 6in. in length and 6ft. in girth and length combined.

NEWSPAPERS.

Published in Queensland.		Published out of Queensland.	
Inland and British New Guinea.	United Kingdom or Foreign.	Inland.	United Kingdom or Foreign.
Each newspaper one halfpenny for every 10oz. or fraction thereof.	Each newspaper not exceeding 4oz. one penny; for every additional 2oz. or fraction thereof one half-penny.	Each newspaper 1d. for every 10oz. or fraction thereof.	Each newspaper not exceeding 4oz. one penny; for every additional 2oz. or fraction thereof one-halfpenny.

Intercolonial.—Each newspaper one half-penny for every 2oz. or fraction thereof.

PACKET POST.

Books.		Printed Papers and Samples.	Commercial Papers.	
Inland and Intercolonial.	Foreign.	All Places.	Inland and Intercolonial.	Foreign.
Not exceeding—	Not exceeding—	Not exceeding—	Not exceeding—	Not exceeding—
4oz. .. 1d.	2oz. .. 1d.	2oz. .. 1d.	2oz. .. 1d.	2oz. .. 3d.
8oz. .. 2d.	4oz. .. 2d.	4oz. .. 2d.	4oz. .. 2d.	4oz. .. 3½d.
12oz. .. 3d.	6oz. .. 3d.	6oz. .. 3d.	6oz. .. 3d.	And so on up to 10oz.; beyond that 1d. for every 2oz. up to a pound
			8oz. .. 4d.	
And so on.	And so on.	And so on.	And so on.	

We Recommend SQUATTER WHISKY.

MONEY ORDERS.

THE RATES OF COMMISSION TO BE CHARGED AS FOLLOWS:—

For Orders Payable in—	Not exceeding £2.	Above £2 and not exceeding £5.	Above £5 and not exceeding £7.	Above £7 and not exceeding £10.
	s. d.	s. d.	s. d.	s. d.
Queensland	0 6	0 6	1 0	1 0
New South Wales, Victoria, South Australia, Western Australia, Tasmania, New Zealand and Fiji	0 6	1 0	1 6	2 2
All other places	6d. for	every £1	or fraction thereof	

For colonies and countries on which single orders may be issued up to £20 the same proportion as above is to be charged for sums exceeding £10.

Money may be remitted by Telegraph to any Money Order Office, which is also a Telegraph Office, in Queensland, New South Wales, Victoria, South Australia, Tasmania, and Western Australia, on payment of the charge for a telegraph message of ten words in addition to the Money Order Commission. The remitter should advise the payee by a telegram paid for in the ordinary manner.

POSTAL NOTES.

Postal Notes are issued and cashed at all Money Order Offices and at other Money Order Offices in New South Wales, Victoria, South Australia and Tasmania. The following are the values of Postal Notes issued and their cost:—

Postal Note.	Poundage.	Postal Note.	Poundage.
s. d.	d.	s. d.	d.
1 0	½	4 0	1
1 6	½	5 0	2
2 0	1	7 6	3
2 6	1	10 0	3
3 0	1	10 6	3
3 6	1	15 0	3
4 0	1	20 0	3

SCALE OF CHARGES FOR TELEGRAMS.

Queensland.

	Ten words.	Each additional word.
	s. d.	s. d.
Between all Stations in Queensland, exclusive of address and signature	1 0	0 1
With the following exceptions:—		
Between Brisbane, Albion, Bulimba, Brunswick-street Railway Station (Brisbane), Fortitude Valley, Roma-street Railway Station (Brisbane), Petrie-terrace, Red Hill, Toowong, Melbourne-street, Woolloongabba, and all stations within a radius of six miles from the General Post Office (exclusive of address and signature)	0 6	0 1
Between any station in Queensland and N.S.W. border stations—viz., Barringun, Hoggabilla, Chinderah, Cudgen, Goodooga, Hungerford, Jennings, Mingoola, Mungindi, Murwillumbah, New Angledool, Parragundy (Telephone), Tumbulgum, Tweed Heads, and Yetman, exclusive of address and signature	1 0	0 1

Telegrams marked "Urgent" double rates. Sunday telegrams inland and intercolonial:—

(a) "Urgent" and ordinary messages, one hundred (100) per cent. more than the usual daily rate. (b) Press and cable messages, at the ordinary rate.

No telegrams will be transmitted after 10 p.m. on Sundays.

From any station in Queensland to any station in:—

	s. d.	s. d.
New South Wales, exclusive of address and signature	3 0	0 2
Victoria " "	3 0	0 3
South Australia (excepting line to Port Darwin) "	3 0	0 3
Tasmania (only ten words allowed free for address and signature)	4 0	0 4
New Zealand (address and signature included in the counting)	4 6	0 6
Western Australia (exclusive of address and signature)	4 0	0 4
New Caledonia (address and signature included in the counting)	9d. per word	

We Recommend SQUATTER WHISKY.

109

DISTANCES OF OCEAN TRAVEL.

MELBOURNE																
564	SYDNEY															
634	70	NEWCASTLE														
1,074	510	440	BRISBANE													
1,424	838	768	328	ROCKHAMPTON												
1,614	1,031	961	521	193	MACKAY											
1,719	1,149	1,079	639	311	118	BOWEN										
1,822	1,252	1,182	742	414	221	103	TOWNSVILLE									
2,082	1,510	1,440	1,000	672	479	361	258	COOKTOWN								
2,522	1,940	1,870	1,430	1,102	909	791	688	430	THURSDAY ISLAND							
4,759	4,195	4,125	3,685	3,357	3,164	3,046	2,943	2,685	2,255	BATAVIA						
8,609	8,045	7,975	7,535	7,307	7,114	6,996	6,893	6,635	6,205	3,950	ADEN					
10,016	9,452	9,382	8,942	8,614	8,421	8,303	8,200	7,942	7,512	5,257	1,307	SUEZ				
10,104	9,540	9,470	9,030	8,702	8,509	8,391	8,288	8,030	7,600	5,345	1,395	88	PORT SAID			
11,219	10,655	10,585	10,145	9,817	9,624	9,506	9,403	9,145	8,715	6,460	2,510	1,203	1,115	NAPLES		
13,229	12,665	12,595	12,155	11,827	11,634	11,516	11,413	11,155	10,725	8,470	4,520	3,125	3,125	2,010	PLYMOUTH	
13,539	12,975	12,905	12,465	12,137	11,944	11,826	11,723	11,465	11,035	8,780	4,830	3,435	3,435	2,320	310	LONDON

Brisbane to San Francisco *via* Sydney 6,900 ; Yokohama 5,800 ; Hong Kong 5,350 ; Vancouver *via* Sydney 7,800 ; New York *via* Sydney 13,470.

RAILWAY INFORMATION.

Time Tables containing the whole of the Regulations affecting Passengers, Fares, Time Tables, etc., throughout the Queensland railway lines, with a plan of the Brisbane and suburban railway lines and a railway map of Queensland, are obtainable at all railway stations; price, one penny. A useful publication for those forwarding large quantities of goods is the "Classification of Goods"; price, threepence.

RAILWAY ITEMS WHICH MAY BE USEFUL.

Children under 3 years travel free.

Between 3 and 12 years of age, half-fare.

Return tickets are of use as follows: —10 miles and under on day of issue only; 11 to 50 miles, two weeks; to 150 miles, one calendar month; 150 miles to 300 miles, three calendar months; over 300 miles, six calendar months.

Passengers holding return tickets may break their journey at any station, but the forward journey must be completed within the period for which single tickets are available.

Holders of single tickets may break their journey under certain conditions.

Special reductions in passenger rates may be granted to the following classes when travelling:—

Teachers of recognised day schools during vacation, single fare for the double journey, 10 miles and over.

Students during vacation, under 16 years of age, half single fare for the double journey; over 16 years, single fare for the double journey.

Press representatives of newspapers published in Queensland or the southern colonies, half the ordinary fare, and season tickets at one-fourth of the full fare, on Queensland lines.

Athletic Clubs travelling in parties of twelve or more, under 100 miles, single fare for the double journey; over 100 miles, half return rates.

School Excursions, numbering not less than 50 adults, single fare for the double journey; scholars, half single fare, irrespective of age.

Scholars' Season Tickets, half full season rates.

Children under 16 residing where there is no public school within 2 miles are granted free tickets by rail to the nearest public school.

Family Season Tickets, two tickets, a reduction of 10 per cent.; three tickets, 15 per cent.; four or more, 20 per cent.

Half rates will be charged to wives of season ticket holders.

Fortnightly Season Tickets may be issued to Sandgate, Wynnum, Manly, Birkdale, Wellington Point, Ormiston, Cleveland, Southport, Pialba, Emu Park, and Broadmount, at half rates for monthly tickets, with 10 per cent. added.

Commercial Travellers' and Insurance Agents' Yearly Season Tickets, a scheduled scale of reductions.

Registered Ministers of Religion, season tickets for 3 months and over, 45 miles and under, one-fourth of the full season ticket rate. Minimum distance charged, 10 miles. Over 45 miles, specially low rates.

Employees under 20 years of age of both sexes, earning less than £65 per annum, two-thirds of full season ticket rates.

Delegates, twelve or more, travelling to attend meetings of religious or other bodies, single fare for the double journey. Minimum distance, 20 miles.

Special Trains, 5s. per mile (minimum charge, £5), in addition to full fares from passengers and full rates for goods, etc., with a concession upon the return journey if the special returns within 12 hours of its arrival at its destination of one-half fares and rate and one-half mileage rate.

Special concessions are made to large traders according to the amount of freight paid to the Commissioner for Railways.

Saloon Reserved Compartments are granted upon payment of ten first-class fares; small compartments, four first-class fares.

Technical College Students' and Teachers' Return Tickets, half rates.

Pleasure Parties must apply three days before the excursion. Minimum, six first-class or ten second-class passengers; return tickets, single fare and a quarter; minimum distance, 10 miles each way. Parties of not less than twenty first-class or thirty second-class passengers travelling not less than 24 miles going and returning, single fare for the double journey.

CLOAK - ROOM CHARGES. — The following charges are payable for parcels and luggage deposited in cloak-rooms:—

Weight of Articles.	Deposited for Periods.			
	Under 24 hours.	Over 24 and under 48 hours.	Over 48 hours and under 7 days.	For every week or part of a week over 7 days.
	s. d.	s. d.	s. d.	s. d.
Under 28lbs	0 2	0 3	0 4	0 2
28lbs and under 56lbs	0 2	0 4	0 6	0 8
56lbs and under 112lbs	0 3	0 5	0 7	0 8
112lbs and under 224lbs	0 4	0 6	0 8	0 4

Theatrical Companies of not less than six travel first-class, between Brisbane and Melbourne, or wholly upon Queensland rail-

ways, on payment of second-class fares, or a discount of 25 per cent. off full fares if they travel second class.

Passengers' Luggage, first-class, 168lbs, free; second-class, 112lbs.

Special rates are scheduled for tricycles, perambulators, and other bulky goods.

Special discounts are scheduled for newspaper parcels, game, fish, meat, vegetables, fruit, ice, and bread; also books from circulating libraries, and cut flowers for shows.

PARCELS RATES, BRISBANE, SYDNEY AND MELBOURNE.—The rates for parcels between Brisbane, Sydney and Melbourne (which shall be carried subject to the conditions prescribed for the carriage of Parcels within the Colony), shall be as follows:—3 lbs. and under, Sydney, 2s.; Melbourne, 4s. 7d. 7 lbs., Sydney, 3s.; Melbourne, 6s. 10d. 14 lbs., Sydney, 4s.; Melbourne, 10s. 2d. 28 lbs., Sydney, 6s.; Melbourne, 13s. 7d. 56 lbs., Sydney, 10s.; Melbourne, 22s. 8d. 84 lbs., Sydney, 13s. 6d.; Melbourne, 27s. 2d. 112 lbs., Sydney, 17s.; Melbourne, 32s. 10d. For each additional 28 lbs. or part thereof, Sydney, 3s. 6d.; Melbourne, 5s. 8d.

WITHIN THE COLONY.

Distance	50 miles and under	51 to 101 miles	102 to 150 miles	151 to 200 miles	201 to 300 miles	301 to 400 miles	401 to 500 miles	501 to 600 miles	601 to 700 miles
Parcels over 112lbs. in weight to be charged for each extra lb. as under.									
Parcels 85 to 112lbs.									
Parcels 57 to 84lbs.									
Parcels 29 to 56lbs.									
Parcels 15 to 28lbs.									
Parcels 8 to 14lbs.									
Parcels 4 to 7lbs.									
Parcels 3lbs. and under									

Fish in cases conveyed from stations on the Southport and Cleveland lines by passenger trains to South Brisbane will be charged as follows:—Up to 15 miles, 4d. per case; 16 to 25 miles, 6d.; 26 to 50 miles, 8d. Milk in bottles (packed in cases) will be charged one-fourth the ordinary parcels rate, and the same for the returned empties. Minimum charge, 6d. for full bottles; and 3d. for the returned empties.

HORSES.—4d. per mile up to 200 miles, 3d. per mile in addition beyond 200 miles; two horses belonging to same owner in one box, 3d. per mile each up to 200 miles, 2d. per mile in addition after. Entires charged as two horses but the owner may send another horse free in the same box at his own risk. Mare and foal at foot will be charged 21 per cent. more than the rate for one horse.

VEHICLES.—5d. per mile for the first 100 miles: to 200 miles 4d. per mile added; to 300 miles 3d. per mile added to the 200 mile rate.

Dogs' rates are specially scheduled, commencing at 3d. for the first 10 miles to 6s. for 800 miles.

GOLD AND SILVER, DUST, COINS, OR BULLION.—Per £100 value up to 50 miles, 6d.; to 100 miles, 1s.; 200 miles, 1s. 6d.; 300 miles, 2s.; 400 miles, 2s. 6d.; 500 miles, 3s. If in charge of a bank official, coin, etc., to the value of £5,000 carried free. If the value exceed £10,000, a compartment will be reserved without extra charge.

MILK RATES.—The rates for the carriage of milk are as follows:—25 miles and under, ½d. per gallon; 26 miles to 50 miles, ¾d. per gallon; 51 miles to 100 miles, 1d. per gallon. Minimum charge, 3d. Empty milk-cans returned free.

RATES FOR CREAM.—The rates for cream will be as under:—25 miles and under, 1d. per gallon; 26 to 50 miles, 1¼d. per gallon; 51 to 100 miles, 1½d. per gallon; 101 to 200 miles, 2d. per gallon; over 200 miles, 2½d. per gallon. Minimum charge, 3d. Empty cream-cans returned free.

CORPSES.—The rate for each corpse is 6d. per mile. Minimum charge, 20s. Corpses will not be received for conveyance unless a medical certificate be produced, setting forth that death was not caused by any infectious or contagious disease.

GOOD AND LIVE STOCK RATES.

The rates for the carriage of all goods, except flour, and timber in logs, shall be calculated upon the actual gross weight thereof, and upon the basis of 2,240 lbs. to the ton.

The rates for the carriage of flour shall be upon the basis of 2,000 lbs. to the ton. The rates for the carriage of timber in logs shall be according to measured weight, as follows:—Pine, cedar, silky oak, ballygum, sassafras and cudgeree, 50 cubic feet = 1 ton; all other timber, 30 cubic feet = 1 ton.

The rates for the carriage of sawn or split timber shall be according to machine or measured weight, at the option of the Commissioner.

Carriage on perishable goods shall (if required) be prepaid.

Dangerous Goods, except lucifer matches and small arm cartridges, 50 miles, 3s. 6d.; 100 miles, 5s. 6d.; 200 miles, 8s.; 300 miles, 10s.; 400 miles, 12s. 6d.; 500 miles, 15s.; over 500 miles, 17s. 6d.

Returned empty bags and bales, in bales or bundles shall be charged 6d. per cwt., or part of a cwt., or at B Class rates (minimum 8d.) if cheaper. Empty fruit cases charged B class rates (minimum 8d.), or 1d. each if cheaper. Empty milk and cream cans will be returned free.

TIMBER RATES.—The minimum charge for the carriage of timber shall be as for the following weights mentioned in connection with each class of truck respectively:—

Description of Truck.	Timber Squared, or in Log.					
	Pine, cedar, silky oak, maple, red cedar, beech, hoop, white, silk wood.	All other timber.				
Timber in trucks of 25½ feet and over	5 tons	4 tons	5 tons	7 tons	4 tons	8 tons	2 tons
Timber in trucks under 25½ feet, except 4-wheeled trucks	4 tons	2½ tons		6 tons		
Timber in 4-wheeled timber trucks	2½ tons			4 tons		

If timber can be loaded in a 4-wheeled goods wagon (F or T class), the minimum charge will be as for the one ton, or at actual weight if cheaper. Guard trucks required for the carriage of long timber will be charged as follows:—25½ feet and over, as for 4 tons; under 25½ feet (except 4-wheelers), as for 8 tons; 4-wheeler, as for 1 ton.

All live stock must be loaded and unloaded by the senders and consignees respectively, but in the event of consignees delaying to unload the trucks on arrival at the delivery station, the Commissioner may proceed to do so, and in that case will be entitled to make a charge at the rate of 2s. 6d. per truck in addition to the carriage, but will not be liable for any loss in respect of stock so unloaded.

A return second-class free pass will be issued to the drover or drovers of live stock being conveyed by train on the basis of one pass to each 50 head of cattle or horses, or 500 sheep, on condition that the drovers accompany and attend to the live stock during their conveyance. Such pass shall include a dog for each drover.

Store sheep and cattle which are required to travel for grass or water, may be conveyed when convenient, by special arrangement with the General Traffic Manager, at a reduction of 33⅓ per cent. less than the ordinary rates; provided always that the trucks used in their conveyance are not required for the carriage of live stock at ordinary rates.

Exhibits sent to Agricultural Shows or Exhibitions will be charged at the full rates. Exhibits belonging to different owners but forwarded in the same truck and from the same station will be charged the same as if they belonged to the same owner. All exhibits shall be loaded and unloaded at the risk and expense of the owner.

Exhibits, if unsold and returned within one week after the closing of the show, will be carried back free of charge to the station from which they were conveyed, on production of a certificate in the form of Schedule XV. hereto. Live stock exhibits returned under these conditions will, in addition, be allowed a rebate of one-half the freight paid on the forward journey.

Exhibits unaccompanied by such a certificate will be charged for at the full rates.

A free pass will be issued to an attendant in charge of stock, provided that not less than one full truck, van, or horse-box is sent, and that the necessary certificates of entry are produced. If the stock be not sold, and a certificate is produced to that effect, a free pass will be issued on the return journey.

QUEENSLAND CUSTOMS TARIFF.

Under "The Customs Duties Act of 1888," "The Customs Duties Act of 1890," "The Customs Duties Act of 1892," and "The Customs Duties Act of 1894," and "The Customs Duties Act of 1896." (Revised to September 14, 1897, by Mr. W. H. Irving, Collector of Customs).

	£ s. d.
Acid, acetic, containing not more than 33 per cent. of acidity, per lb	0 8
For every extra 10 per cent. or part thereof of acidity, per lb	0 1
Acid, sulphuric, per cwt	5 0
Ale, Beer, Porter, Cider, and Perry, per gallon	1 3
Ale, Beer, Porter, Cider, and Perry, for six reputed quart bottles	1 6
For twelve reputed pint bottles	1 6
Arrowroot, per reputed lb	0 1
Axle and Lubricating Grease, per cwt	6 0
Bacon, per lb	0 3
Barley, per bushel	0 9
Barley (malting), per bushel	1 6
Beans and Peas, per bushel	1 0
Biscuits, per lb	0 2
Bitters, if containing not more than 25 per cent. of proof spirit, per gallon	6 0
Bitters, if containing more than 25 per cent. of proof spirit, per gallon	14 0
Blue, per lb	0 2
Boots and Shoes, except indiarubber shoes (present English sizes to be the standard)—	
Men's, No. 6 and upwards, per doz. pairs	33 0
Youths', Nos. 2 to 5, per doz. pairs	21 0
Boys', Nos. 7 to 1, per doz. pairs	17 6
Women's No. 3 and upwards, per doz. pairs	19 6
Girls', Nos. 11 to 2, per doz. pairs	16 0
Girls', Nos. 7 to 10, per doz. pairs	11 6
Boot Uppers, Men's, per doz. pairs	18 0
Bran and Pollard, per bushel	0 4
Brandy (foreign), per proof gallon	14 6
Butter, per lb	0 3
Butterine, & other similar products, per lb	0 3
Cakes, per lb	0 2
Candles, per reputed lb	0 2
Carriages—	
Tilburys, Dog-carts, Gigs, Boston Chaises, and other wheeled vehicles, with or without springs or thorough braces, each	£10 0 0
Express Waggons and Waggons for carrying goods, or Single or Double-seated Waggons and Four-wheeled Buggies, without tops, mounted on springs and braces, and Hansom Cabs, each	£12 0 0
Single and Double-seated Waggons, Waggonettes, and Four-wheeled Buggies, with tops, each	£15 0 0
Omnibuses and Coaches, for carrying mails or passengers, each	£20 0 0
Barouches, Broughams, Mail Phaetons, Drags, Landaus, and similar vehicles, each	£30 0 0
Cement, per barrel	2 0
Chaff, per ton	15 0
Cheese, per lb	0 3

	£ s. d.
Chicory, per lb	0 6
Chicory Root (kiln dried), per lb	0 3
Chocolate Confectionery, per lb	0 4
Cigarettes (including wrappers), per lb	6 0
Cigars, per lb	6 0
Coal, per ton	2 0
Cocoa and Chocolate, per lb	0 4
Coffee (raw), per lb	0 4
Coffee (roasted), per lb	0 6
Condensed Milk, per reputed lb	0 2
Confectionery and Succades, per lb	0 4
Cordage and Rope, per cwt.	8 0
Cordials, per gallon	14 0
Corn Flour, per reputed lb	0 2
Doors (wood), each	4 0
Farinaceous Food, prepared, not being wheaten flour, or otherwise specified, per lb	0 2
Fish (pickled or salted, in casks), per lb	0 1
Fish (dried), per lb	0 1
Fish (preserved, not salted), per doz. reputed lbs	2 0
And in same proportion for larger or smaller contents	
Flour, per ton of 2,000 lbs	20 0 0
Fruit, Pulp, and Fruit preserved by acids, per cwt.	5 0
Fruits (bottled, or in tins or jars), per doz. reputed pints	1 6
And in same proportion for larger or smaller contents.	
Fruits (dried), per lb	0 3
Geneva, per proof gallon	14 0
Ginger (preserved and dried), per lb.	0 4
Glucose, per cwt	10 0
Glue, per lb	0 2
Grease, lubricating, per cwt.	6 0
Groats, patent, per lb.	0 2
Hams, per lb	0 3
Harmoniums, each	£3 0 0
Hay, per ton	15 0
Honey, per lb	0 3
Hook and Eye Hinges, per cwt.	6 0
Hops, per lb	0 6
Iron Castings for building purposes, and malleable Iron Castings, per cwt	3 0
Iron (corrugated), per cwt	2 0
Iron (galvanised), per cwt	2 0
Jams and Jellies, per doz. reputed lbs	2 0
And in same proportion for larger or smaller contents.	
Lard, per lb	0 1½
Lead (piping and sheet), per cwt	2 0
Lead (white and red), per cwt	3 0
Leather (except otherwise enumerated), per lb	0 4
Macaroni, per reputed lb	0 2

113

Crown Jams—The Best. VERNEYS, Makers.

QUEENSLAND MODEL DAIRY deliver Butter daily throughout City and Suburbs.

Article	£ s. d.
Maize, per bushel	0 8
Maizemeal, per reputed lb	0 2
Maizena, per reputed lb.	0 2
Malt, per bushel	4 6
Methylated Spirits (foreign), per liquid gallon	5 0
Milk, condensed, per reputed lb.	0 2
Molasses and Syrups—In packages containing 1 gallon or under, per cwt	10 0
In any other packages, per cwt	7 6
Mustard, per lb.	0 3
Nails, per cwt	3 0
Nuts (all sorts except cocoanuts), per lb	0 3
Oatmeal, per cwt	4 0
Oats, per bushel	0 8
Oils—	
Castor, packed in bottles, jars, and other vessels (not exceeding one gallon in size) as under:—	
Quarter-pints and smaller sizes, per doz.	0 6
Half-pints and over quarter-pints, per doz.	1 0
Pints and over half-a-pint, per doz.	2 0
Quarts and over a pint, per doz.	4 0
Over a quart and not exceeding a gallon, per doz.	12 0
Chinese (in bulk), per gallon	1 0
Cod Liver Oil (in bottle), per doz. reputed pints	2 0
And in same proportion for larger or smaller contents.	
Cod Liver Oil (in bulk), per gallon	1 0
Colza Oil (in bulk), per gallon	1 0
Linseed and other vegetable oils (in bulk) per gallon	1 0
Mineral, and all other oils not otherwise enumerated (except perfumed oils) and Turpentine, per gallon	0 6
Neatsfoot Oil (in bulk), per gallon	1 0
Salad Oil packed in bottles, jars, and other vessels (not exceeding one gallon in size), as under—	
Quarter-pints and smaller sizes, per doz.	0 6
Half-pints and over quarter-pints, per doz.	1 0
Pints and over half-a-pint, per doz.	2 0
Quarts and over a pint, per doz.	4 0
Over a quart and not exceeding a gallon, per doz.	12 0
Old Tom, per proof gallon	14 0
Onions, per ton	20 0
Opium, per lb	20 0
Organs (cabinet), each	60 0
Paints (wet and dry), per cwt	3 0
Paper Bags (not printed), per cwt	8 0
Paper Bags (printed), per cwt	12 6
Patent Groats, per lb	0 2
Pearl Barley, per lb	0 1
Peel (dry and drained), per lb	0 2
Pepper, per lb	0 8
Pianos (upright), each	£6 0 0
Pianos (horizontal, square, grand, or semi-grand), each	£12 0 0
Pickles, packed in bottles, jars, and other vessels (not exceeding one gallon in size) as under:—	
Quarter-pints and smaller sizes, per doz.	0 6
Half-pints and over quarter-pints „	1 0
Pints and over half-a-pint „	2 0
Quarts and over a pint „	4 0

Article	£ s. d.
Over a quart and not exceeding a gallon, per doz.	12 0
Pork (mess), per lb	0 1
Pork (not including mess pork), per lb	0 2
Potatoes, per ton	15 0
Preserved Meat (not salted), and Extract of Meat, per doz. reputed lbs	4 0
And in same proportion for larger or smaller contents.	
Rice, per lb	0 1
Rope, per cwt.	8 0
Rum, excise duty per proof gallon	12 0
Rum (foreign), per proof gallon	14 0
Sago, per lb	0 1
Salt Beef, per lb	0 1
Sarsaparilla (if containing not more than 25 per cent. of proof spirit), per gallon	6 0
Sarsaparilla (if containing more than 25 per cent. of proof spirit), per gallon	14 0
Sashes, per pair	4 0
Sauces, packed in bottles, jars, and other vessels (not exceeding one gallon in size), as under—	
Quarter-pints and smaller sizes, per doz.	0 6
Half-pints and over quarter-pints, per doz.	1 0
Pints and over half-a-pint, per doz.	2 0
Quarts and over a pint, per doz.	4 0
Over a quart and not exceeding a gallon, per doz.	12 0
Snuff, per lb	5 0
Soap, per cwt	10 0
Soap and Washing Powders, per lb	0 2
Soap (perfumed, fancy, and toilet), per lb	0 3
Soda, bicarbonate, per cwt	1 0
Soda Crystals, per cwt	2 0
Spices, per lb	0 3
Split Peas, per lb	0 1
Spirits (perfumed), per liquid gallon	20 0
Spirits (all other), per gallon	14 0
Starch, per lb	0 2
Starch, in cardboard and other boxes, containing as under—	
Under half-a-pound, per doz.	1 0
One pound and over half-a-pound, per doz.	2 0
Two pounds and over one pound, per doz.	4 0
Four pounds and over two pounds, per doz.	8 0
Stearine, per lb	0 1½
Sugar (raw), per cwt	5 0
Sugar (refined), per cwt	6 8
Tapioca, per lb	0 1
Tallow, per lb	0 1½
Tanks (iron), each	8 0
Tea, in paper, cardboard, or other packets, made up for sale by retail—	
Half-pound and under, per packet	0 4
Over half-pound, per lb	0 8
Tea, per lb	0 6
Timber, Logs, per 100 superficial feet	1 6
Timber, undressed, of a scantling 96 square inches and over, per 100 superficial feet	1 6
Timber, dressed and sawn, of a scantling under 96 square inches, per 100 superficial feet	3 0

(The duty on timber to be estimated as of a thickness of one inch, and to be in proportion for any greater thickness. Any thickness under one inch to be reckoned as one inch).

We Recommend SQUATTER WHISKY.

	£ s. d
Tobacco (manufactured), per lb ..	1 0
Tobacco (unmanufactured), entered to be manufactured in the colony. At the time of removal from a Customs bond, or from an importing ship to any licensed manufactory for manufacturing purposes only into tobacco, cigars, and cigarettes, per lb ..	2 0
Turpentine, per gallon ..	0 6
Twine, per lb ..	0 1½
Vermicelli, per reputed lb ..	0 2
Vinegar (in bottle)—	
For six reputed quarts..	1 0
For twelve reputed pints ..	1 0
Vinegar (in wood), per gallon ..	0 0
Wheat, per bushel ..	0 4
Whiting, per ton ..	7 6
Whisky, per proof gallon ..	14 0
Wine (sparkling), per gallon ..	16 0
Wine (other kinds), per gallon ..	6 0
Writing Paper (cut), per lb ..	0 2

	£ s. d
Case Spirits— Reputed contents of two, three, or four gallons shall be charged on and after the first day of March, 1889, as follows :—Two gallons and under, as two gallons; and not exceeding three, as three gallons; over three, and not exceeding four, as four gallons.	

EXCISE DUTY.

	£ s. d
Beer, per gallon..	0 3
Spirits, per proof gallon ..	12 0
Methylated Spirits, per liquid gallon ..	2 0
Tobacco, per lb ..	1 0
Cigars, per lb ...	2 0
Cigarettes, per lb ..	2 0
Snuffs, per lb..	1 0

EXPORT DUTY.

	£ s. d
Log Cedar, per 100 superficial feet ..	2 0
Sawn Cedar, over 4 inches in thickness, per 100 superficial feet ..	2 0

ARTICLES EXEMPTED FROM DUTY.

FROM 31st MARCH, 1897.

Agricultural Implements and Machines, namely:—Acme Harrows, Cane Shavers, Chaff-cutting Machines, Cheese Pressers, Circular Coulters, Clod Crushers, Corn Crushers, Cultivators, Dairy Refrigerators, Disc Harrows, Drill-wheel Hoe Cultivator, Earth Scoops, Fertilizer and Drill combined, Field and Garden Rollers; Furrower, Marker, Hiller, and Ridger combined; Gang Ploughs, Grain Cleaners and Dressing Machines, Grain Mills, Grain Separators, Grain Sowers, Hay Presses, Hedge Cutting and Trimming, Horse Hoe and Cultivator combined, Horse Hoes, Horse Rakes, Huskers and Shellers, Mowing Machines, Potato Raisors, Rake and Plough combined, Reapers, Root Cutters, Scarifiers, Screening, Seed Drills, Sifting, Smutters, Spading Harrows, Strawsonisors, Straw Stackers, Stubble Diggers, Stump-Extractors, Stump-Jumping Ploughs, Sulky Ploughs, Thatch Making, Threshers, Winnowing Machines
Alkaline Earth
Alumina
American oak for staves.
Animals, alive.
Anchors over 3 cwt.
Antifermentine
Art materials and mediums, including canvasses mounted or in rolls, brushes, &c.
Art pictures, printed, used as studies or copies by artists: including Oleographs, Chromographs and Lithographs
Artists' colours
Asbestos, unmanufactured
Ash timber, in plank
Asphalt
Backs (wooden) for brushes
Bagging and wool-bagging
Ballast, being stone unsuitable for building purposes, gravel, sand, or earth
Bark for tanning
Bark (long) in bundles
Bass and bristles

Bicycle and tricycle parts and accessories, rough and unfinished, namely:—Brackets, lugs, fork sides, rims, chain wheels and chain rings, hubs, handle bars, stems and T pieces, seat pillar stems and T pieces, crowns and crown plates, spokes, fork and tube strengtheners, steel stamping and forgings, and any other part or parts which may come in rough and unfinished, as may be specified from time to time by the Treasurer and published in the Gazette
Birthday cards
Blocks
Bloomer, used in colouring sugar
Boiler plates, boiler tubes
Bolts and Nuts
Books, copy (for schools) with printed headings
Books (printed), except for advertising purposes
Bookbinders' leather and cloth
Bottles, empty
Bottling wire
Boots, children's, 0 to 6
Braces, rachet
Brass—bar, sheet, and rolled
Brass cocks and valves; Brass, ingot; Brass screw wire, wove wire, and gauze
Brimstone
Buckles of every description
Bunting, in the piece
Buttons, braids, tapes, waddings, pins, needles; and such minor articles required in the making up of apparel, boots, shoes, hats, caps, saddlery, upholstery, carriage and other vehicles, umbrellas, parasols and sunshades, as may be enumerated in any order of the Treasurer and published in the Government Gazette.

Cabbage-tree leaf
Candlewick
Cane shredders
Canvas
Capsules for bottles
Capsules, earthenware
Cartridges for sporting purposes, filled and unfilled

Cartridge fillers and re-cappers

Carriage and cart makers' materials, namely:—Axles, axle-boxes, and whip-sockets, carriage shafts, spokes, felloes, naves, hubs, bent wheel rims, spring steel, brass hinges, tacks, tire-bolts, shackle-holders, rubber cloth and American cloth.

Castor-oil seeds, Castor-oil in bulk

Chaff-cutting knives

Chalk

Chloride of lime

Christmas cards

Chromographs

Cocoanuts

Coin—gold, silver, and bronze

Copper—sheet, plain, ingot, rod, wire

Copper nails, piping, and wire (thread covered)

Copper, perforated, and copper gauze

Copper, bar and scrap

Copper-wire rope, Copper tacks, Copper rivets, Copper clouts, and Flemish nails

Copperas

Corks, cork, and cork socking

Corn sacks (jute), to contain 8 bushels

Cotton wicks, cotton waste, and cotton wool

Cotton-seed oil

Cotton and linen thread, sewing, knitting, embroidery, crotchet, crotchet thread, sewing silks and twists.

Cream separators, Cream testers

Curiosities, antique.

Cylinders and tubes containing gas or ammonia

Diving pumps and dresses

Diving dress parts, namely:—Helmets, corsets, cup leathers, valves, springs and screws, corset screws, nuts and keys, pump spanners, pipe couplings, face glasses, repairing cloth in solution

Dredgers and steam tugs to be used in execution of harbour works

Droppers and Standards for wire fencing

Drugs and chemicals, namely:—Acetate of soda, Boracic acid, Benzoic acid, Carbolic acid, Citric acid, Oxalic acid, Phosphoric acid, Pyrogallic acid, Salicylic acid, Sulphurous acid, Tannic acid, Tartaric acid, Albertine, Aloes, Alum, Ammonia, Antitoxin serums, Arsenic, Bisulphide of carbon, Borax, Calumba root, Camphor, Carbolate of lime, Carbonate of potash, Cascara bark, Caustic potash, Chloride of gold and tin, Cinchona bark, Collodion, Cream of tartar, Cyanide of potassium

Ergot

Garfield Tea

Gentian root, Glacialine, Glycerine, Iodine, Ipecacuanha root, Lithofuge, Nitrate of silver, Nut galls, Nux vomica, Pearl ash, Phosphorus, Saltpetre, Senega root

Silicate of soda, Soda nitrate, Soda sulphate

Soda caustic, Sulphur, Sulphate of copper or blue stone

Sulphate of barytes, Sulphate of iron

Sulphate of ammonia

Sulphate of magnesia, Sulphate of potash

Sulphate of quinine

Sulphide of sodium

Superphosphate of lime, Strychnine

Dye

Elastic

Electro-plating materials, namely:—Nickel anodes, nickel salts, rouge composition, Tripoli composition, wire scratch brushes, polishing mops, wheels, felt, and leather

Engine packing

Engravers' prepared plates or process blocks

Explosives, bellit, roburite, sporting powder, and percussion caps, dynamite, gelatine dynamite, lithofracteur, blasting powder, fuse, detonators, and other explosives

Eyelet punches and eyelets

Family portraits and clothing (old)

Felt and felt sheathing

Fibre, coconnut

Fire engines

Fish oil in bulk ; fish, frozen and fresh

Flax

Flock

Fruit, green

Flowers, cut

Game, frozen and fresh

Garden seeds, bulbs, trees, and shrubs

Gimp, silk or cotton

Glaziers' tools

Gold, unmanufactured

Gold leaf

Graining combs

Grass yarn or grass rope, twisted

Grindstones

Gutta percha

Hand Stamps for numbering and paging.

Hatmakers' materials, namely:—Felt hoods, shellac, galloons, spale-boards for hat-boxes, black silk plush

Hatmakers' cap-peaks, straps and hat leathers, cork tips and sides, corrugated cork and vents

Heirlooms, which have been in use and which have been left by will to, or inherited by, the importer, provided that such articles are not imported for sale, and that the intrinsic value thereof does not exceed 75 per centum of the value of new articles of a similar description

Hemp

Hessian

Hides, raw

Hooks and eyes

Hose, india-rubber and canvas

Hydraulic lifts

India-rubber

India-rubber insertion, India-rubber in solution

Infusorial earth

Ink, ruling

Ink, printing

Insulating materials

Iron ore; Iron, plain sheet (not including galvanised); Iron, pig; Iron, bar; Iron, rod—from 3 16ths to ¼ inch; channel iron, angle and tee iron, rolled iron joists up to 10 inches by 5 inches; Iron, scrap; Iron, hoop, iron sleepers, fish plates, points and crossings, switch-box for portable railways and clutch bolts; iron, sheet, chequered and gauze; iron pipes, cast

Ivory

Jewellers' tools—bellows, broachers or rimers, burnishers, doming punches and dies, draw-plates ; drawtongs, bench and hand ; emery wheels : felt, wool, leather polishing wheels ; furnace bodies, gauges, gravers and scoopers, ingot moulds, mallets, nippers, pliers, polishing lathe heads, polishing lathes, saw-frames, screwdrivers, triblets for rings, tweezers, watch and clock brushes

Jute

Kapock

Lead, pig
Leather — patent, enamelled, kid, hogskins, levant, morocco and imitations thereof; grained, Russia, chamois, chrome, and glace
Liebig condensers
Linotype metal
Linseed
Liquid stain for leather
Lithographs
Lithographic stones, lithographic ink and colours
Locomotives under ten inch cylinders
Machinery of the following descriptions, not including engines and boilers—Flour-milling; Bookbinding and ruling machines; Yaryan evaporators; Canning machines; Steam-threshing machinery
Machinery for carding, spinning, weaving, and finishing the manufacture of fibrous material, and cards for such machinery
Machinery used in the manufacture of paper and felting
Machinery—Centrifugals, multiple effets; dry air (for refrigerating), without engine; freezing machines, not including engine power; gas engines, portable engines, sewing machines, traction engines and steam ploughs, tubing for artesian wells
Machines, namely:—Planting machines and machines for joinery, hot air machinery for drying timber, hydraulic hat moulds, knitting machines, printing machines and presses, but not the motive power (if any) for same
Machinery for telegraphic purposes
Machines and machinery, not including boilers and engines, namely:—American band-saw frames, bag-folding, bark-cutting; biscuit, for cutting and stamping designs; bone crushing, bootmaking, bottle washing, brick and tile making; burring, used by fellmongers; burring, used in woollen factories; button fastening, button-making, cash registering and numbering, cloth cutting, condensers, corrugated iron curving, darning, drilling, drying (Cummer style), oleatric and fittings, electrotyping, embossing, engine governors, eyelet, felting, flock making, fret saw, fruit paring, fruit preserving, honeycomb making, horse clippers, label cutting, lathes, manure, mincing, oil expressing, patent brakes for locomotives and motors, pill making, plate bending, platform weighbridges, printers' and bookbinders', punching, punching and flaring hoops, rice dressing and cleaning, rubber stamp making, shaping, shearing for iron; sheep shearing, and all parts thereof; slotting, soda water, steam hammers; stone breakers; stone grinding (for printers), tinsmiths, tobacco cutting, twine balling; washing and scouring, for manufacture of blankets and rugs; washing and wringing, all kinds, wire net making, woodworkers', boring
Mining machinery, namely:—Air compressors, ball mills for crushing quartz, rock drills, roller mills for crushing quartz, steel rings for quartz mills, screens and gratings, tanners, ventilating fans
Machines and machinery, and parts thereof, required for mining purposes, agricultural, pastoral, or other purposes, which are not specified, and are of new invention, and of a description not heretofore made in

Queensland, as may be exempted from time to time by the Governor in Council, and published in the *Gazette*
Machine belting, not leather
Magic lanterns and slides
Malleable iron piping
Manure, guano
Maps, charts, and globes
Marble, unwrought
Materials, for scientific purposes, of china earthenware, and porcelain
Metal fittings for portmanteaus, travelling bags, and leggings
Metal frames for bags and satchels
Metal tubing, except tin, zinc welded, and lead
Millet straw
Mould boards and shears, steel for ploughs and steel beams
Mill stones
Mill silk
Muffles, Earthenware
Muntz metal
Music
Myrabolans, unground

Naval and military stores imported for the service of the Colonial Governments, or for the use of Her Majesty's land or sea forces
Newspapers, printed
Newlandite

Oakum
Oars
Oil of rhodium
Oil engines and fittings which can be only used for oil engines
Opticians' materials:—Optical tools, lenses (rough-edged), spectacle and eye-glass frames, empty, and repairing parts, spectacle and eye-glass cases, empty
Ores
Outside packages, in which goods are ordinarily imported, and which are of no commercial value except as covering for goods
Packages returned empty in which Queensland produce has been exported, namely:— Crates, bales and bags, provided that the number of such articles re-imported by any person or firm is not greater than that exported by them, and are of similar size and kind
Paint brushes
Paper patterns
Paper, hand-made or machine-made, book or writing, of sizes not less than the size known as "demy," when in original wrappers, and with uncut edges as it leaves the mill
Paper, printing
Palette knives
Passengers' cabin furniture and baggage, and passengers' personal effects (not including vehicles, musical instruments, glassware, chinaware, silver and gold plate and plated goods, and furniture other than cabin furniture), which are imported with and by passengers *bond fide* for their own personal use and not imported for the purpose of sale
Patent porcelain or steel roller for flour mills
Persons coming to reside permanently in Queensland may import with them their furniture and effects which have been in use, and are not imported for sale, up to the value of one hundred pounds (£100) duty free
Phormium tenax

Phosphorized pollard and distributing carts for same

Photographic materials — Cameras, sensitised plates, lenses and mounts

Picture cards for schools

Plated nails

Pottery materials, namely:—Potters' lead, Paris white, ground body manganese, oxides of chrome, copper, zinc, tin, black cobalt and uranium; suboxide of copper, carbonate of iron, bichromate of potash, white fluor-spar, ball clay, and Brandon mineral paint, ground flint, Cornish stone, china clay, ground glass, felspar, granite shavings, glaze for porcelain or china

Preservitas

Precious stones, unset

Pumps

Quicksilver

Rattans, canes and willows

Regalia for Friendly Societies

Resin

Reaper and binder—combined, strippers

Saddlers' tools

Saddlers' ironmongery, such as hames, and mounts for harness, straining, surcingle, brace, girth, and roller webs; collar check; saddle serge

Saddle-trees, saddle binding

Safety matches

Salt

Scientific instruments, being metal or glass-ware

Seaming twine

Sheep dip, sheep lick

Shoe pegs, peg wood

Shoemakers' nails, viz.: — Sparrow-bills, wrought and cast tips, bright and black malleable hobs, wrought hobs, nuggets, Hungarian cut sprigs, steel bills, tingles, iron and brass rivets

Shot

Silver—bar, ingot, and sheet

Silver, unmanufactured

Silver leaf

Skins, raw

Slates (school), slate pencils

Soda-ash

Sizeoline and hytra size

Soap colourings

Specimens of natural history

Split wood staves

Staymakers' binding, eyelet-holes, corset-fasteners, jean, lasting, and coutil

Starch, manufactured in bond from imported rice, under such restrictions and regulations as the Treasurer may impose

Staples for wire fencing

Steel wire rope, steel rails

Steel—unwrought, sheet, bar, angle, and tee

Straw, mill, and paste boards

Straw plaits, palm-leaf plaits, Tuscan plaits

Surgical and dental appliances and instruments, namely:—Aspirators, atomizers for surgical purposes only, bandages, basins (pus), batteries, galvanic belts, surgical binders, bistouries, bottles, injection bougies, brushes (throat), catheters, chairs (dental, complete), chairs (operating, surgical), dilators, elevators, bed clothes encases, exhausters, breast forceps, head-rests, dentals, inhalers, injectors, instruments, namely: Aspirating, cupping, dissecting, ear, eye, midwifery, tooth, uterine, and

veterinary, instruments and engines used in dental operations; lancets, lamps (used solely for surgical or dental purposes) laryngoscopes, pessaries, probes, protectors (chest), pumps (stomach), specula, splints, stethoscopes, stockings (elastic, silk), suspenders, syringes, trocars, trusses, tubes, and urinometers

Tailors' trimmings, namely:—French canvas, buckram, wadding, padding; silk worsted, and cotton bindings and braids; stay-binding

Tar, Stockholm

Thimbles (ship's gear)

Tinfoil

Tin plates

Tools, namely:—Grindery tools, edge planes, kit, peg, shaves, and welt-trimmers: Adze, anvils, augers, screw and shell and auger bits; Awls, awl pads, and hafts, Axes, hatchets, tomahawks; Bevels, blowpipes; Braces and bits, and breast drills; Bruzzes for wheelwrights; Bung borers; Brushes, patent roller for blockmaking; Chisels and gouges; Choppers and cleavers—butchers'; Compasses, dividers; Compasses—carpenters' and coopers'; Diamonds—glaziers'; Files and rasps; Forks —digging, hay, and stable Hoes, garden, plantation; Knives—butchers', hay, pruning, putty, saddlers', shoemakers', cane; Needles of all sorts: Palms, leather; Planes and plane irons, Rules, tapes, and chains—measuring; Saws of all kinds, but not the machinery (if any) connected therewith; Scissors, scrapers (ship); Screws—bench, brass, coach, galvanised, hand, table, wood; Scythes and scythe-handles; Shears —garden, hedge, sheep, tailors', tinmen's; Shovels--iron or wood; Sickles, spades; Spokeshaves, shaves and spoke-trimmers; Squares; Squeezers, cork; Steels, butchers'; Stocks and dies, and taps for same; Saddlers' tools, namely:— Rein rounders, claw, carving, French edge, patent leather tools, wheels, rosette cutters; Trowels; Vices, and patent saw-vices.

Tools—Hammers (mining), picks (mining)

Trace and plough chains, and iron hames

Traps, iron and steel

Twine, for net-making, only when imported by net-makers

Type, typewriters

Umbrella-makers' materials, namely:—Sticks, runners, notches, caps, ferrules, cups, ribs, stretchers, tips, and rings, for use in the making of umbrellas, parasols, and sunshades; reversible and Levantine silk mixtures of not less than 44 inches in width

Valonia, unground

Whalebone

Wheels and axles, steel

Wire, iron –plain, barbed, and galvanised

Wire, steel

Wire, heel

Wire netting

Wooden hoops for casks

Wool, unmanufactured

Wool packs

Works of art, namely: Paintings, engravings, and statuary

Yarn Russian, Italian, and coir

Yarn—jute and hemp

ARTICLES EXEMPTED FROM DUTY—*Continued.*

Zinc

Zinc plates polished, known as process blocks, stereotypes and woodcuts, as printing blocks.

Articles and materials (as may from time to time be specified by the Treasurer) which are suited only for, and are to be used and applied solely in, the fabrication of goods within the colony. All decisions of the Treasurer in reference to articles so admitted free to be published from time to time in the *Government Gazette.*

AD VALOREM DUTIES.

For every £100 of the value thereof, a duty of £5.

Alpaca cloth, with border
Cotton piece goods
Crimean flannel, in the piece
Furniture springs
Linen piece goods

Moleskin, in the piece
Paper, except otherwise enumerated
Tailors' trimmings :—Italians
Union ticks, in the piece
Zanella cloth, with border

For every £100 of the value thereof, a duty of £15.

Bags and sacks, being bran, corn sacks (except jute corn sacks to contain 3 bushels, free, 31st March, 1897), flour, gunny, ore, woolpacks, and sugar bags and mats
Bicycles and tricycles
Boot cloth
Burnishing ink
Castors for furniture
Carriage-makers' materials, viz.:— Carriage springs, carriage trimmings, carriage cloth in the piece
Casks, and staves and heads imported in shooks
Cigarette papers
Cocoa-beans, raw
Cotton, raw
Cutlery
Curled hair
Drapery and Millinery, viz.:—Bonnet shapes; Cotton blind nets; Cords—cotton, linen; Worsted—in hanks, coils and reels
Piece goods, viz.,- Baize; Bedford cord; Cloths; Dress Goods; Flannel; Linseys; Mosquito nets and valance nets; Ribbons; Serges and ostamenes; Silks; Trimmings (mantle and dress) Tweeds; Velvets and velveteens; Woollens
Wool (Berlin and knitting)
Carpeting, druggeting, floorcloth, oilcloth (in the piece)
Lace (cotton and silk)
Straw hats and bonnets (untrimmed and unlined; paper and glazed calico not to be considered lining)

Gilt mouldings for pictures
Glass stoppers for soda-water bottles
Hair-seating for furniture
Ironmongery and hardware, viz.:—Door-knobs —glass, brass, and china; emery cloth, emery paper, emery powder; hammers, except mining; hinges, except otherwise enumerated; holystones; irons — hatters', Italian, smoothing, and tailors'; latches, locks, mortice furniture, all kinds; patent door springs, pencils — carpenters', sash-fasteners, tinned rivets, weighing machines of all kinds (except platform weighbridges), and weights for same
Isinglass
Lamp chimneys and globes
Lemon peel in brine
Ostrich feathers, raw
Paperhangings
Pens
Saddlers' materials, viz.:— Saddle-cloths and saddle-girths made up
Sponge
Stone, unwrought
Watches, clocks, and all parts thereof
Window and plate glass

Upon all goods, wares, and merchandise, imported into Queensland other than those mentioned in the foregoing schedules, for every £100 of the value thereof, a duty of £25

DIVIDEND DUTY ACT.

A duty is levied of 5 per cent. on all dividends paid by any company except Insurance only having their chief place or head office in Queensland, or a proportionate amount of the average capital employed if the Head Office or chief place is out of the colony.

Mining companies pay dividend duty only when the amount they have expended on development, etc., is repaid.

Insurance companies pay a duty of 5 per cent. on the gross premiums received.

LICENSES.

For High-class Butter, Telephone 379.

	£	s.	d.
Apothecary, chemist, or other person to use a still of not more than 8 gallons, for any scientific purpose, or making perfume	2	0	0
Auctioneer, General .. .. per ann.	15	0	0
" (for Police district only) "	5	0	0
Bagatelle license, each table, per annum	5	0	0
Bagatelle license (temporary) for a special district, each table	2	0	0
Billiard license, each table, per ann...	10	0	0
Billiard license (temporary) for a special district, each table	5	0	0
Brewer	25	0	0
Brickmaker (for each mould) per ann.	4	0	0
Carrier (for each vehicle)	0	2	6
Club license (not less than 50 persons in Brisbane, nor 25 elsewhere), fee of £5 at registration.			
Distiller (for distilling, rectifying, or compounding spirits from sugar cane grown in Queensland), per ann.	25	0	0
Rectifying and Compounding Spirits	10	0	0
Distillation of Spirits from any material	10	0	0
License for removing stone, gravel, &c., from off Crown lands	5	0	0
Hawker and Pedler .. per ann.	10	0	0
Miner's right .. .. .. "	0	10	0
Business license .. .. .. "	4	0	0
Licensed victualler within a town or municipality, or within a distance of 5 miles from the boundaries thereof	30	0	0
Licensed victualler, if at a distance of more than five miles from the boundaries of a town or municipality	15	0	0
For a second bar or counter over which liquor is sold under a Licensed Victualler's license	10	0	0
Temporary License to retail wine or fermented and spirituous liquors in a special district (for not more than six months)	15	0	0
For railway station bar, from £5 to £30 per annum			
Packet license to retail fermented or spirituous liquors while the vessel is actually on her passage, or one half-hour before her departure, for every 200 tons or part of the registered tonnage of the vessel £5, but not to exceed £20			
Pawnbroker	10	0	0
Slaughter-house	0	2	6
Timber—To cut and remove Hardwood from off Crown lands per annum	5	0	0
Pine, Beech, or any Timber defined as rare	7	0	0
Cedar	10	0	0
To cut and split slabs, fencing stuff, or shingles, per annum	3	0	0

	£	s.	d.
To cut firewood, strip bark, or burn charcoal, per annum	2	0	0
To manufacture tobacco, cigars, and cigarettes—For every factory according to the weight per annum manufactured—			
Not exceeding 5,000lbs.	5	0	0
Above 5,000lb. but not ex. 10,000lb.	10	0	0
" 10,000lb. " 20,000lb.	20	0	0
" 20,000lb. " 50,000lb.	50	0	0
" 50,000lb. " 100,000lb.	100	0	0
" 100,000lb. " 200,000lb.	150	0	0
" 200,000lb. " 350,000lb.	200	0	0
Exceeding 350,000lb.	250	0	0
License, annual, to sell or deal in tobacco, cigars and cigarettes ..	0	5	0
License to sell poisons	1	0	0
Annual fee for renewal	0	5	0
Spirit Merchant (Registration and description of premises), if within City of Brisbane	30	0	0
If situated elsewhere	20	0	0
Wine-maker, to keep and use a still of not more than 50 gallons nor less than 15 gallons, for the purpose of distilling brandy from wine, to fortify wines the produce of his own vineyard	1	0	0
Wine-seller's license	10	0	0
Sale of Queensland-made wine only, not stronger than 33%	5	0	0
Stage Carriage	0	5	0
License for Oystering	0	10	0
To collect oysters for sale	0	10	0
For men employed	0	10	0
For each boat or vessel not exceeding 3 tons employed in collecting, obtaining or carrying away bank oysters for sale	1	0	0
For every ton, or part of a ton, over 3 tons	0	10	0
License to occupy land between high water mark and two feet below the level of low water mark, for the purpose of making oyster beds or layings	5	0	0
Fishing License, for each boat	1	0	0
For catching fish with net	0	10	0
Pearl Fishing License (to occupy Crown lands for the purpose of pearl shell and bêche-de-mer fishing) ..	5	0	0
And for every boat employed ..	0	10	0
For every ship of 10 tons or under ..	3	0	0
Above 10 tons, per ton or part ..	0	10	0
but not exceeding in all	20	0	0
Person in charge of a ship or diver using diving apparatus	1	0	0
To deal in Pearls	25	0	0

Auctioneers', Distillation Licenses, &c., on December 31; Brewers' and Publicans' Licenses, &c., on June 30, in each year; Pawnbroker, Carriers', Hawkers', and Pedlers' Licenses expire ... year from date of issue.

STAMP DUTIES.

Under *"The Stamp Duties Act of 1894."*

[CAME INTO OPERATION, NOVEMBER 1, 1894.]

NOTE.—All Stamp Duties must be denoted by IMPRESSED STAMPS except the following for which ADHESIVE STAMPS can be used :—Agreement under hand ; Bills of Exchange payable on demand or at sight ; Bills of Exchange and Promissory Notes drawn or made out of Queensland ; Bank Draft payable outside Queensland when issued from a locality where there is no stamp office ; Charter Party ; Drafts from outside the colony received by a bank for acceptance and payment within the colony ; Policies of Insurance ; Receipts or discharges for the payment of money ; Transfers of shares or stocks ; All documents requiring to be registered at the office of a Clerk of Petty Sessions, Warden, Mineral Land Commissioner, or Mining Registrar.

	£	s.	d.
AGREEMENT or CONTRACT accompanied with a deposit, *see* Mortgage, Bond, and Covenant			
AGREEMENT for a lease, or for any letting, *see* Lease			
AGREEMENT for sale of property, *see* Conveyance on Sale			
AGREEMENT, or any MEMORANDUM of an AGREEMENT, under hand only, and not otherwise specifically charged with any duty, whether the same be only evidence of a contract or obligatory upon the parties from its being a written instrument	0	2	6
Exemptions.—Agreement or Memorandum, the matter whereof is not of the value of £5. Agreement made between the Government and parties tendering for the performance of work and labour, or the supply of materials for use by the Government.			
ANNUITY—			
Conveyance in consideration of, *see* Conveyance on Sale.			
Purchase of, *see* Conveyance on Sale.			
Creation of, by way of security, *see* Mortgage, Bond, and Covenant.			
APPOINTMENT of a new trustee and appointment in execution of a power of any property or of any use, share, or interest in any property by any instrument not being a will	0	10	0
APPRENTICESHIP, Instrument of	1	1	0
ARTICLES OF CLERKSHIP whereby any person first becomes bound to serve as a clerk in order to his admission as a solicitor of the Supreme Court	10	10	0
ARTICLES OF CLERKSHIP whereby any person having been bound by previous duly stamped articles to serve as a clerk for his admission in the Supreme Court, and not having completed his service so as to be entitled to such admission, becomes bound afresh for the same purpose	1	0	0

	£	s.	d.
ASSIGNMENT—			
By way of security or of any security, *see* Mortgage, Bond, and Covenant.			
Upon a sale or otherwise, *see* Conveyance.			
ASSURANCE, *see* Policy of Insurance.			
AWARD in any case in which an amount or value is the matter in dispute—			
Where no amount is awarded or the amount or value awarded does not exceed £50	0	2	6
Where the amount or value awarded exceeds—			
£50 and does not exceed £100	0	5	0
£100 " " £200	0	10	0
£200 " " £500	1	0	0
£500 " " £750	1	10	0
£750 " " £1,000	2	0	0
For every additional £100, and also for any fractional part of £100	0	5	0
BILL OF EXCHANGE—			
Payable on demand or at sight, or on presentation, or in which no time for payment is expressed	0	0	1
BILL OF EXCHANGE of any other kind whatsoever (except a bank note), and promissory note of any kind whatsoever (except a bank note), drawn or expressed to be payable or actually paid or endorsed, or in any manner negotiated in the Colony of Queensland—			
Where the amount or value of the money for which the bill or note is drawn or made does not exceed £50	0	1	0
Exceeds £50, and does not exceed £100	0	2	0
And where the same shall exceed £100, then for every £50, and also for any fractional part of £50	0	1	0
Exemptions.—Draft or order drawn by any bank in the Colony of Queensland, upon any other bank in the Colony of Queensland, not payable to bearer or to order, and used solely for the			

Corona Culinary Essences. VERNEYS, Agents.

For High-class Butter, Telephone 379.

purpose of settling or clearing any account between such banks. Letter written by a bank in the Colony of Queensland to any other bank in the Colony of Queensland, directing the payment of any sum of money, the same not being payable to bearer or to order, and such letter not being sent or delivered to the person to whom payment is to be made, or to any person on his behalf. Letter of credit granted in the Colony of Queensland authorising drafts to be drawn out of the Colony of Queensland payable in the Colony of Queensland. All debentures, Treasury bills, and promissory notes for the payment of money, on demand, issued by the Government of Queensland. All bills of exchange or promissory notes issued by any bank for Government purposes to the Colonial Treasurer. All promissory notes for the payment of money on demand, issued within the Colony of Queensland by any bank or banking company legally incorporated and carrying on business in the said Colony.

BILL OF LADING or RECEIPT of or for any goods, merchandise, or effects to be carried beyond the Colony—
Bill of Lading and each copy .. 0 1 0
Receipt and each copy 0 0 6
Exemption—Copy of Bills of Lading given to Sub-Collector in accordance with "The Duty on Cedar Act of 1880."

BILL OF SALE—
Absolute, see Conveyance on Sale
By way of security, see Mortgage, Bond, and Covenant.
BOND given as a security for the due execution of an office, and for the accounting for money received by virtue thereof 0 10 0
BOND of any kind whatever not otherwise charged nor expressly exempted from all stamp duty .. 0 10 0
Exemptions — Bond given by the parent or friends of any lunatic for the maintenance of such lunatic in any asylum for the relief or cure of lunacy. Bond given by any person on obtaining letters of administration. Bond given pursuant to an Act of Parliament or by direction of the Collector of Customs in and for the Colony of Queensland, or any of his officers, upon or with relation to any duty of Customs for or in respect of any goods, wares, or merchandise exported or shipped to be exported from the said Colony or imported into the said Colony. And also any bond given as aforesaid for or in relation to any other matter or thing in connection with the levy

and collection of duties of Customs in the said Colony. Renewal of any such bond by reason of the death or insolvency of the sureties, or either of them, or otherwise.

CHARTER PARTY—
When the charter does not amount to £20 .. .. 0 10 0
When it amounts to more than £20 and less than £100 .. .. 0 15 0
When it exceeds £100 .. .. 1 0 0
COMPANIES(Queensland) on registration 1s. per cent. on the nominal share capital or increase of capital.
COMPANIES (Foreign), capital not exceeding £1000, 10s.; for every £1000 after the first up to £200,000, 1s. per £100 of nominal capital.
CONVEYANCE or TRANSFER on sale of any share or shares in the stock or funds of any company or corporation—
For every £10, and also for any fractional part of £10 of the then value of shares or stock transferred 0 0 6
CONVEYANCE or TRANSFER on sale or any property (except such shares of stock as aforesaid, and runs or stations held under lease or promise of lease or license from the Crown, or any interest therein)—
Where the amount or value of the consideration for the sale does not exceed £50 .. .. 0 7 6
Exceeds £50 and does not exceed £100 .. .. 0 15 0
Exceeds £100—For every £100, and also for any fractional part of £100 of such amount or value 0 15 0
Exemptions — All conveyances or transfers of lands to the Government for public purposes. Any grant from the Crown under the hand of the Governor, for the time being, of the Colony of Queensland, to any purchaser of Crown lands in Queensland. Transfer under the Gold Fields Acts or Mineral Lands Acts of a claim or share in a claim where the consideration paid does not exceed £50.
CONVEYANCE or TRANSFER, by way of security, of any property (except such shares of stock as aforesaid) or of any security, see Mortgage, Bond, and Covenant.
CONVEYANCE or TRANSFER of any kind not hereinbefore described .. 0 10 0
DEED of any kind whatsoever not described in this Schedule 0 10 0
LEASE or AGREEMENT for a LEASE or any written document for the tenancy or occupancy of any lands, tenements, or hereditaments, the following duties in respect of the rent at the rate per annum —
Where the rent shall not exceed £50 at the rate per annum .. 0 2 6

We Recommend SQUATTER WHISKY.

Crown Jams—The Best. VERNEYS, Makers.

	£	s.	d.

Where the same shall exceed £50 and not exceed £100 .. .. 0 5 0
Above £100, for every fractional part of £100 .. .. .. 0 5 0
Exemption—Leases from the Crown.

LEASE of any lands, tenements, or hereditaments, granted in consideration of a sum of money by way of premium and also of a yearly rent amounting to £20 and upwards (Both the *ad valorem* duties payable upon a conveyance according to the consideration therein expressed, and for a lease in consideration of a rent of the same amount).

For every transfer or cancellation of any lease (other than a transfer of any run or station held under lease or promise of lease or license from the Crown, or of any interest therein) one-half the amount originally paid or in the case of leases made prior to the passing of this Act, one-half the amount which would have been paid thereon had they been made subsequent to the passing of this Act.

MORTGAGE of stock or marketable security, under hand only, *see* Agreement.

MORTGAGE, BOND, and COVENANT—
(1) Being the only or principal or primary security for the payment or repayment of money—
Not exceeding £50 .. .. 0 2 6
For every additional £50, and also for any fractional part of £50 0 2 6
(2) Transfer or assignment of any mortgage, bond, or covenant, or of any money or stock secured by any such instrument—
For every £50, and also for any fractional part of £50 of the amount transferred or assigned, exclusive of interest which is not in arrear .. 0 1 3
And also where any further money is added to the money already secured. (The same duty as a principal security for such further money).
(3) Re-conveyance, release, or discharge of any such security as aforesaid, or of the benefit thereof, or of the money thereby secured 0 2 6

POLICIES OF INSURANCE—
Upon any policy or instrument of guarantee or indemnity against loss or damage by fire or other casualty to any property on land—
For every £100 or fractional part of £100 insured for any period exceeding six months 0 1 0
For every £100 or fractional part of £100 insured for any period not exceeding six months 0 0 6
Upon any one policy or instrument of guarantee or indemnity whereby any insurance is made upon

any ship or vessel, or upon any goods, merchandise, or other property on board of any ship or vessel, or upon the freight thereof, for any period or voyage, for every £100 or every fractional part of £100 .. .. 0 0 3
For every renewal 0 0 8
Upon any policy of insurance on wool, tallow, skins, meats, or sugar to be carried both on sea and land 0 0 8
Upon any policy or instrument of guarantee or indemnity against accident or fidelity or want of honesty, for every £100 or any fractional part of £100 .. 0 1 0
Upon all other policies, for every £100 or fractional part of £100 .. 0 1 0
Exemptions.—Life policies issued under the Act 29 Vic. No. 15. Life policies not exceeding £50. Policies effected and expressed to be effected by way of re-insurance. Cover notes and interim receipts issued pending inspection and acceptance of any risk or issue of policy.

PROMISSORY NOTE, *see* Bill of Exchange.
RECEIPT given for or upon the payment of money amounting to twenty shillings or upwards 0 0 1
Exemptions.—Receipt given for or upon the payment of money to or for the use of Her Majesty. Receipts endorsed upon any instrument duly stamped under this Act acknowledging the receipt of the consideration money therein expressed. Receipt given for money deposited in any bank to be accounted for. All receipts for money withdrawn by depositors from the Government Savings Banks. All receipts or discharges given by any seaman, labourer, or menial servant for the payment of wages.

RELEASE OR RENUNCIATION of any property, or any right or interest in any property—
Upon a sale, *see* Conveyance on Sale.
By way of security, *see* Mortgage, Bond, and Covenant.
In any other case 0 10 0
REQUEST for the registration or the entering of any instrument under the provisions of the Real Property Acts not otherwise stamped 0 2 0
SETTLEMENT—Any instrument whether voluntary or upon any good or valuable consideration other than a *bona fide* pecuniary consideration, whereby any definite and certain principal sum of money (which charged or chargeable on lands or other hereditaments or not, or to be laid out in the purchase of lands or other hereditaments or not, or any definite and certain amount of stock or any security is settled or agreed to be settled in any manner whatsoever—

We Recommend SQUATTER WHISKY.

QUEENSLAND MODEL DAIRY, Turbot Street. Telephone 379.

123

	£ s. d.
For every £100, and also for any fractional part of £100 of the amount or value of the property settled or agreed to be settled	0 5 0

Exemption.—Instrument of appointment relating to any property in favour of persons specially named or described as the objects of a power of appointment where duty has been duly paid in respect of the same property upon the settlement creating the power, or the grant of representation of any will or testamentary instrument creating the power.

TRANSFER of any run or station held under lease or promise of lease or

	£ s. d.
license from the Crown, or of any interest therein, where the declared value of such property or interest, or the value thereof assessed as in this Act provided, shall not exceed £100	0 10 0
And where such value shall exceed £100, then for every £100 and any fractional part of £100	0 10 0

Exemption.—Any transfer from the mortgagee to the mortgagor of any run or station held under lease or promise of lease or license from the Crown, or of any interest therein.

SUCCESSION DUTIES.

Where the whole amount passing by death to any person amounts			
to less than £200		No duty.	
£200 and less than £1000		2 per cent.	
1000 " " 2500		3	"
2500 " " 5000		4	"
5000 " " 10,000		6	"
10,000 " " 20,000		8	"
20,000 and upwards		10	"

(Under the "Amendment Act of 1895.")

To the wife or husband or children of the deceased the duty shall be one-half of the foregoing rates.

Where the legatee is a stranger in blood to the deceased the duty shall be double the above rates.

Any succession which in the whole is of less value than £200 is exempt from duty.

Where a man dies intestate leaving a widow but no issue, and no mother who is a widow surviving him, where net value of his real and personal property shall not exceed £500, it shall belong to his widow absolutely and exclusively.

Where the value exceeds £500, widow is entitled to £500 in addition and without prejudice to her interest and share in the residue of the property.

PROBATE AND LETTERS OF ADMINISTRATION.

			Probate.	Administration.
			£ s. d.	£ s. d.
Where the net value of the property of the deceased person does not exceed		£50	Nil.	Nil.
Where it exceeds £50 but does not exceed		100	0 10 0	1 0 0
" 100 "	200		1 0 0	2 0 0
" 200 "	500		2 0 0	4 0 0
" 500 "	1000		5 0 0	10 0 0

—o—

TOTALISATOR TAX.

On all moneys received by the conductor of any authorised Totalisator by way of stakes, wagers, or bets, or agreed to be paid by him, for every 20s., 6d.

Macaroni Pudding.—Partly boil the macaroni, grease a pudding-basin and curl the macaroni carefully until it is well covered. Fill the inside with minced meat and one onion, and some parsley chopped fine; season with pepper and salt, place a buttered paper on the top, and bake for an hour. Turn on a dish, and serve with tomato sauce poured round it.

We Recommend SQUATTER WHISKY.

DIRECTIONS FOR MAKING A WILL.

A WILL should be made in the plainest language possible; it must be written with ink on paper or parchment, and must be signed at the end of each sheet (if there be more than one) by the Testator (the person who makes the Will) in the presence of TWO or more witnesses.

The Witnesses *must not be in any way beneficially interested in the will*, as in such case any gift or legacy to that witness is void. For example, a son to whom anything is left, or who might benefit under the will, should not witness his father's will; nor should a wife who benefits thereunder, witness her husband's will. The witnesses must strictly comply with every particular required by the Attestation Clause, at the end of which clause they must sign their names.

A witness need not know the contents of the will, as the will may be so folded, that the signature and Attestation Clause alone can be seen.

FORM OF A WILL.

LEAVING EVERYTHING TO A WIFE.

This is the last Will and Testament of me (name)   of (address)   made this   day of   One thousand eight hundred and ninety-   as follows:—I give, devise, and bequeath all my messuages, lands, tenements, and hereditaments, and all my household furniture, ready money, money secured by life assurance, goods and chattels and all other my real and personal estate and effects whatsoever, unto my dear wife for her own sole and separate use absolutely. And I appoint my said wife executrix of this my Will, and hereby revoke all other Wills.

In witness whereof I have hereunto set my hand this day and year above written.

ATTESTATION CLAUSE.

Signed and acknowledged by the said   as and for his last Will and Testament, in the presence of us, who in his presence and at his request, and in the presence of each other, have subscribed our names as witnesses.

In the event of a person wishing to make some alteration in his Will, it can be done by the addition thereto of what is known as a Codicil.

A CODICIL TO A WILL.

A Codicil is to be made with the same regulations as the Will itself, and may be written thus:—

This is a Codicil to my last Will and Testament, bearing date the   day of   189   and which I direct to be taken as part thereof. I give, devise, and bequeath, &c.

As witness my hand this   day of   189

NOTE.—Obliterations and alterations of any sort in the Will ought, if possible, to be avoided; when they have to be made, each one of them must be signed or initialled by the Testator and witnesses on the margin, or as near to the alteration as possible.

NOTE.—Marriage after making a Will renders the Will void, and necessitates another being made.

If a person wishes to dispose of all his property in one gift, the words, "all my real and personal estate," may be used.

In many cases the death of an executor or unwillingness to act, leads to considerable trouble, which can be altogether avoided by employing the Queensland Trustees, Ltd., to act as Executor and Trustee. The advantages of appointing an institution such as this, having a local directorate and being of good standing, are manifest, independently of the fact that a company never dies like a private executor or trustee. The expenses of the company acting are no greater than those of a private individual. In such case the following form of appointment of the Queensland Trustees, Limited, may be substituted in the above form in lieu of individual persons:—

"I APPOINT the Queensland Trustees, Limited, "executor and trustee of this my Will and I "DECLARE that the said Company by its officers "may execute any of the trusts or powers "therein contained."

125

REGISTRATION OF BIRTHS, MARRIAGES, AND DEATHS.

Every Birth must be registered within sixty days, and every death within thirty days next thereafter respectively; any neglect of this regulation renders the parties whose duty it is to register, liable to a fine not exceeding £10. If sixty days have elapsed from the date of birth, the law requires the parent, or other person making the application to register such birth, to pay a fee of two shillings and sixpence, and to make a solemn declaration of the facts before a Justice of the Peace, prior to the registration. The father or mother ought to sign as informant. If unable to write, let a mark be made. No birth can be registered after three years have elapsed from the date thereof; but a record will be made in the Registrar-General's Office if reliable information be supplied by the parents respecting such a birth.

Every Minister who has celebrated a marriage must, within one month thereafter, transmit (in accordance with the Act 28 Victoria No. 15) the original certificate to the Registrar of the District in which the marriage was celebrated, and every Minister who fails to transmit the certificate to the District Registrar, is liable to a fine of NOT LESS THAN £10 and not exceeding £50. Marriages must be solemnized between the hours of 8 a.m. and 8 p.m. Persons under age must produce the written authority of parents or guardians, signed by them in the presence of a Justice of the Peace, Registered Minister, or District Registrar, or the marriage cannot take place.

In every case of Burial, the Minister or person officiating at any religious service at such burial, ought to receive from the undertaker or person having charge of the funeral, a certificate from the District Registrar, certifying the registration of the death, unless in the case of inquest, when a certificate from the Coroner or Magistrate holding the inquest, will be sufficient; and if any dead body shall be buried without such certificate, the person who may bury the same, or perform any funeral or religious service for the burial, or who shall in any way dispose of the body, shall forthwith give notice of the facts to the District Registrar. Undertakers are bound, under a penalty not exceeding £10, to lodge with the District Registrar, IMMEDIATELY after the burial, a Certificate of such burial signed by themselves and COUNTERSIGNED BY TWO WITNESSES.

REGISTRY DISTRICTS AND NAMES OF REGISTRARS.

ARAMAC—Edmund Filmer Craven, Muttaburra
BALONNE—John Macalister, St. George
BLACKALL—R. T. Taylor, Blackall
BOWEN—Martin O'Donohue, Bowen
BRISBANE—The Registrar-General, Jos. Hughes; and Deputy Registrar-General, Richard Baron Howard
BUNDABERG—Cæsar E. Power, Bundaberg
BURKE—A. H. Zillman, Normanton
BURNETT—Thomas Illidge, Gayndah
CABOOLTURE—Thos. Bryce, Burnside, Stony Ck.
CAIRNS—Hubert Morris, Cairns
CARDWELL—Wm. C. Miller, Ingham
CHARLEVILLE—Marcus Gallagher, Charleville
CLERMONT—W. G. F. King, Clermont
CLONCURRY—Thos. Hy. Boddington, Cloncurry
COOK—Arthur Dean, Cooktown
CUNNAMULLA—Christopher Francis, Cunnamulla
DALBY AND DARLING DOWNS NORTH—Frederick William Roche, Dalby
DARLING DOWNS WEST—Octavius Armstrong, Goondiwindi
DARLING DOWNS EAST AND WARWICK—W. G. Hanbury, Warwick
DIAMENTINA—Reginald Edwd. Halloran, Islsford
DRAYTON AND TOOWOOMBA, DARLING DOWNS, CENTRAL AND HIGHFIELDS—G. E. Evans, Toowoomba
ENOGGERA—G. H. Cole, Paddington
ETHERIDGE—P. M. Hishon, Georgetown
FASSIFERN—Geo. Whitney, Fassifern
GLADSTONE—R. B. Hetherington, Gladstone

GYMPIE—John Farrelly, Gympie
HERBERTON—J. S. Berge, Herberton
HUGHENDEN—B. C. MacGroarty, Hughenden
IPSWICH & MORETON WEST—R. Miller, Ipswich
KENNEDY—Frank Russell, Charters Towers
LEICHHARDT—Jas. McDonald, Banana
LOGAN—J. A. Macarthur, Beenleigh
MACKAY—Adolph Hasenkamp, Mackay
MARANOA—Frederick Vaughan, Roma
MITRATHON—Ernest Eglinton, Winton
MARYBOROUGH AND WIDE BAY—John Blaine, Maryborough
MORETON, EAST—Henri Willson Haseler, South Brisbane
NUNDAU—John Henry Nicholson, Albion
OXLEY—John Moffatt, Sherwood
PALMER—George Sydney Pegus, Maytown
PEAK DOWNS—Hugh Jas. Johnston, Blackwater
ROCKHAMPTON AND WESTWOOD—F. R. Chester-Master, Rockhampton
SOMERSET—Wm. Grace Moran, Thursday Island
SPRINGSURE—C. A. Collard, Springsure
STANLEY—Richard Frederick John Gore, Esk
STANTHORPE—F. H. Hyde, Stanthorpe
ST. LAWRENCE—Alexander Blyth
TAMBO—R. W. Moran, Tambo
TAROOM—Alfred Scott, Taroom
TIARO—Jonathan Pickering, Tiaro
TOOWONG—H. C. Luck, Toowong
TOWNSVILLE—John Nicholson, Townsville
WARREGO—J. W. W. Jackson, Thargomindah
WOOTHAKATA—James Williams, Thornborough

126

TRADE MARKS.

THE Laws of Queensland relating to the registration of Trade Marks requires a mark to consist of or contain at least one of the following essential particulars :—

(a) A name of an individual or firm printed, impressed, or woven in some particular and distinctive manner ; or

(b) A written signature, a copy of a written signature of the individual or firm applying for registration thereof as a trade mark ; or

(c) A distinctive device, mark, brand, heading, label, or ticket ; or

(d) An invented word or invented words ; or

(e) A word or words having no reference to the character or quality of the goods, and not being a geographical name.

Trade marks that were in force prior to 13th Act, 1884, can be registered under somewhat more lenient conditions.

From the number and character of the marks registered by Queensland firms, it would seem that a vast number of the commercial population of Queensland do not appreciate the value of a trade mark or the reputation that can be built up and defended thereon. Many who do understand, to some extent, the advantages of registering their trade marks, often seek to register all sorts of matter that the law does not permit to be registered, and many marks that have been registered in the past would not stand the test of a law suit.

In Great Britain many marks of great value to the owners have been expunged from the Register, after being years in use, because they did not meet the requirements of the law.

Merchants and others desiring to avail themselves of the trade mark laws of this country, or any other country, require the assistance of an expert in trade marks as much as they would an architect in connection with the building or enlargement of their premises.

---o---

PATENTS.

IN the early days monopolies were granted by the sovereign to the people for the sale of any kind of goods without any reference to inventions or discoveries. Monopolies were granted for the sale of salt, cloth, oils, paper, etc., etc., and the monopolists became so exhorbitant in their demands that they raised prices until the burdens on the people became most grievous. Parliament at different times sought to take from the sovereign this power to grant monopolies, but it was not until the reign of James I , in 1624, that the famous Statute of Monopolies (21 Jac 1., c. 3), was passed. This Act swept away the old monopolies, leaving only the grants of privileges and letters patent, " for the term of fourteen years or under, thereafter to be made, for the sole working or making of any manner of new manufactures within the realm, to the true and first inventor or inventors, which others at the time of making such letters patent shall not use, so as they be not contrary to the law, nor mischievous to the State."

MITCHELL

CHARLEVILLE.

Upon this foundation has been built up the present laws under which letters patent are granted in Great Britain. Queensland has in many respects the same law, but with one or two variations, which are not considered improvements by those comptent to judge. Plainly stated, letters patent are granted in this colony to any person for a *new* invention. A well known authority states that—

(a) The application of old materials or methods to the production of new and useful results;

(b) The modification of one element in an old combination;

(c) A slight alteration in the shape of an old instrument, being new and very useful;

(d) A new addition to an existing machine;

(e) A combination of old materials, by which a new, or a better, or a cheaper article is given to the public—may be patented.

By the word *new* is meant, that the invention must be unknown to the public. In other words, the inventor cannot use or publish the invention and then apply for a patent, when the value of the invention is clear, but must leave at the Patents Office his application (properly prepared) before he can make public his invention. The law allows a certain latitude for experimenting, and when owing to the nature of the invention this cannot be kept secret, the exposure is been held not to be publication. Besides the fact that an invention must be new to be protected by letters patent, it is also equally important for the inventor's protection that he should lodge with his application a properly prepared specification; it must be couched in correct language, and sufficiently clear (and illustrated with plans if necessary) to enable any one, versed in the Art to which the invention relates, to thoroughly understand it, and able to carry it out, without experimenting, when the period for which the patent is granted shall have expired. It will, therefore, be clear that the specification should be prepared by a competent person, for although the inventor may know all about his invention, he does not know all the difficulties that surround him, or how to put his papers into legal form to avoid future trouble. Many inventors have lost valuable rights through trying to be their own expert for the preparation of the patent applications.

The cost of a patent in this country compares fairly favourably with other British colonies, and is certainly within the reach of most inventors. The sum to be paid to Government for fourteen years is only £18, but payment of this is spread over a number of years.

Dried Green Peas Soup.—Ingredients: One and a-half pints of dried green peas, half a pint of boiled spinach, one lettuce, four ounces of butter, and one teaspoonful of flour. After steeping the peas in soft water twelve hours, set them on the fire in a quart of boiling soft water, with a teaspoonful of salt, a piece of soda the size of a large pea, and two ounces of butter. Simmer gently till the peas are perfectly soft and rub them through a fine colander or wire sieve. Add the lettuce and boiled spinach. Put all together into the pan, with two quarts of boiling water; simmer till nearly ready. Take out the lettuce, and add some heads of asparagus or a few leaves and young stalks of spinach, cut in very small pieces. Stir in a teaspoonful of flour, with two ounces of butter; season with pepper and salt, add a piece of sugar the size of a walnut, and boil the soup twenty minutes.

We Recommend SQUATTER WHISKY.

NEWSPAPERS IN QUEENSLAND.

ALLORA: "Guardian"; Saturday

AYR: "The Chronicle"

BAROALDINE: "Western Champion"; Tuesday

BLACKALL: "Barcoo Independent"; Wednesday

BOWEN: "The Port Denison Times" (established March, 1864); Saturday. "Mirror' Friday

BRISBANE.—*Daily*:—"The Courier" (established June, 1846); morning; office, Queen-street. "The Evening Observer"; office, Queen-street. "The Telegraph" (established October 1, 1872); evening; office, Queen-street

Weekly:—"The Queenslander" (established February, 1866); Saturday; office, "Courier" Office, Queen-street. "The Week" (established January 1, 1876); Friday morning; office, "Telegraph," Queen-street. "The Queensland Government Gazette" is issued from the Government Printing Office, William-street, Saturday at noon. "The Nord Australische Zeitung"; Saturday; office, Mary street. "The Australian"; Saturday, office, Gotha-street. Fortitude Valley. "The Australian Christian World") office, George-street. "The Worker"; office, Turbot-street. "The Age"; Saturday; office, 79 Elizabeth-street. "War Cry"; office, Ann-street. "Flashes"; office, Queen-street. "Queensland Figaro"; Friday; office, Elizabeth-street. "Ithaca and Toowong Record," Saturday; office, George-street. "Queensland Farmer and Grazier," Friday, office, Edward-street. "Queenslander Herald," German; office, Elizabeth-street. "Moreton Mail," Friday; office, Ann-street. "Queensland Sportsman," Friday; office, Queen-street. "Queensland Law Journal"; office, Elizabeth-street. "Saturday Night," Saturday; office, Edward street. "The Street," office, Mary street. "Queensland Sporting and Dramatic News," office, Queen-street. "Queensland Grazier, Wool and Produce Journal," Friday; office, Eagle-street. "Queensland Agricultural Journal," office, Government Treasury. "Hall's Mercantile Gazette," Saturday. "The White Mercantile Gazette."

Monthly:—A.B.C. Guide; office, Adelaide-street. "Australian Agriculturist"; office, Queen-street. "Australian Tropiculturist," office, Queen-street. "Australian Pastoralist"; office, 398 Queen-street. "The Queensland Mercantile Gazette and General Advertiser"; office, Adelaide-street. "Queensland Baptist"; office, Queen-street. "Queensland Railway Times"; office, Edward-street. "Queensland Electric Telegraph Gazette." "Austral Star," office, Eagle-street. "Church Chronicle"; office, Diocesan Chambers, George-street.

BUNDABERG: "The Bundaberg Star" (established December 24, 1874); Tuesday, Thursday, and Saturday. "The Bundaberg Mail"; Monday, Wednesday, and Friday.

BURKETOWN: "Burke Telegraph"; Friday

CAIRNS: "Argus"; Wednesday and Saturday. "Morning Post"; Thursday. "Advocate," Wednesday

CHARLEVILLE: "Charleville Times" (established December 25, 1883); Saturday. "Charleville Courier"; Saturday

CHILDERS: "Isis Standard"; Wednesday and Saturday

CHARTERS TOWERS: "The Northern Miner" (established 1872); daily. "The Towers Herald," (established 1877); daily. "North Queensland Register," Wednesday; "Eagle," Saturday. "North Queensland Figaro," Saturday; "Mining Standard"; daily, evening. "Queenton Advertiser," weekly

CLERMONT: "The Peak Downs Telegram" (established in October, 1864); Tuesday

CLONCURRY: "Cloncurry Advocate"; Friday

COOKTOWN: "Cooktown Independent" (established June 6, 1884); Wednesday and Saturday; "The Endeavour Beacon and Cook District Advertiser," Monday and Thursday

CROYDON: "Golden Age"; Tuesday evening. "Croydon Mining News"; Friday.

CUNNAMULLA: "Warrego Watchman"; Saturday. "Comet"; Saturday.

DALBY: "The Dalby Herald" (established in September, 1865); Wednesday and Saturday

FASSIFERN: "Chronicle"; Saturday

GEORGETOWN: "Mundic Miner"; Saturday

GERALDTON: "Advocate"; Wednesday

GLADSTONE: "The Gladstone Observer" (established 1880); Tuesday

GOONDIWINDI: "The McIntyre Herald" (established January 7, 1886); Tuesday

GYMPIE: "The Gympie Times"; Tuesday, Thursday, and Saturday. "The Gympie Miner"; Monday, Wednesday, and Friday evening. "Truth"; Saturday

HALIFAX: "Northern Age"; Saturday

HERBERTON: "Wild River Times"; Tuesday

HUGHENDEN: "Hughenden Observer"; Wednesday

INGHAM: "Ingham Planter"; Tuesday.

IPSWICH: "The Queensland Times" (established as the "Ipswich Herald" in July, 1859). Tuesday, Thursday, and Saturday; office, Ellenborough-street. "The Standard"; Saturday "Queensland Railway Times," Martin street

LAIDLEY: "The Lockyer Star"; Tuesday, Thursday and Saturday

LOGAN: "Albert Leader" (Beenleigh); Saturday. "Despatch" (Beaudesert); Saturday.

LONGREACH: "Standard"; Saturday

MACKAY (PIONEER RIVER): "The Mackay Mercury" (established in 1866); Tuesday, Thursday, and Saturday. "The Mackay Standard" (established in December, 1877); Monday, Wednesday, and Friday. "The Mackay Chronicle"; Monday, Wednesday and Friday. "The Sugar Journal and Tropical Agriculturist"; monthly

MARYBOROUGH: "The Maryborough Chronicle" (established in November, 1860); morning, daily. "The Wide Bay and Burnett News" (established July 2, 1870); Tuesday, Thursday, and Saturday. "The Colonist" (established March 29, 1884); Saturday. "The Patriot"; Saturday

MOUNT MORGAN: "Mount Morgan Chronicle"; Saturday. "Herald"; Thursday. "Truth"; Saturday

NORMANTON: "Norman Chronicle" (established October, 1885); Wednesday and Saturday,

PORT DOUGLAS—"Port Douglas and Mosman Gazette" (established 1896); Friday

RAVENSWOOD: "Mining Journal"; Saturday

ROCKHAMPTON: "The Morning Bulletin" (established in July, 1861); daily. "The Capricornian" (established January 2, 1875); Saturday; office, "Bulletin" Office. "The Daily Record"; evening. "The Patriot"; Saturday. "People's Newspaper," Friday

ROCKHAMPTON, NORTH: "North Rockhampton Times"; Saturday

ROMA: "The Western Star" (established March 21, 1875); Wednesday and Saturday. "Maranoa Advocate"; Tuesday and Friday

SOUTHPORT: "Southern Queensland Bulletin" (established March, 1885); Saturday

ST. GEORGE: "St. George Standard"; Friday

STANTHORPE: "The Border Post" (established July 20, 1872); Saturday

TAMBOURINE: "Logan and Albert Advocate"; Saturday

THARGOMINDAH: "Thargomindah Herald and Cooper's Creek Advertiser" (established August, 1884); Tuesday

THURSDAY ISLAND: "Torres Straits Pilot"; Saturday

TOOWOOMBA: "The Darling Downs Gazette" (established in June, 1858); Monday, Wednesday and Saturday. "The Toowoomba Chronicle" (established in July, 1861); Tuesday, Thursday, and Saturday. "Settler and South Queensland Pioneer"; Saturday. "Darling Downs Democrat," Saturday

TOWNSVILLE: "The Townsville Bulletin"; daily. "The Townsville Herald"; Wednesday. "Evening Star"; daily. "North Queensland Illustrated Weekly Herald." "Church Chronicle." "The Townsville Grammar School Magazine," half-yearly.

WARWICK: "The Warwick Argus" (established in November, 1864); Tuesday and Saturday, "Examiner and Times" (established 1866); Wednesday and Saturday

WINTON: "The Winton Herald and Western Queensland Gazette"; Wednesday

---

LEARNING makes a man fit company for himself.

MODESTY is a guard to virtue.

NOT to hear conscience is the way to silence it.

ONE hour to-day is worth two to-morrow.

PROUD looks makes foul work in fair faces.

QUIET conscience gives quiet sleep.

We Recommend SQUATTER WHISKY.

WEIGHTS AND MEASURES.

—o—

Liquid Measures.

60 Minims..	..	1 Drachm
8 Drachms	.. ,,	1 Ounce
20 Ounces ..	.. ,,	1 Pint
8 Pints ..	.. ,,	1 Gallon
1 Minim	.. ,,	1 Drop
1 Drachm	.. ,,	1 Teaspoonful
2 ,,	.. .. ,,	1 Dessert ,,
4 ,,	.. .. ,,	1 Table ,,

1 Gal. Pure Water at 62° Fah.
Bar. at 30 = 10lb.

4 Gills = 1 Pint   = 34·66 cubic inch
2 Pints ,, 1 Quart ,, 69·318   ,,
4 Qts. ,, 1 Gallon ,, 277·274 ,,

Beer, &c., Measure.

9 Gals. = 1 Firkin	54 Gals. = 1 Hhd.
18 ,, ,, 1 Kldkn	108 ,, ,, 1 Butt
36 ,, ,, 1 Barrel	216 ,, ,, 1 Tun

Wine Measure.

A Hogshead = ½ a Pipe or Butt, or 2 Qr. Casks, or about 52½ Gallons.

A Pipe of Port = 115 Gallons, or about 56 dozen Bottles.

A Butt of Sherry = 108 Gallons, or about 52 dozen Bottles.

A Hogshead of French Wine = 46 Gallons, or about 22 dozen Bottles.

An Aum of Rhenish = 30 Gallons, or about 15 dozen Bottles.

Dry Measure.

4 Qts. = 1 Gallon	12 Sacks = 1 Char.
2 Galls. ,, 1 Peck	8 Bush. ,, 1 Qur.
4 Pecks ,, 1 Bush'l	5 Qtrs. ,, 1 Load
8 Bush. ,, 1 Sack	

A Bushel of Wheat is on an average 60 lbs. ; Barley, 47 lbs. ; Oats, 38 to 40 lbs. A Truss of Straw weighs 36lbs ; Old Hay, 56lbs ; New Hay (until 1st Sept), 60lbs. A load is 36 Trusses.

Avoirdupois Weight.

27¹⁰⁄₃₂ Grains	1 Drachm
16 Drachms	,, 1 Ounce = 437½ grains
16 Ounces	,, 1 Pound (16) = 7,000 ,,
14 Pounds	,, 1 Stone
28 Pounds	,, 1 Quarter (qr.)
8 Stones	,, 1 Hundredweight (cwt.)
20 Cwts.	,, 1 Ton

A Central = 100lbs.

1cwt.	= Small Sack	Coal
2cwt.	,, Dble. ,,	Wgts.
20cwt. or 10 Dble. Sacks 1 Ton	

3 Bushels of Coke = 1 Sack
12 Sacks   ,, 1 Chaldron
21 Chaldrons   ,, 1 Score

Wool Weight.

			cwt.	qrs.	lb.
7 Pounds	1 Clove	=	0	0	7
2 Cloves	,, 1 Stone	,,	0	0	14
2 Stones	,, 1 Tod	,,	0	1	0
6½ Tods	,, 1 Wey	,,	1	2	14
2 Weys	,, 1 Sack	,,	3	1	0
12 Sacks	,, 1 Last	,,	39	0	0
240 lbs.	,, 1 Pack				

Troy Weight.

3·17 Grains	1 Carat
24 Grains	,, 1 Pennywt. = 24 grs.
20 Pennywts.	,, 1 Ounce ,, 480 ,,
12 Ounces	,, 1 Pound ,, 5760 ,,

Standard Gold consists of 22 parts pure gold, alloyed with 2 parts of copper or other metal, and according to the quantity of alloy is called 9, 12, 15, or 18 carat, i.e., that quantity of pure gold out of the twenty-four.

Measure of Surface.

144 Square Inches	1 Square Foot
9 Square Feet	,, 1 Square Yard
30¼ Square Yards	,, 1 Rod, Pole or Perch
16 Poles	,, 1 Chain
40 Square Poles	,, 1 Rood (1,210 yards)
4 Roods or 10 Sq. Chains	,, 1 Acre (4,840 yds)
640 Square Acres	,, 1 Square Mile

We Recommend SQUATTER WHISKY.

Measure of Length.

12 Lines	: 1 Inch	5½ Yds	{ 1 Rod, Pole
12 Ins.	,, 1 Foot		or Perch
18 Ins.	,, 1 Cubit	4 Poles = 1 Chain
3 Feet	,. 1 Yard	40 Poles ,, 1 Furl'ng
6 Feet	,, 1 Fthm.	8 Fur. ,, 1 Mile
	3 Miles = 1 League.

60 Nautical Miles = 1 Degree
69½ Geograph. ,,   ,, 1 Degree

The English Mile is 1,760 yards; Scotch 1,984; Irish 2,240.

Measure of Solidity.

1,728 Cubic Inches = 1 Cubic Foot
  27 Cubic Feet   ,, 1 Cubic Yard
A Load of Earth is 27 Cubic Feet
A Load of Bricks is 500
40 Cubic Feet is 1 Shipping Ton

WORKSHOP NOTES.

Brass buried in sand kept moist will soon become of a handsome brown colour, which will take a high polish. Brown in all its shades can also be procured by dipping the brass articles in solutions of nitrates or chlorides of iron, after having been dipped in diluted nitric acid, cleaned with sand and water, and carefully dried. The depth of the tint depends on the strength of the solution.

• • •

Raw Hydrochloric Acid (Spirits of Salts) is used in soldering galvanised iron, while for tinned articles the same acid is used; but zinc strips must be added to neutralise the liquid.

• • •

Wood enclosed in a close chamber, and submitted to the action of steam for a limited time, may be rendered so pliant that it may be bent in almost any direction. The same process will also eliminate the sap from the wood, and promote rapid seasoning.

• • •

Mortar.—The proportions of cement or of lime to sand should not exceed two and a-half of clean sharp sand to one by measure of ground Portland cement or lias lime. If clean furnace ashes or slag is available, there may be two of sand and one-half of ashes or slag, the whole to be mixed in a revolving pan, each panful to have 20 minutes' grinding. When mortar is used with bricks, the beds and joints should be spread thick and full over the entire area of both bed and joint. leaving, when pressed into place, a bed and joint never less than ⅜in. in thickness of mortar. In four cubic yards of completed brickwork there should be not less than one cubic yard of mortar incorporated. In making mortar or concrete, it will be of the utmost importance to use clean materials, and to preserve them clean. Concrete and mortar should also be used on clean surfaces.

• •

Cement for Leather Belting.—Common glue and isinglass, in equal parts, soaked for ten hours in just enough water to cover them. Bring gradually to a boiling heat, and add pure tannin until the whole becomes soapy, or appears like the white of an egg. Buff off the surface to be joined; apply the cement warm, and clamp.

Canned Fruits. VERNEYS, Preservers.

Belts.—To clean belts which are dirty from drop oil and dust, first wash the belts with warm water and soap, using a sharp stiff brush, and while still moist rub them with a solution of sal ammoniac, which saponifies the oil in them. Immediately thereafter the belts must be rinsed well with lukewarm water, and then dried with sufficient tension. While they are still moist the belts are to be rubbed well on the inside, and less on the outside, with the following :—2lb. ½oz. of indiarubber heated to 122deg. Fah., and mixed with 2lb. ½oz. of rectified turpentine oil. After the solution is complete, 27oz of bright resin are added, and when it is dissolved 26½oz. of yellow wax. This mixture, by diligent stirring, is mixed with 6lb. 10oz. of fish oil and 2lb. 12oz. of tallow, previously dissolved in the former. In the further treatment of the belt, rub the inside only and the outside only the first time as stated. The unguent also replaces the tannin extracted from the leather, prevents the dragging of the belt, and imparts elasticity to it.

* * *

The Composition of Feed water is very often so bad as seriously to affect the boiler, either by acidity or the deposition of scale. In the former case, pitting and grooving is likely to take place, and in the latter, scale is formed, which sometimes leads to overheating of flues, and is always a loss of power. To counteract acidity, a little lime or caustic soda, added to the feed water, will be effective. Where water contains carbonate of lime only, the addition of a mixture of three grains of caustic soda for each four grains of carbonate is sufficient ; and, where sulphate of lime is present, four grains of soda ash to each five grains of sulphate will precipitate. In the event of both salts being present, a sufficient quantity of caustic soda will precipitate them.

* * *

A Lubricant, which becomes gummy on exposure to the air or acidifies when subjected to heat, is unsuitable for use. A test of an oil for gumminess can be made by allowing a few drops to flow down an inclined plane and noting the rapidity with which they set. Rape and linseed oils gum rapidly ; sperm and gallipoli oils less rapidly. Lard oil oxidises slowly.

* * *

Sperm contains less free fatty acid than any other animal or vegetable oil, olive oil being the worst ; the order in point of freedom being—Southern sperm, Arctic sperm, white whale, refined rape, neatsfoot, lard, and olive.

* * *

Solder for Sealing Tops of Canned Goods.—1¼lb. lead, 2lb. tin, 2oz. bismuth ; the lead is melted first, the tin added next, and finally the bismuth stirred in well just before pouring. This makes a soft solder, and the cans do not take much heat to open them.

* * *

To Bronze Gun Barrels.—Dilute nitric acid with water, and rub the gun barrels with it ; lay them by for a few days, then rub them with oil and polish them with beeswax.

* * *

To Distinguish Steel from Iron.—Pour on the object to be tested a drop of nitric acid of 1·2sp.gr., let it act for one minute, then rinse with water. On iron the acid will cause a whitish grey, on steel a black stain.

* * *

Testing Water.—To test the purity of water there has been no better or simpler way than to fill a clean bottle three-fourths full of the water to be tested, and dissolve in the water half a teaspoonful of the purest sugar - loaf or granulated will answer—cork the bottle, and place it in a warm position for two days. If in twenty-four or forty-eight hours the water becomes cloudy or milky, ii is unfit for domestic use.

We Recommend SQUATTER WHISKY.

To Prevent Boots From Cracking.—To prevent new boots cracking take some boiled linseed oil, and with a piece of flannel or rag wetted in it, rub over the soles and round the edges of boots, turn the soles upwards until they are quite dry. This method not only keeps the boots from cracking but renders them more impervious to damp.

* * *

To Clean Felt Hats.—Dirty black felt hats should first be thoroughly brushed with a stiff brush to remove all the dust, and then wiped over with benzine; this will remove all the dirt and grease. The smell of benzine is much disliked by many people, so it is a good plan to leave the hats in the openair for some time afterward.

Fighting the White Ant.

By W. STREET.

I T is safe to say that the majority of owners of wooden houses in Queensland live in daily dread of the industrious white ant. Most buildings are subject to attack at some time or other; nothing in the form of wood can resist them for long, and even metal sometimes succumbs to their powerful jaws. We have now in our possession a revolver cartridge (/380 bore), the bullet of which has been completely eaten through by white ants. A photograph of the bullet showing the hole is reproduced in this issue. The specimen comes from Mr. W. Hutson, of Vanrook Station, in the Gulf District. We have heard many strange stories of the voracity of the Northern white ant, but have never had such indisputable evidence of their destructive powers. Housecowners in the North are naturally deeply interested in means of exterminating their foe, consequently the following practical hints, prepared by Mr. W. Street, the well-known white ant expert, will be of special interest to readers in that part of the colony.

The Termite, usually known as the white ant, causes such a large amount of destruction in tropical climates that it has prominently forced itself (like the tick) into notice, and set man to work to find means to protect property from its ravages. Hundreds who have suffered by this innocent-looking little insect, and fought it for years unsuccessfully, have lost all heart and believe there is no defeating it. If books by the first authorities are consulted, it is singular how very little aid can be got from them. They tell everything but the one thing which the searcher wants to know—how to get rid of the white ants. What good is it to a person who sees his home being devoured day by day, to tell him all about the birth, habits, and daily life of the pest? Such information only exasperates. This paper is for those who want to put an end to destruction, or entirely prevent it. In Australia some houses have their foundations resting upon the ground, of concrete, brick, stone, &c., under the walls of each room; others upon arches, and great numbers in the tropical part rest upon stumps or brick piers. If it is desired to make a building ant proof, the entire foundation and all timbers resting thereon are syringed or brushed over with white ant "cure." Care must be taken that steps, chimney foundations, or any upright of any description leading from the ground to the floor of the house, be also brushed or syringed. It is much easier and less expensive to do this before the erection of the building than after; an ounce of prevention costs far less than a pound of cure. The white ant requires timber for food, and regards foundations of every description simply as ladders to enable it to reach the desired prey. The termites, when leaving their ground tunnels, build others upon the foundations. This gives them protection from their many enemies, and also acts as a guide to the

We Recommend SQUATTER WHISKY.

feeding-places of the blind white ant. When exterminating the pest from a building, search is ...ade over the entire foundations for these roads. If the cure is used in the form of powder a tiny opening is made in the run, and a small quantity of the powder placed within, the tunnel being otherwise untouched, so that it may act as a trap to the ants. If the liquid cure is used, clear the run right away, and brush or syringe the part over which the track ran ; also where the tunnel enters the ground give an ex..ra quantity. Should the termites have their road within the stump, bore till the auger reaches the heart of the run ; or, with a knife or trowel pierce through the clay, till the ants are seen ; then apply the cure right amongst them and down the throat of the run. The same course is followed if ants are in the heart of walls of any description. The foundations of chimneys are favourite homes of the white ants, and they usually come out where plates enter the wall, and ascend between the stud and the brickwork. With a knife clear a little of the mortar from around plates and woodwork, touching chimney foundation at any part, drive the liquid in as far as the plates go, and soak well between the stud and any woodwork touching the chimney. Should a nest be suspected in the heart of the foundation, lift a brick or two of the inner hearth, and let a gallon or two soak down. There is no need whatever to take the chimney down. Do not waste time looking for the ants above the floor. Search them out under the floors, and deal with the pest there, which will ensure safety for all parts of the building above. If a brick or stone building has to be cured of white ants, get underneath the floors if possible from outside ; failing that, cut a trapdoor in one corner of the room. Take a reflecting lamp or ordinary candle and search around the entire foundation for the roads of the pest. To exterminate the ants and make the building ant proof, clear away the dust or mortar from plates, joists, or any other timber against or entering the wall ; then syringe the liquid in as far as the timber goes ; also syringe a foot wide strip around the whole wall from the floor downwards. If joists are side on to wall, the liquid must be syringed between wall and joist from above. If powder is used it can be shot into position with an "insect gun." If the whole building is to be made ant proof, the above treatment must be thoroughly carried out ; no half measures will succeed. If there is no room for an operator under the floor, sufficient of the floor boards against the wall and over the piers must be taken up to permit of the application of the cure. Ends of flooring abutting against walls should be well soaked to prevent the pest entering. If a wooden building is close to the ground the same treatment must be given. The outer walls are often effectually got at by taking the bottom board off, which will lay the joists and plates bare to the operator, who should paint or brush with the cure these and the inside of the board just taken off. If the building is high enough for a person to crawl under, search all the uprights leading from the ground to the floor, steps and chimneys included. A patient search and good light will discover the white ant runs. Treat these with either powder or liquid cure, and all the ants in the building, from the ridge downwards, will be destroyed. There is no need whatever to tear the house about, not a single board need be disturbed unless repairs are to be done. Where repairs are made, paint the exposed faces of the joists or plates before nailing the boards on.

If a wooden house is to be made white ant proof, cut the sapwood from the stumps to about 6in. above the ground. With a knife or trowel make a way for the

137

cure to run into the ground at the foot of steps, chimneys, or other uprights. Apply the cure ungrudgingly at foot of stumps, chimneys, steps, &c., with a syringe; also on top of all stumps (lifting caps a little, if necessary) at the junction of all wood with foundations of chimneys and at the top of all steps, or anything else going from the ground to the house. With a brush then paint thoroughly the entire stumps, also timbers resting upon them, to about 6in. beyond the face of the stumps. If the pest is in the heart of the stump, bore till ants are seen, or pierce the veins of clay with a knife, then apply the cure liberally. If the building is without caps to the stumps, there will be no need to apply caps. Soaking the tops of stumps well with the cure is of far more value than caps, which are of very little service indeed in preventing the pest from entering the house. At best, when without holes, they only make the ants show their roads, nothing more. Do not trust to caps on stumps, as loss and disappointment will result. Tar, salt, ammonia, gas lime, kerosene, turps, creosote, and carbolic acid are useless as a permanent cure.

Now, a word to punt and ship owners. The white ants are fond of river and sea life; they enter a vessel in coal, sand, firewood, or logs, and make comfortable homes between the outer and inner walls. Nests are generally up against the gunwale; from here the ants descend to the bottom for fluid and dust to carry out roads, and spread themselves from stem to stern, doing enormous damage to timber work. To exterminate them, take an inner plank off, or bore through it as close to the gunwale as possible, and syringe cure on from end to end until the sides and ends are coated with it. By taking the plank off there is the great advantage of seeing things, and also of being able to take out nests.

To protect trees, mix powder or liquid with flour and sugar, or honey or treacle, form pine sandwiches, with the cure between, and bury 4in. in the ground about a couple of feet from the tree.

RICHEST is he that wants least.
SMALL faults indulged in are little thieves that let in greater.
THE boughs that bear most hang lowest.
UPRIGHT walking is sure walking.

Calendar for 1899.

	JANUARY.					APRIL.						JULY.						OCTOBER.				
S	1	8	15	22	29	2	9	16	23	30		2	9	16	23	30		1	8	15	22	29
M	2	9	16	23	30	3	10	17	24	..		3	10	17	24	31		2	9	16	23	30
Tu	3	10	17	24	31	4	11	18	25	..		4	11	18	25	..		3	10	17	24	31
W	4	11	18	25	...	5	12	19	26	...		5	12	19	26	...		4	11	18	25	...
Th	5	12	19	26	...	6	13	20	27	...		6	13	20	27	...		5	12	19	26	...
F	6	13	20	27	...	7	14	21	28	..		7	14	21	28	...		6	13	20	27	..
S	7	14	21	28	...	1	8	15	22	29		1	8	15	22	29	...	7	14	21	28	...

	FEBRUARY.					MAY.						AUGUST.						NOVEMBER.				
S	...	5	12	19	26	..	7	14	21	28		...	6	13	20	27		...	5	12	19	26
M	...	6	13	20	27	1	8	15	22	29		..	7	14	21	28		...	6	13	20	27
Tu	...	7	14	21	28	2	9	16	23	30		1	8	15	22	29		...	7	14	21	28
W	1	8	15	22	..	3	10	17	24	31		2	9	16	23	30		1	8	15	22	29
Th	2	9	16	23	..	4	11	18	25	..		3	10	17	24	31		2	9	16	23	30
F	3	10	17	24	..	5	12	19	26			4	11	18	25	..		3	10	17	24	..
S	4	11	18	25	...	6	13	20	27	...		5	12	19	26	..		4	11	18	25	..

	MARCH.					JUNE.						SEPTEMBER.						DECEMBER.				
S	...	5	12	19	26	...	4	11	18	25		...	3	10	17	24	...		3	10	17	24	31
M	...	6	13	20	27	...	5	12	19	26		...	4	11	18	25	..		4	11	18	25	...
Tu	...	7	14	21	28	...	6	13	20	27		...	5	12	19	26	..		5	12	19	26	...
W	1	8	15	22	29	...	7	14	21	28		...	6	13	20	27	..		6	13	20	27	...
Th	2	9	16	23	30	1	8	15	22	29		...	7	14	21	28	..		7	14	21	28	...
F	3	10	17	24	31	2	9	16	23	30		1	8	15	22	29	...	1	8	15	22	29	...
S	4	11	18	25	..	3	10	17	24			2	9	16	23	30		2	9	16	23	30	..

Calendar for 1900.

	JANUARY.					APRIL.						JULY.						OCTOBER.				
S	..	7	14	21	28	1	8	15	22	29		1	8	15	22	29		...	7	14	21	28
M	1	8	15	22	29	2	9	16	23	30		2	9	16	23	30		1	8	15	22	29
Tu	2	9	16	23	30	3	10	17	24	..		3	10	17	24	31		2	9	16	23	30
W	3	10	17	24	31	4	11	18	25	...		4	11	18	25	...		3	10	17	24	31
Th	4	11	18	25	..	5	12	19	26	..		5	12	19	26	...		4	11	18	25	..
F	5	12	19	26	..	6	13	20	27	..		6	13	20	27	..		5	12	19	26	..
S	6	13	20	27	..	7	14	21	28	..		7	14	21	28	...		6	13	20	27	..

	FEBRUARY.					MAY.						AUGUST.						NOVEMBER.				
S	..	4	11	18	25	..	6	13	20	27		..	5	12	19	26		..	4	11	18	25
M	..	5	12	19	26	..	7	14	21	28		6	13	20	27			..	5	12	19	26
Tu	..	6	13	20	27	1	8	15	22	29		..	7	14	21	28		..	6	13	20	27
W	..	7	14	21	28	2	9	16	23	30		1	8	15	22	29		..	7	14	21	28
Th	1	8	15	22	..	3	10	17	24	31		2	9	16	23	30		1	8	15	22	29
F	2	9	16	23	..	4	11	18	25	..		3	10	17	24	31		2	9	16	23	30
S	3	10	17	24	..	5	12	19	26	...		4	11	18	25	..		3	10	17	24	..

	MARCH.					JUNE.						SEPTEMBER.						DECEMBER.				
S	...	4	11	18	25	..	3	10	17	24		..	2	9	16	23	30	2	9	16	23	30
M	...	5	12	19	26	..	4	11	18	25		..	3	10	17	24			3	10	17	24	31
Tu	...	6	13	20	27	..	5	12	19	26		..	4	11	18	25	..		4	11	18	25	..
W	...	7	14	21	28	..	6	13	20	27		..	5	12	19	26	..		5	12	19	26	..
Th	1	8	15	22	29	..	7	14	21	28		..	6	13	20	27	..		6	13	20	27	..
F	2	9	16	23	30	1	8	15	22	29		..	7	14	21	28	..		7	14	21	28	..
S	3	10	17	24	31	2	9	16	23	30		1	8	15	22	29		1	8	15	22	29	

R. W. THURLOW & CO.

General Merchants.

Proprietors of the CRESCENT PACKING CO., Manufacturers and Packers of:

OO=PACK TEA

KOOLANA TEA

TURKISH COFFEE

FRENCH COFFEE

ROYAL

BAKING POWDER

The BEST GOODS of their class yet offered to the Queensland Public.

Brewers of the celebrated

CRESCENT VINEGAR

Guaranteed brewed from Malt, and EQUAL TO THE BEST IMPORTED BRANDS. Sold by all Merchants and Grocers throughout the Colony.